AAL- 6161

THE ENVIRONMENTAL
CRISIS
OPPOSING VIEWPOINTS®

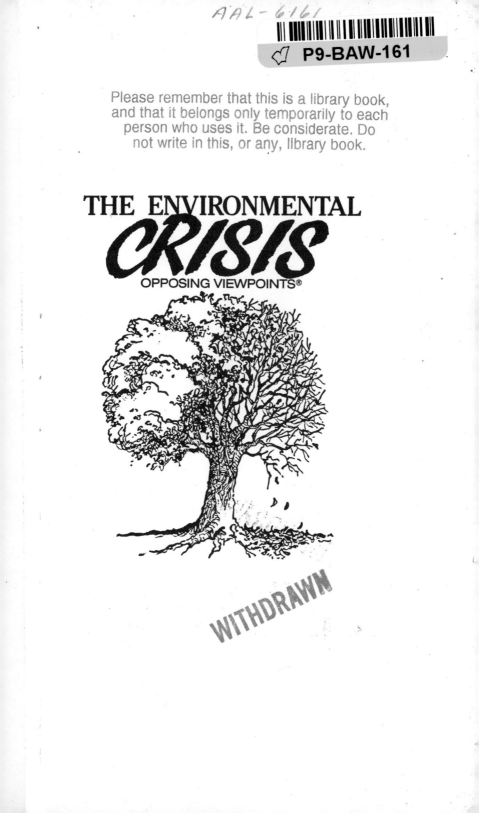

Other Books of Related Interest in the Opposing Viewpoints Series:

Central America
Economics in America
Genetic Engineering
Global Resources
The Health Crisis
Immigration
The Third World
Trade
War on Drugs

THE ENVIRONMENTAL
CRISIS
OPPOSING VIEWPOINTS®

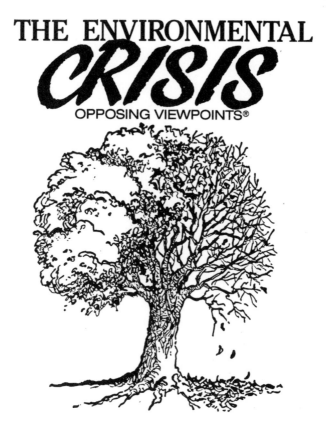

David L. Bender & Bruno Leone, *Series Editors*

Neal Bernards, *Book Editor*

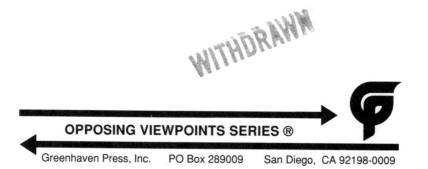

OPPOSING VIEWPOINTS SERIES ®

Greenhaven Press, Inc.   PO Box 289009   San Diego, CA 92198-0009

Library of Congress Cataloging-in-Publication Data

The Environmental crisis—opposing viewpoints / Neal Bernards, book editor.
    p.   cm. — (Opposing viewpoints series)
  Includes bibliographical references and index.
  Summary: Presents opposing views on questions of environmental protection and damage resulting from air and water pollution, toxic wastes, pesticides, and the ever-growing tide of refuse.
  ISBN 0-89908-150-9 (pbk.). — ISBN 0-89908-175-4 (lib. bdg.)
  1. Environmental policy—United States. [1. Environmental protection.] I. Bernards, Neal, 1963-   . II. Series: Opposing viewpoints series (Unnumbered)
HC110.E5E49835   1991
363.7—dc20   90-24086

"Congress shall make no law . . .
abridging the freedom of speech,
or of the press."

First Amendment to the U.S. Constitution

The basic foundation of our democracy is the first amendment
guarantee of freedom of expression. The Opposing Viewpoints
Series is dedicated to the concept of this basic freedom and the
idea that it is more important to practice it than to enshrine it.

Contents

Why Consider Opposing Viewpoints?

"It is better to debate a question without settling it than to settle a question without debating it."

Joseph Joubert (1754-1824)

The Importance of Examining Opposing Viewpoints

The purpose of the Opposing Viewpoints Series, and this book in particular, is to present balanced, and often difficult to find, opposing points of view on complex and sensitive issues.

Probably the best way to become informed is to analyze the positions of those who are regarded as experts and well studied on issues. It is important to consider every variety of opinion in an attempt to determine the truth. Opinions from the mainstream of society should be examined. But also important are opinions that are considered radical, reactionary, or minority as well as those stigmatized by some other uncomplimentary label. An important lesson of history is the eventual acceptance of many unpopular and even despised opinions. The ideas of Socrates, Jesus, and Galileo are good examples of this.

Readers will approach this book with their own opinions on the issues debated within it. However, to have a good grasp of one's own viewpoint, it is necessary to understand the arguments of those with whom one disagrees. It can be said that those who do not completely understand their adversary's point of view do not fully understand their own.

A persuasive case for considering opposing viewpoints has been presented by John Stuart Mill in his work *On Liberty*. When examining controversial issues it may be helpful to reflect on this suggestion:

The only way in which a human being can make some approach to knowing the whole of a subject, is by hearing what can be said about it by persons of every variety of opinion, and studying all modes in which it can be looked at by every character of mind. No wise man ever acquired his wisdom in any mode but this.

Analyzing Sources of Information

The Opposing Viewpoints Series includes diverse materials taken from magazines, journals, books, and newspapers, as well as statements and position papers from a wide range of individuals, organizations, and governments. This broad spectrum of sources helps to develop patterns of thinking which are open to the consideration of a variety of opinions.

Pitfalls to Avoid

A pitfall to avoid in considering opposing points of view is that of regarding one's own opinion as being common sense and the most rational stance, and the point of view of others as being only opinion and naturally wrong. It may be that another's opinion is correct and one's own is in error.

Another pitfall to avoid is that of closing one's mind to the opinions of those with whom one disagrees. The best way to approach a dialogue is to make one's primary purpose that of understanding the mind and arguments of the other person and not that of enlightening him or her with one's own solutions. More can be learned by listening than speaking.

It is my hope that after reading this book the reader will have a deeper understanding of the issues debated and will appreciate the complexity of even seemingly simple issues on which good and honest people disagree. This awareness is particularly important in a democratic society such as ours where people enter into public debate to determine the common good. Those with whom one disagrees should not necessarily be regarded as enemies, but perhaps simply as people who suggest different paths to a common goal.

Developing Basic Reading and Thinking Skills

In this book, carefully edited opposing viewpoints are purposely placed back to back to create a running debate; each viewpoint is preceded by a short quotation that best expresses the author's main argument. This format instantly plunges the reader into the midst of a controversial issue and greatly aids that reader in mastering the basic skill of recognizing an author's point of view.

A number of basic skills for critical thinking are practiced in the activities that appear throughout the books in the series. Some of the skills are:

Evaluating Sources of Information. The ability to choose from among alternative sources the most reliable and accurate source in relation to a given subject.

Separating Fact from Opinion. The ability to make the basic distinction between factual statements (those that can be demonstrated or verified empirically) and statements of opinion (those that are beliefs or attitudes that cannot be proved).

Identifying Stereotypes. The ability to identify oversimplified, exaggerated descriptions (favorable or unfavorable) about people and insulting statements about racial, religious, or national groups, based upon misinformation or lack of information.

Recognizing Ethnocentrism. The ability to recognize attitudes or opinions that express the view that one's own race, culture, or group is inherently superior, or those attitudes that judge another culture or group in terms of one's own.

It is important to consider opposing viewpoints and equally important to be able to critically analyze those viewpoints. The activities in this book are designed to help the reader master these thinking skills. Statements are taken from the book's viewpoints and the reader is asked to analyze them. This technique aids the reader in developing skills that not only can be applied to the viewpoints in this book, but also to situations where opinionated spokespersons comment on controversial issues. Although the activities are helpful to the solitary reader, they are most useful when the reader can benefit from the interaction of group discussion.

Using this book and others in the series should help readers develop basic reading and thinking skills. These skills should improve the reader's ability to understand what is read. Readers should be better able to separate fact from opinion, substance from rhetoric, and become better consumers of information in our media-centered culture.

This volume of the Opposing Viewpoints Series does not advocate a particular point of view. Quite the contrary! The very nature of the book leaves it to the reader to formulate the opinions he or she finds most suitable. My purpose as publisher is to see that this is made possible by offering a wide range of viewpoints that are fairly presented.

David L. Bender
Publisher

11

Introduction

"A new generation of Americans has come to recognize more clearly than ever before the importance of our global environment."

Frederick A. Bernthal, assistant secretary of state for oceans and international and scientific affairs

Concern for the environment influences countless decisions in Americans' daily lives. From breakfast to bedtime Americans face hundreds of choices: Recycle the morning paper? Pay extra for organic fruits and vegetables? Bring a bag lunch or eat fast food? Use paper or plastic bags? Drive miles for entertainment or stay home? Often the question arises whether these individual choices are the best way to solve environmental problems, or must private industry and government shoulder the burden of ecological preservation?

President George Bush and others believe private industry can protect the environment. Bush cites Minnesota Mining and Manufacturing's (3M) "Pollution Protection Pays" program as a prime example of corporate environmental responsibility. 3M's program includes reducing the need for toxic ingredients in production, using waste heat to warm its offices, installing smokestack and pipe discharge filters, and recycling the company's reusable wastes. Bush states that the program "has saved well over half a billion dollars since 1975—prevented 112,000 tons of air pollutants, 15,000 tons of water pollutants, and almost 400,000 tons of sludge and solid waste from being released into the environment." Bush believes industry can be the best environmental protector because it can bring to bear the latest technologies, the newest inventions, and the brightest entrepreneurs to solve the problems.

Most environmental groups vehemently disagree with this approach. Barry Commoner, a noted environmental author and director of the Center for the Biology of Natural Systems at Queens College in New York, argues that private industry cannot be trusted to preserve the environment. He maintains that industry's only motive is profit, not society's interests, and must therefore give way to government as the environment's protector. Commoner believes the environment can be saved by allowing the general public, via government elections and legislation, an opportunity to control natural resources.

Finally, many argue that trusting either the government or private industry to protect the environment is foolish. Citizen activists contend that every individual must work to save the earth's resources. Environmentalists like author and naturalist Lester R. Brown maintain that by forfeiting the issue to large, faceless institutions, individuals shirk their duty to conserve global resources. Brown, president of the Worldwatch Institute, writes, "Ultimate responsibility for the future rests with individuals. Our values, choices, and behaviors shape social and political change." Proof of citizen power can be found in the reduction of gasoline use during energy crises, the demand for more energy-efficient cars, and the nationwide interest in community recycling. Brown lauds these examples of citizen action and foresees change through continued personal commitment to the protection of the environment.

The answer to the question Who should take responsibility? may ultimately lie in all three groups pooling their talents to protect the environment. This book presents a wide spectrum of political, social, and economic thought. Viewpoints were taken from briefing papers, editorial pages, scientific journals, environmental newsletters, books, business magazines, and pamphlets. The six topics covered in *The Environmental Crisis: Opposing Viewpoints* are: Is There an Environmental Crisis? How Should Pesticides Be Handled? How Can the Garbage Problem Be Reduced? How Should America Dispose of Toxic Waste? How Serious Is Air and Water Pollution? and How Can the Environment Be Protected? As the world's population expands and technology advances, environmental protection will remain in the forefront of pressing global concerns. The diverse viewpoints offered in this book should give readers a better understanding of the issues at hand.

Is There an Environmental Crisis?

Chapter Preface

Despite more than two decades of well-intentioned environmental laws designed to reduce pollutants, America's air and water quality has not improved as rapidly as experts had hoped. For example, laws were enacted in 1970 aiming to reduce auto emissions. And, in fact, new cars emit less than one-quarter of the pollutants given off by cars built before 1970. Unfortunately, 386 million cars ply the world's roads today, up considerably from the pre-1970 era. This increase negates the improvements the pollution control laws seemed to ensure. Environmentalists say this is only one of many examples that prove environmental laws are not keeping pace with rising population, rapid Third World development, and expanding industrialization. These problems deserve serious long-range planning and international cooperation in order to develop laws that work, many scientists and environmentalists argue.

Others are not convinced there is enough of a problem to warrant this type of concern. Julian Simon, author of *The Resourceful Earth* is one among a small but growing faction that believes environmental problems are exaggerated by the media and vitriolic environmentalists. Environmental problems are simply not serious enough to require people to spend the time and money to find alternatives, he contends. For example, using fossil fuels, (which admittedly cause a certain amount of pollution) is significantly less expensive than using any of the highly touted alternatives such as solar or hydroelectric power. Simon predicts that people will act only when the earth runs out of cheap fossil fuels, quite possibly within the next two hundred years. This is not necessarily bad, he argues, for history has shown that when people do act, they are usually capable of solving extraordinary problems. Simon and others do not believe there is a current environmental crisis, and they conclude that when and if one does materialize, people will solve it.

The debate over whether environmental problems deserve immediate attention is one that is sure to continue into the future. The authors of this chapter hold strong opinions on this issue.

"Humanity stands in the shadow of global catastrophe. "

There Is an Environmental Crisis

Roger L. DiSilvestro

Since the first Earth Day in 1970, ecologists have warned that the world teeters on the edge of an environmental disaster. Roger L. DiSilvestro, the author of the following viewpoint, agrees with this assessment. In this excerpt DiSilvestro argues that catastrophe awaits humanity if nothing is done to improve the environment. He writes that global warming, acid rain, reduction of the ozone layer, and overpopulation threaten to cut worldwide food production and cause serious health problems. DiSilvestro is the chief staff writer for television specials sponsored by the Audubon Society and is the author of *The Endangered Kingdom*.

As you read, consider the following questions:

1. According to the author, how will global warming affect the planet?
2. In DiSilvestro's opinion, what are the consequences of acid rain?
3. Why does the author warn against depleting the ozone layer?

Roger L. DiSilvestro, *Fight for Survival.* Copyright © 1990 by the National Audubon Society. Reprinted by permission of John Wiley & Sons, Inc.

Please think for just a bit about what we have wrought in North America within the past 500 years. We have journeyed from a time in which our forebears stood on the eastern edge of an uncharted Atlantic and pondered its invisible, distant reaches, and come to a time in which the vast ocean has been so humbled that it seems to be rotting from the touch of human industry and waste. Through a combination of advanced technology and precipitously increasing populations, we have become a force capable of shaping the face of the globe. We have altered natural environments so drastically and so often and in so many places that the Earth and the atmosphere that surrounds it are becoming less and less protective and nurturing of living things. Humanity stands in the shadow of global catastrophe.

Looming Catastrophe

The signs of that looming catastrophe have been around a long, long time. They were there thousands of years ago, when salts from irrigation water poisoned farmlands in the Fertile Crescent of the Tigris and Euphrates valley. They were there in biblical times when deforestation and overgrazing turned verdant lands in the Middle East into deserts. The signs are with us now, and becoming more urgent. We can see them in Asia, where the cutting of mountain forests in Tibet, Nepal, Bhutan, and northern India since the 1970s has removed the trees and other vegetation that absorbed the monsoon rains. Now the annual floods that once nourished the croplands of Bangladesh with fresh soil and nutrients have turned with increasing frequency into deadly torrents that rush out of the denuded mountains, leaving millions homeless and many dead.

We see other signs in Africa, Asia, and Latin America, where the cutting of forests is leading to erosion of topsoil and creating new deserts, where overgrazing by livestock in arid regions is laying waste to grass lands. Worldwide, desertification is eating up nearly 15 million acres a year, land needed for food production in starving countries.

We see more signs in the United States. Toxic runoff channeled from western agricultural lands into national wildlife refuges, where it kills the birds the refuges were created to protect, is one of the signs. The tumors on the sea turtles of Florida's Indian River and the corroded skins of the dolphins off New Jersey are also signs.

In the past we could ignore the signs and still escape the more tragic effects of our work. We always had more land to move to, new worlds to settle. But as we carry history into the twenty-first century, we are beginning to learn that we have crowded the limits of the Earth. . . .

We have already seen the first indications of what we will face

18

in the near future. Meteorological data indicate that the Earth is warming, the warmth a byproduct of the greenhouse effect. The greenhouse effect begins when tons and tons of carbon are poured into the atmosphere by the burning of coal, oil, and natural gas and by the burning of tropical rain forests to clear land for agriculture. In 1988 alone, the burning of fossil fuels added 5.5 billion tons of carbon to the atmosphere. From the scorched rain forests came as much as 2.5 billion tons. Within the next twenty years, carbon entering the atmosphere from the burning of fossil fuels could rocket to 10 billion tons yearly.

Failing the Physical

In giving the earth a physical examination, checking its vital signs, we find that the readings are not reassuring: The planet's forests are shrinking, its deserts expanding, and its soils eroding—all at record rates.

Each year, thousands of plant and animal species disappear, many before they are named or cataloged. The ozone layer in the upper atmosphere that protects us from ultraviolet radiation is thinning. The temperature of the earth appears to be rising, posing a threat of unknown dimensions to virtually all the life-support systems on which humanity depends.

Lester R. Brown, Christopher Flavin, and Edward C. Wolf, *The Futurist*, July/August 1988.

Over the past thirty years, the amount of carbon dioxide in the air has increased from 315 parts per million to 352, by far the highest concentration of the past 160,000 years. As atmospheric carbon builds up it acts like the glass of a greenhouse, holding in heat from the sun and keeping it from radiating back into space as much of it normally does. The greater the carbon concentration, the greater the amount of heat the atmosphere retains. This greenhouse effect threatens to raise the average temperature of the globe by as much as eight degrees Fahrenheit by the year 2050, warmer than the Earth has been for some 2 million years.

The damage will be tremendous. A change in average temperature of less than one degree every ten years in northern regions will move the range of some tree species northward 60 to 100 miles. But since trees cannot adapt as quickly as the Earth apparently is warming, whole species are likely to die off. Trees that die ultimately might be replaced by others adapted to warmer weather, but replacement will take centuries. Meanwhile, as the dead trees die and rot, the carbon they contain in their cells will escape into the atmosphere as a gas and speed the warming process. The problems of global warming will be compounded for wildlife species living in national parks and refuges that are surrounded by developed lands. With no pathway to new habitat, they will be locked within the confines of the withering preserves. Say the authors of *The State of the World 1989*, an excellent handbook on the Earth's environmental status and the source for much of this [viewpoint], "Indeed, various biological reserves created in the past decade to protect species diversity could become virtual death traps as wildlife attempt to survive in conditions for which they are poorly suited. Accelerated species extinction is an inevitable consequence of a rapid warming."

The Consequences

Sea levels will rise, and the salt seas will invade the drinking-water sources of coastal cities such as New York and Miami. Agricultural lands and coastal towns in nations such as Bangladesh and Egypt will flood, forcing more than 25 million people from their homes in just those two nations. Weather will change. Warming is likely to cause severe and unpredictable droughts and heat waves. Vast crop-growing regions of the Earth will fail as rainfall declines. The unusually hot summer of 1988 foreshadowed what in the future may be the norm. In that year, the U.S. grain harvest fell below consumption for the first time in recent history. The reverberations of such a disaster extend beyond U.S. boundaries: The 100 million tons of grain usually available for export each year were lost. If current warming trends continue, the grain and corn-producing regions of the midwestern United States will become semi-arid, cutting crop production in some areas by 50 to 100 percent. In parts of Canada a longer winter growing season will increase the amount of croplands, but summer corn crops will probably decline. Crop failures in Third World nations, home to some 4 billion people, will bring starvation to millions upon millions.

Despite the relative speed, in geologic terms, with which the temperature increase apparently is occurring—the five hottest years of the past century occurred in the 1980s—it has scarcely been noticed by the average person. Most people may not perceive the change until sometime in the 1990s, when the burning heat waves and prolonged droughts that may soon typify the average summer will begin. But that does not mean that global warming is not already taking place. Scientists who monitor annual average temperatures have found an alarmingly consistent increase in the past two decades.

Global warming is an international problem. It requires an international solution, just as the protection of wide-ranging species such as dolphins, sea turtles, and sharks requires an international solution. As our environmental problems have become global in extent, they have diminished the role that any one nation can hope to play in solving them. This is shown not by global warming alone. We see it in the pollution of our seas. We see it elsewhere. We see it in acid precipitation.

Acid precipitation is another product of the use of fossil fuels. When coal high in sulfur is burned, the sulfur is released into the atmosphere. When gasoline is burned in automobile engines, nitrogen compounds flow into the atmosphere. The sulfur and the nitrogen compounds each combine with oxygen to form acids. These acids are washed from the atmosphere by rain and snow, and thus enter lakes and streams. In Canada, New York State, New England, and the northern European nations, acid precipitation has killed tens of thousands of lakes by raising their acidity to levels that are deadly to the microscopic animals, insects, and smaller fish that most freshwater wildlife species need to survive. Lakes in which fish once thrived are now barren.

Reprinted by permission: Tribune Media Services.

Acid precipitation damages cities, too. It has damaged historic buildings in Europe, slowly dissolving metal and stone sculptures. It is slowly eroding the Lincoln Memorial in Washington, D.C. It is costing billions of dollars yearly in building repairs. And increasing evidence indicates that the pollutants that cause acid precipitation are affecting human health by increasing the intensity and frequency of asthma attacks and by working deep into our lungs to gnaw at our tissues, perhaps increasing the incidence of certain types of cancer.

Like the greenhouse effect, acid precipitation is a global problem. More than half of Canada's acid precipitation originates in the United States, and acids that originate over the Soviet Union travel into Europe and the arctic. To stop the spread of acid precipitation will cost billions of dollars and require the cooperation of many nations. But throughout the 1980s, prospects for change were slim. For example, the midwestern U.S. power plants that produce most of the acidity that wafts into Canada have refused to accept the burden of moderating Canada's acid-rain problem, and the U.S. government has repeatedly fumbled every offer from Canada for a two-nation effort to limit acid precipitation. In a time when environmental problems have become international in scope, human society has remained heedlessly regional in its commitments.

A Hole in the Ozone Layer

Another global catastrophe is in the making in the Earth's ozone layer. Ozone gas is relatively rare in the atmosphere—at its highest concentrations some eight to sixteen miles above the Earth's surface it amounts to only a few parts per million. Nevertheless, it is vital to all life because it is the only atmospheric gas that keeps the sun's deadly ultraviolet rays away from us. But human-made chemicals are destroying the ozone layer.

The primary ozone-destroying chemicals are called chlorofluorocarbons, or CFCs. They were invented in the 1930s and marketed for use as coolants in refrigerator and air conditioning systems. One CFC coolant was given the trade name Freon by its manufacturer, E. I. du Pont de Nemours & Company. CFCs also are used to make some types of foam insulation, popularly called Styrofoam, a trade name originated by Dow Chemical Company. Some forms of the chemicals were also widely used to make aerosol cans work.

CFCs released into the atmosphere, for example through leaks in air conditioners or through the use of aerosol sprays, can, through a series of chemical reactions, cause ozone to break down. This was first discovered over Antarctica, where environmental and atmospheric conditions speed ozone destruction, creating huge holes in which ozone concentrations are cut in half. One hole late in the 1980s was twice the size of the United States.

Ozone holes have been discovered over the arctic, too, and ozone concentrations are quite likely declining in areas all over the globe. As the ozone drops off, the amount of ultraviolet light reaching the Earth's surface increases. Ultraviolet light causes drying of human skin and increases the incidence of skin cancers, including melanoma, which kills about a third of its victims. Ultraviolet light has other harmful effects as well. The Environmental Protection Agency estimates that during the next ninety years, increased ultraviolet radiation will cause as many as 2.8 million cases of cataracts, which is a blurring of vision caused by a clouding of the lens of the eye. Some evidence suggests that ultraviolet radiation suppresses the human body's immune responses, making people more susceptible to disease.

A Growing Crisis

In the summer of 1988, medical waste floated onto public beaches in North Jersey, Long Island, Connecticut, Massachusetts, and as far north as Maine. That same summer, a drought persisted in the Midwest agriculture belt with a severity not seen since the Dust Bowl phenomenon of the 1930s. The drought coincided with a record heat wave throughout much of the country, which climatologists suspect is part of a trend in global warming. We are told by NASA that the ozone layer over Antarctica is being depleted at a faster rate than any experts had forecast. This news caused the Environmental Protection Agency (EPA) to admit that the new international treaty to limit ozone-depleting chemicals, the 1987 Montreal Protocol, is already outdated. Hardly a day has passed. . . when the daily newspapers I read have failed to carry stories of the crisis in solid waste, with landfills rapidly filling up and their alternative—municipal incinerators—generating dioxins.

H. Patricia Hynes, *Earth Right*, 1990.

Ultraviolet rays will also affect plants and animals. One soybean species important as a food crop declined in productivity when experimentally exposed to the amount of ultraviolet radiation that would occur if the concentration of the ozone layer dropped 25 percent. The microscopic plants, called phytoplankton, that float at the ocean's surface and form the basis of the marine food chain could become more than a third less productive under the same level of ozone depletion. This would affect the fish populations that feed on them, and the animals that feed on the fish. Everything from crustaceans to whales would be jeopardized. Some commercially important fish species, such as anchovies, would decline significantly at even a 9 percent level of ozone depletion.

The problem underlying such massive threats as ozone depletion and acid precipitation is overpopulation. In 1950 the globe supported 2.5 billion people. By 1987 that number had more than doubled. Within the next four decades it is expected to reach nearly 9 billion. As populations grow, nations have to draw upon their resources with increasing intensity. As part of the process, they create more wastes and toxic emissions, compounding the environmental problems that face the world today. In some cases, burgeoning populations, and the economic problems they create, force nations to adopt virtually suicidal policies. One example is the destruction of rain forests in Latin America, Southeast Asia, and Africa. In many areas the forests are being cut and burned at unprecedented rates in an effort to create croplands. However, because rain-forest soils generally are not fertile enough to be turned into productive farmland, the populations of these areas are ultimately faced with a crisis in the availability of foods and other needs. Meanwhile, in return for the quick profits made by converting the forests to crops, these nations destroy a valuable resource that could provide income indefinitely if properly husbanded.

A Global Problem

Similarly, as populations in major cities grow, air pollution from industry and automobiles increases. Waste disposal becomes a more and more difficult challenge, especially in an era in which the oceans seem no longer able to hold all the garbage that is dumped into them. Even in affluent nations such as the United States, increasing amounts of wildlife habitat are being lost as cities and suburbs sprawl into surrounding countrysides. Moreover, demand for energy and other resources is sending human development into all corners of the globe. . . .

In the 1940s we saw nations unite to fight a merciless common enemy that threatened millions of lives. The environmental enemies we face today are no less merciless. Every year in the United States, particulate pollution alone kills an estimated 100,000 people—about 1.25 times the number of U.S. military personnel killed in battle in each year of World War II. This is just a prelude to what lies ahead if problems such as ozone depletion are not solved or reduced. We are, in effect, fighting an invisible invasion force, and the battle is truly on the level of a world war.

"It is a fact that effluents no longer pour unchecked from the stacks and chimneys and waste pipes of industry. "

There Is No Environmental Crisis

Dixy Lee Ray and Lou Guzzo

Dixy Lee Ray is the former governor of Washington, chairperson of the Atomic Energy Commission, and a long-time member of the zoology faculty at the University of Washington in Seattle. Lou Guzzo is a radio and TV commentator and author in Seattle. In the following viewpoint, Ray and Guzzo contend that humanity has a minimal effect on the environment. They maintain that the earth is resilient and has rebounded from much worse treatment than it presently receives. Ray and Guzzo believe that humans have been good stewards of the earth and possess the intellectual capability to clear up any past environmental mistakes.

As you read, consider the following questions:

1. In the opinion of Ray and Guzzo, what separates humans from other animals?
2. According to the authors, what effect does humanity have on the weather?
3. Why do Ray and Guzzo believe that environmentalists' efforts to clean up the environment are counterproductive?

As we approach the twenty-first century, we're given more than ever to reflecting upon what our society is all about, what our country means, what modern civilization has achieved, and, most of all, what the future promises to bring.

Our nation, which, to me, is the greatest the human race has conceived, is just a bit more than 200 years old. We can expect an endless supply of problems; some people have doubts about our science, our technology, and the way we use our knowledge. We have some hopes and many fears. We must wonder a little about our age. How old are we, anyway?

The Thinking Animal

Human society has been around a long time, but recorded history goes back only about 6,000 years. The earth has been around between four and five billion years, and every generation of human beings that lives on it thinks its problems are the worst and that humankind has never faced such difficulties before. Most of us believe that unless we solve our problems now, all will be lost.

It's sobering to dwell upon how long humans have survived in a frequently hostile environment. We don't have claws, talons, or fangs. We have no barbs or poison glands to protect ourselves. We don't even have any fur or feathers to keep us warm when the ambient temperature drops; indeed, in our birthday suits, we are ill-adapted to live anywhere, except in the rather warm tropics. Our eyesight is not so good as that of most birds; our hearing is less keen than that of almost all of the higher animals; and our sense of smell is nothing compared to that of most fish and mammals. We can be outrun on land and outswum in the seas.

Yet, with all these difficulties, we've made it somehow. We have managed to penetrate every ecological niche, and we are able to survive in every environmental climate and condition anywhere on earth.

No other species of higher life can do so. You don't find polar bears swimming in a tropical sea; cactus does not grow in a rain forest. Plants and animals have their own ecological and environmental niches, and they are restricted to them. What, then, are our advantages?

First, we have a brain—a brain the likes of which is not seen in any other higher animal. That brain is capable of abstract thought; that brain can solve problems. We have developed a means of communication through human language that so far exceeds communication among other animals as to be in a completely different category. We are learning a good deal more about animal language and animal communication, but to compare even that of the higher primates or of whales and dolphins to the language capabilities of human beings is to overlook the enormous diversity of expression, the implications and nuances of words in the thousands of languages that exist among human beings. Abstract thought and language lead to systematized thinking, which leads to learning, the highest activity human beings engage in.

Learning and teaching, the buildup of knowledge, the questioning of truth, the development of philosophical systems, the practical applications of ideas—these are the things that distinguish humans from all other living things. When we join thoughts, speech, and learning to the peculiar capability to walk on two legs—thus freeing our arms—and the development of dextrous hands, we have a physical form that is truly remarkable in the animal kingdom. These gifts give us the ability to manufacture tools and gadgets of all kinds. They give us the ability to create engines and machines that utilize non-living energy, making the muscle power of slaves and beasts of burden unnecessary in modern society.

It is through our technology that we have been able to fly far away from earth to learn, in truth, how precious it is. It is no coincidence that our awakening to the special nature of our world and to its uniquely balanced environment and its limitations coincided with our first glimpse of earth from outer space, through the eyes of astronauts, television cameras, and photographic equipment. It was through technology that we saw ourselves as we really are, alone on one living, precious globe in space, a human family dependent on the resources of our minds and of our home planet, Earth.

Considering what we humans have accomplished, what we've done to build the modern high-tech society in which we live, and how we've swarmed across the land and changed its face—at least in the temperate region—some critics appear to be fearful that we are now about to destroy nature itself.

Are they right?

A Renewable Planet

Without doubt, humans have been hard on the environment in many discrete places. Whenever mankind has cleared land to build a city or to farm or to manufacture something, the naturalness of nature has been changed. From a longer perspective, civilizations have come and gone since antiquity. Sometimes, in areas that were once inhabited and then abandoned, nature has taken over. On a shorter time scale, it has been demonstrated again and again that areas once despoiled by pollutants can return to being a healthy abode for many species.

True, humans can be and have been destructive, but humans also learn. The ways to live in harmony with nature while maintaining a comfortable, even high-tech, lifestyle are far better understood today. And more and more they are being practiced. There is no reason to believe that, inevitably, everything will get worse.

But activist environmentalists charge that man has gone beyond having an effect on the immediate vicinity of his activities and is now damaging the entire planet. They say man's industrial activities are changing the composition of the atmosphere, presumably irreversibly, through increased production of CO_2 and other greenhouse gases. As already pointed out, until the predictions of human-caused, global atmospheric alterations can be accepted as certain, there must be a satisfactory explanation for the increases in greenhouse gases 300 years ago, 150,000 years ago, and in the geological past. And it must be established that the ozone-destroying chloride ion really does, in fact, come from CFCs [chlorofluorocarbons] and not from any of a number of natural sources.

In the light of the enormous size of the atmosphere and the hydrosphere, and the colossal natural forces involved, it would appear that man's puny activities are being vastly exaggerated.

The fact is that weather will be what it is and that man's influence, if any, is trivial and relatively local. In the long term, climates, too, will change, as they have done in the past, determined not by man but by immense natural forces. Neither the sun nor the earth is immortal. Each will grow old and die. Inevitably, the sun will burn itself out, slipping first into that stage called a "red giant," where its size will become so huge that it will encompass the inner planets. Our earth will be swallowed up and cease to exist. Fortunately for us, the time scale for this is fairly long—about two billion years or so from now. That gives us a pretty good cushion of time to become better stewards of the environment. We are not ever going to control it on a worldwide scale.

Environmentalism

Still, there are those who believe that we are threatening earth with intolerable stresses, born of just exactly those same things that have made us unique—human knowledge and technology. This belief finds expression in the modern environmental movement.

Now aside from unrivaled success in obtaining favorable publicity for its positions, how is it that environmentalism became so successful? Part of the answer is fairly clear. There were two essential ingredients. One was national legislation that gave the activists access to the federal courts and standing before the law (the National Environmental Protection Act). [Since 1975,] more than 100 environmental laws have been passed. The other was the creation of many governmental agencies, including the Environmental Protection Agency, the Occupational Safety and Health Administration (OSHA), and the Nuclear Regulatory Commission.

Environmentalism, as we have come to know it in the waning years of the twentieth century, is a new and complex phenomenon. It is new in the sense that it goes far beyond the traditional conservation movement—be kind to animals, support good stewardship of the earth, and so on—a philosophy of nature that we have known from the past. It is complex in that it incorporates a strongly negative element of anti-development, anti-progress, anti-technology, anti-business, anti-established institutions, and, above all, anti-capitalism. Its positive side, if that is what it can be called, is that it seeks development of a society totally devoid of industry and technology.

As a movement, it is activist, adversarial, punitive, and coercive. It is quick to resort to force, generally through the courts or through legislation, although some of its more zealous adherents engage in physical violence (Earth First! and Greenpeace, for example). Finally, the environmentalist movement today has an agenda that goes far beyond a mere concern for nature, as shown by its links to and common cause with other leftist radical movements—such as are incorporated in the Green parties of Europe.

29

This is not to suggest that everyone who supports more responsible policies for cleaner air and water, who believes in restraining pollution, and who cares about how the earth's resources are used is a wild-eyed extremist. Far from it. The great majority of those who make up the membership of the Audubon Society, Sierra Club, National Wildlife Federation, Wilderness Society, Nature Conservancy, and countless other groups are fine, decent citizens. They are honest, honorable supporters of a good, clean environment and responsible human actions. However, the leaders of some of their organizations—such as the Natural Resources Defense Council, Friends of the Earth, Earth First!, Greenpeace, Government Accountability Project, Institute for Policy Studies, and many others—are determinedly leftist, radical, and dedicated to blocking industrial progress and unraveling industrial society.

Healthier by Far

In terms of what has been measured by the Environmental Protection Agency, the environment is healthier than it used to be by far. Pollution has diminished in fairly direct proportion to the amount of money spent to diminish it.

Ben Wattenberg, *The Washington Times*, November 2, 1989.

These activist leaders and spokesmen are referred to as "political environmentalists" to distinguish them from the rest of us, who believe that using scientific data, not scare tactics, is the correct way to deal with environmental issues.

Modern environmentalism arose in response to real and widely recognized problems, among them: growing human pressures on natural resources, accumulation of wastes, and increased pollution of land, air, and water. Remember, for example, accounts from Cleveland about the alarming condition of the Cuyahoga River, which flows through the heart of Cleveland's industrial corridor into Lake Erie and was once called the world's most polluted river. So many gallons of industrial and chemical waste, oil, and other flammables had been dumped into it over the years that the river actually caught fire and blazed for a time. The Cuyahoga has since been cleaned up, and so has Lake Erie.

Without question, by the 1960s it was time to curb the excesses of a throwaway society. It was time to face up to the fact that there simply wasn't any "away" to throw things any more; "vacant" land and open space were limited. It was also time to recognize that there is a human tendency to overuse a good product, whether it's a vitamin, antibiotic, fertilizer, pesticide, or wilderness. It was time to redress many environmental wrongs. But, perhaps inevitably, the movement has gone beyond correcting past abuses and now poses real obstacles to industrial and technological progress.

Leave Well Enough Alone

Under the slogan of protecting the environment, political environmentalists now oppose and cause delay in the construction of important facilities, even those that are obviously necessary and have wide support. It is now next to impossible and certainly far more expensive than in the past to build a sewage treatment plant, garbage incinerators, a power plant, a dam, or to open a new landfill. Industrial facilities, even when they are expected to produce useful commodities, hardly fare better. Liability for anything that might go wrong and the threat of litigation are effective deterrents used by political environmentalists against industry.

After achieving so much—establishing government agencies with oversight authority and regulatory power, armed with such laws as the National Environmental Protection Act, the Clean Air Act, the Clean Water Act, the Waste Management Act, and more than 100 other environmental laws—environmentalist groups apparently cannot leave well enough alone. They seem to be unable to let these laws and statutory agencies work to continue the significant progress of the last two decades. Instead, they press for ever more stringent and punitive controls. They continue to push for and insist on an unachievable pristine perfection, whatever the cost. Never mind that humans never survived without altering nature.

It is a fact that effluents no longer pour unchecked from the stacks and chimneys and waste pipes of industry. Open hearth furnaces and other industrial processes that depend on burning fuel have been largely replaced by electric furnaces and much of our foundry and smelting capacity has been shut down. Open burning of garbage no longer occurs and discharge of untreated sewage and waste water is becoming rare. It is certainly illegal.

Responsible timber companies have revised their logging practices and more trees are growing now than 50 years ago, an increase of more than three and a half times since 1920. Reforestation is a usual, not an occasional, practice. Coupled with modern agricultural procedures that require less land for food production, we now have at least as much wooded and forested acreage in America as existed in Colonial times, and probably more. . . .

Humans cannot live on earth without altering it and without using natural resources. Our responsibility is to be good stewards of the environment and to remember that a well-tended garden is better than a neglected woodlot. It is demeaning beyond belief to consider mankind simply another species of animal, no better and no worse than wild beasts.

We human beings are what we are—imperfect but well-meaning and capable of improvement. We learn from mistakes. We have the ability to think rationally; and we should do so more often. We also have the gift to make conscious choices; and we should choose to pursue knowledge and understanding that will better the lot of all species on the planet.

A Struggle for Salvation

In Goethe's *Faust*, Faust, jaded with every conceivable worldly experience, finally finds, in a land reclamation project, the contentment that has eluded him all his life.

Now it may seem strange that Faust should find his greatest happiness in a prosaic engineering project. But in nineteenth century Europe, the clearing of swamps had clear human benefits. (Swamps had not been graduated to the status of "wetlands," and no environmental impact studies were required.) Faust's soul was saved, not because he reclaimed land, but because, in Goethe's immortal words, "whosoever, aspiring, struggles on, for him there is salvation."

In this sense and in the knowledge that we who believe in technology are engaged in the struggle to improve the lot of every human being, we can still share Goethe's enthusiasm and have a taste of Faust's salvation.

"Since the first Earth Day in 1970 most measures of U.S. ecological quality have improved, not declined."

The Environment Is Improving

Gregg Easterbrook

Most environmental writers predict a grim future for the planet Earth. They foresee increasing smog, deteriorating water quality, and an upsurge in environment-related illness. However, some commentators, like Gregg Easterbrook, envision a brighter future. In the following viewpoint, Easterbrook argues that major environmental improvements have been made in the last twenty years. He also claims that humanity's contribution to global pollution is not as great as most people believe. Easterbrook is a contributing editor at *Newsweek* and *The Atlantic Monthly.*

As you read, consider the following questions:

1. What reason does Easterbrook give for lower sulfur dioxide emissions?
2. According to the author, how does humanity's contribution to global warming compare to nature's contribution?
3. Why does Easterbrook question the effects of ozone depletion?

Gregg Easterbrook, "Everything You Know About the Environment Is Wrong," *The New Republic,* April 30, 1990. Reprinted with the author's permission.

The air and water are getting cleaner, not dirtier. Acid rain may be preventing global warming. Smog protects you from ozone depletion. Family farmers dump more chemicals than toxic waste sites. The "poisoning of America" is already over. Nature kills more species than humanity. The Third World is a greater threat to the ecology than the West. Some environmentalists actually long for the environment to get worse. Some business leaders want it to get better. OK, OK. That last taxes credence, though occasionally it's true. All the others are bang-on actual.

There is a growing sense that the only socially respectable attitude toward the environment is pushing the panic button. Fashionable alarmism may eventually create a Chicken Little backlash: as the years pass and nature doesn't end, people may stop listening when environmentalists issue warnings. The tough-minded case for environmental protection is ultimately more persuasive than the folk song and flowers approach. For liberals, being tough-minded means shedding some cherished preconceived notions, but it also means creating more rigorous arguments in favor of ecological respect as a human value, and, perhaps, of pointing the way toward finding humankind a constructive role in creation's scheme. Herewith a guide to what's really going on in the environment.

Acid Rain

After a decade of Reaganesque mumbling about further study and congressional Democratic stalling, action finally seems assured. (Democrats stalled because the high-sulfur coals that are the chief cause of acid rain come from underground mines staffed by the United Mine Workers; low-sulfur coals come mainly from non-union surface mines in the West.) The new Clean Air Act will reduce national sulfur dioxide emissions by about half and cut a related acid rain source, nitrogen oxide. Probably it will include a "cap" mandating that no matter how much future electricity production grows, total acid rain emissions may never exceed the new (reduced) level. This provision, brainchild of Environmental Protection Agency administrator William Reilly, is a far-reaching barrier against future new pollution.

Little-known note: in the past fifteen years national sulfur dioxide emissions have already fallen by about one-quarter even as coal use increased nearly fifty percent, owing to controls under the old Clean Air Act and to the construction of new power plants with superior technology. Second note: studies, including a ten-year, $500 million federal project, show acid rain effects to be considerably less than theory predicts. Only high-altitude red spruce trees, not forests generally, so far display acid rain damage; and though some enviros projected that a majority of

Eastern U.S. lakes would by now be too acidic for most life, the federal study found that only four percent have crossed this threshold. . . .

In the 1970s my first job as a journalist was with *Waste Age* (its real name), the trade magazine of the garbage industry. One of my first stories quoted various luminaries warning that a "garbage crisis" was about to strike. Fifteen years later it's still about to strike.

Improvements

In 1970, DDT was killing all ocean life. The population "bomb" was set to explode and worldwide famine was just around the corner. All across the country, colleges held massive "teach-ins" to save the earth. Earnest young men and women vowed they would bring no more children into an already overpopulated world.

Congress responded with legislation designed to protect the environment: the National Environmental Policy Act that mandated environmental-impact statements and an enhanced Clean Air Act that set superstrict emission standards for private automobiles. These laws have on the whole helped the environment: over the years, emissions of major noxious pollutants have decreased, rivers and lakes have been cleaned up and industries have become more aware of the effects of pollution.

Fred Singer, *Newsweek*, September 14, 1987.

Except in a few densely populated cities, it's nutty to maintain that a country as vast as America is "running out" of space for landfills. There is room to landfill our trash till the Lord's return. What we are running out of is willingness to tolerate landfills. That's as it should be. Though landfills can be built with reasonable environmental safety, they are fundamentally bad ideas: enablers of an irresponsible attitude toward resource consumption. What are responsible alternatives? Enviros say recycling. Supposedly it's about to take off. Fifteen years ago I wrote story after story saying recycling was about to take off.

Grumps maintain that recycling is a fraud, noting that more recycled newsprint is already available than processors will buy. But don't markets always take time to develop? There's no reason the United States can't eventually recycle a quarter of its trash, considering that the advanced economy of Japan recycles more. Though separation of aluminum cans and newspaper, the two most viable recycling commodities, is a big pain for homeowners, it's a good idea for society.

But recycling won't ever solve all disposal problems; and reductions in the packaging content of products aren't going to make more than a tiny nick in the problem. Municipal waste is probably best managed with a combination of moderate recycling, waste-to-energy plants burning the bulk of the trash, and some landfills (there's no scheme that eliminates them) for ash from the burners. . . .

Global Warming

Data are dueling over two aspects of this subject: whether warming has already been detected, and whether computers can project temperatures for the next century. Widescale climate effects are so little understood that there are currently scientific debates on matters as basic as whether warming would cause increased rainfall or drought; whether plants would flourish in more carbon dioxide or gag on the stuff.

There's even a faction that thinks global warming might be acceptable. Under this theory, my hometown of Buffalo would become a vacation paradise. The United Nations Intergovernmental Panel on Climate Change, the same outfit George Bush was blasted for failing to deliver a doomsday speech to, has estimated that a world warming of 3.5 degrees Fahrenheit would increase agricultural output in the Soviet Union by forty percent and in China by twenty percent (currently chill latitudes would suddenly have growing seasons), while aiding reforestation worldwide. One IPCC committee projected that on balance gains in agriculture and forest growth would outweigh losses of coastal areas owing to sea-level rises.

Perhaps the most important question, raised by Pat Michaels of the University of Virginia, is why the industrial era's output of greenhouse gas hasn't yet triggered runaway heat.

One possibility is that scientific understanding of the greenhouse effect is fundamentally mistaken. Another is that nature's climate control systems are more resilient than currently assumed. Nature manages greenhouse gases by having carbon dioxide inhaled by plants and absorbed by ocean life; research increasingly suggests that biologically moderated greenhouse cycles help keep Earth's climate steady and temperate. Plant decay, volcanic seepage, and other natural processes annually add about 200 billion tons of carbon dioxide to the atmosphere; human activity accounts for 7 billion tons, perhaps a small enough amount that nature can for the moment handle it.

A third possibility is that we haven't reached the greenhouse tipping point. Environmentalists urgently warn that atmospheric carbon dioxide has increased by twenty-five percent in the last century, which sounds like a guarantee of woe. They don't add that the carbon dioxide background level is about 290 parts per million (0.029 percent), so that even a huge relative increase in carbon dioxide has little absolute effect on the amount in the air.

Next, it's possible a greenhouse would be occurring but is being held in check by some other influence. One candidate is "smog block." Industrial activity has put lots of smudgy pollutants into the air, which may be blocking some of the sunlight that would otherwise reach the ground—a kind of nuclear frost. Evidence to support this view comes from data suggesting that temperatures in the Northern Hemisphere, where the industrial activity is, have not risen, while those in the Southern Hemisphere have. Emissions from volcanic activity, up recently, might also be creating a natural block.

Or maybe warming is being temporarily inhibited by the oceans, whose enormous mass tends to smooth out global temperature swings. Since the middle decades of this century were chilly, this line holds, the oceans cooled; now they are giving up their coolness by drawing extra heat from the air, and once they become warm—look out.

Then there is the incredibly annoying possibility that acid rain prevents global warming. Thomas Wigley and other scientists have produced studies suggesting that aerosol particles of sulfur dioxide increase the "albedo," or reflectivity, of Earth's cloud layer, causing more solar heat to bounce back into space. If this theory is correct, acid rain reductions without greenhouse gas control might backfire.

Finally, it's possible that global temperatures can be skewed in either direction by small variations in the output of the sun. Our star is nearing the peak of an unusual sunspot cycle; whether that has any relationship to its energy production, no one knows. In fact precious little is known about the internal processes of the sun. A paper by the astronomer-SDI [Strategic Defense Initiative] salesman Robert Jastrow suggesting that solar variability is the driving force in climate change has had considerable influence in the Bush White House. . . .

A Healthy Nation

Though environmentalists predicted it would get much, much worse, U.S. public health has shown steady improvement in recent decades. AIDS aside, incidence of stroke, heart disease, and hypertension have declined while the life expectancy continues to lengthen. A revealing statistic is that if the mortality rates from 1940 applied to 1988, 4 million Americans would have passed on in 1989. Instead, 2.2 million died. This represents a spectacular net public health improvement occurring during the very period when the manufacture and use of toxic chemicals, dangerous machines, and nuclear materials expanded exponentially.

Considering that gross industrial pollution was far worse in the past than it is today, if the repeatedly predicted pollution-induced health crisis were going to occur, it should already be in evidence: a huge demographic cohort of Americans exposed to gross pollution from the turn of the century through the 1960s having reached the point in life where disease is typical. Yet the age-adjusted incidence of cancer has increased only slightly. Would public health have improved even more with greater environmental regulation? Almost certainly. This, in fact, is the best argument for substantial new investments in pollution control. . . .

No one has ever been killed by a nuclear power plant in the U.S. Using coal for electric power annually condemns to death 101 U.S. miners, the average for the last decade; the mining leaves huge gashes in the Earth. Nuclear generators emit no greenhouse gases, acid rain, or smog; they displace fossil fuels, which we ought to be conserving for our grandchildren.

Nuclear power has many problems. But this is a reason to shut down the bad plants, not to oppose new, technically improved facilities, with passive-safety and waste-reducing features. The cost of nuclear plants may soon be reduced by an overdue shift on the part of American manufacturers to standard modular designs, rather than making every installation one of a kind.

Waste remains an indelible concern. Even Energy Secretary James Watkins, an old nuclear hard-liner, has said that because of waste, contemporary fission reactors are only acceptable as a transitional power source, till alternatives like fusion or perhaps solar energy collected in space become available in the next century. In theory, fusion reactors could burn seawater, producing almost no byproducts; space solar power could be entirely benign. So how about this for a compromise liberal position on nuclear power: live with fission reactors till we know for sure about the greenhouse effect, or something better comes along.

Ozone Depletion

It's real. Even Margaret Thatcher, whose high-latitude nation lies near the North Pole ozone breach, is worried. Stratospheric ozone screens out ultraviolet radiation, which can cause skin cancer and birth defects. Satellite data show that ozone over Antarctica seasonally declines forty percent or more compared with a decade ago. Unanswered is: What does this mean? First, it's far from proven that the current degree of ozone depletion harms anyone. Holes have only been observed over the poles, where there's hardly any life anyway; and it's not clear that even the UV [ultraviolet radiation] at the poles reaches a level that is dangerous, though some researchers think this will be proved eventually. *Nature* published a study suggesting that regardless of what the ozone layer is doing, observed UV levels at the ground have declined in recent years.

Second, though CFCs [chlorofluorocarbons] unquestionably create a breakdown product that depletes ozone, it's not yet proved they are solely responsible for the holes. Little is known about natural ozone cycles. The destructive CFC by-product is chlorine; natural emissions of chlorine (mainly from volcanos) far exceed artificial quantities. For technical reasons CFC chlorine is more likely to reach the stratosphere than chlorine from volcanos. But with world volcanic activity up in recent years, there may be some relationship between that and the sudden holes.

Cleaner Lakes and Rivers

America has made demonstrable progress against water pollution. In the late sixties, lakes were choked with algae, and rivers stank with the carcasses of fish that had been killed by chemicals; one of the era's most potent symbols was an industrial pipe discharging poison into a river. Then, in 1972, Congress passed the Clean Water Act, which blocked many of those pipes, and thousands of rivers, streams and lakes are appreciably cleaner. Among other things, Lake Erie is no longer a virtual cesspool, and even some urban rivers, such as the Potomac, near Washington, D.C., are again safe for swimming in many sections.

Betsy Carpenter, *The State of the Earth*, April 1990.

Third, there may be a solar ozone cycle. Stratospheric ozone is thought to be made when solar energies (including the very ultraviolet radiation we want blocked) strike normal two-atom oxygen molecules, converting them to three-atom ozone variations. Do sun output changes create ozone depletion and restoration cycles? Nobody knows.

This said, humanity can ban CFCs but it can't plug volcanos. The Western nations are committed to a fifty percent reduction of CFC manufacturing by the year 2000. (A bigger deal across the Atlantic since European countries never banned CFCs as a spray-can propellant, as the United States did twenty years ago.) [In 1989] Bush said he would seek a total CFC halt, though he has yet to introduce legislation to this effect. Du Pont, the principal CFC manufacturer, says it will cease production by 2000, offering a new substitute. If CFCs someday prove not to be the ozone villain, we can always go back to them. . . .

Concern about synthetic pesticides is now well out of proportion, though it's easy to see why this happened, since memories remain fresh of DDT and other "hard" pesticides that did enormous damage before being banned. The public seems to have forgotten that most pesticides are there for legit reasons: increasing yields so food is cheap, killing off microbes that otherwise would make consumers sick. Those stories about people getting ill from what they bought at the health food store are no joke. That said, it's crazy not to ban any suspect food chemical that

39

does not have some strong compensating virtue. Alar was an easy choice—who cares if apples are shiny red or only sorta red? Others may be tricky. In the wake of the Alar flap the EPA also banned EDBC, a common fungicide that causes cancer in lab animals. The lowly fungus produces most of nature's deadliest poisons and carcinogens—aflatoxin and a list of others. The net carcinogen content of the U.S. food supply may increase as a result of the EDBC decision.

One positive sign is that the trend in pesticide chemistry is toward compounds that can be used in small quantities ("microdose" pesticides), have narrow ranges of toxicity, and lose their potency rapidly. Great promise is held by the fledgling science of altering plants so that they do not require pesticides. If you're horrified by the thought of genetic engineering, bear in mind that one of its likely first effects on society is a reduction in food chemicals.

Pollution Scorecard

Since the first Earth Day in 1970 most measures of U.S. ecological quality have improved, not declined. Direct industrial water pollution is down significantly; the Great Lakes and some other water bodies are recovering. (Groundwater pollution is more of a question.) Though old toxic waste dumps identified under the Superfund program continue to bedevil everyone, creation of new dumps has essentially ceased—an easily overlooked accomplishment. Development of wetlands has slowed; growth, in general, is less likely to come at the expense of land or vistas better preserved. Airborne sulfur and particulates, the two leading varieties of air pollution in 1970, have fallen sharply; lead, the worst atmospheric poison, has nearly disappeared from the U.S. sky; though smog, an index of American prosperity as measured by per capita auto ownership, has increased slightly, the rate of increase is below that of the increase in autos and economic output, indicating that with further effort smog can be bested, too. . . .

Though commentators often claim human abuses cause aspects of the environment to be "destroyed," nearly every environmental mistake is reversible—except extinction. Sometimes reverses can come surprisingly fast. Lake Erie and the Thames River, both pronounced "dead" in the 1960s, are already nearly thriving again merely through moderate pollution control. The bald eagle may be taken off the endangered species list a decade after many said there was no hope of averting extinction. Within ten years it should be impossible to determine where the *Exxon Valdez* spill even occurred. Whenever the ecology is pronounced "destroyed" by a transitory event, bear in mind nature is an elaborately defended fortress that has been repelling assaults for four billion years.

40

"There is inescapable evidence that the massive national effort to restore the quality of the environment has failed."

The Environment Is Deteriorating

Barry Commoner

Barry Commoner is one of America's leading commentators on environmental issues. He currently directs the Center for the Biology of Natural Systems at Queens College in Flushing, New York and is the author of several books, including *Science and Survival*. In the following viewpoint, Commoner argues that instead of improving, the environment has actually worsened since the first Earth Day in 1970. He writes that the well-intended laws since then have had little success in cleaning up the environment. Commoner cites numerous tests and studies that indicate a rise in air and water contamination.

As you read, consider the following questions:

1. In Commoner's opinion, how does smog affect health?
2. What does the author say is chiefly responsible for water contamination?
3. According to Commoner, which chemicals were found in the Environmental Protection Agency's study of human fat?

If the environmental crisis is generated by the clash between the ecosphere and the technosphere, it becomes imperative that we learn how they interact and what can be done to harmonize them. A useful way to analyze such a relationship is to alter one of the interacting systems and then observe what changes occur in the other. Such a test has, in fact, been carried out in the United States and a number of other countries on a grand scale for the last twenty years. Beginning in 1970, numerous measures were adopted to improve the quality of the environment. Major components of the technosphere —automobiles, power plants, and petrochemical factories— were changed; they were required to adopt control devices in order to reduce their impact on the ecosphere. A good deal can be learned, therefore, by examining the ecological improvement generated by these technological alterations. Such a review has the secondary benefit of evaluating the effectiveness of the movement that has urged this campaign. The modern environmental movement is old enough now—its birth can also be dated from the enthusiastic outburst of Earth Day in April 1970— to be accountable for its successes and failures. Having made a serious claim on public attention and the nation's resources, the movement's supporters and the responsible government agencies cannot now evade the troublesome, potentially embarrassing question: What has been accomplished?. . .

Air Pollution

Information about the trends in air pollution is available from annual reports published by the Environmental Protection Agency (EPA) since 1975. (Data earlier than 1975 tend to be unreliable because measurements were not standardized.) The reports describe changes in the emissions and local concentrations of the major airborne pollutants: particulates (dust), sulfur dioxide, lead, nitrogen oxides, volatile organic compounds, and ozone, a key ingredient of photochemical smog. . . .

Photochemical smog is a complex mixture, created when nitrogen oxides emitted from automobile exhausts and power plants are converted by sunlight into highly reactive molecules that then combine with waste fuel and other hydrocarbons to form ozone and other noxious chemicals. The total emissions of nitrogen oxides *increased* by 2 percent between 1975 and 1987. Ozone is not emitted as such but is formed in the air during the smog reactions.

The noxious smog chemicals are responsible for serious health hazards; people with heart or respiratory problems are routinely warned to stay indoors during "smog alerts." This hazard is now more or less accepted as an apparently unavoidable aspect of urban life. In some places, improvements in smog levels have been achieved by reducing traffic. Yet smog continues to threaten health. For example, in Los Angeles, the worst-afflicted city, between 1973 and 1977 residents were subjected each year to an average of 250 days on which smog was at levels classified as "unhealthful"; 150 days were classified as "very unhealthful." In most U.S. cities, residents are still exposed to unhealthful smog levels for 50 to 150 days each year. On sunny, windless days the telltale brown haze of smog can be seen hanging in the air over nearly every American city. Smog is a continuing hazard to the health of urban residents.

Joel Pett/*The Lexington Herald-Leader.* Reprinted with permission.

One of the consequences of the unsolved problems of air pollution is acid rain. In keeping with the ecological law "Everything has to go somewhere," once emitted into the air, sulfur dioxide and nitrogen oxides are picked up by rain and snow and brought down to earth in the form of sulfate and nitrate. Both of these substances increase acidity, and in recent years, many lakes, especially in the northeastern United States and Canada, as well as in Europe, have become more acid. In some of these lakes, there have been serious biological changes, often involving the virtual elimination of fish populations. Forest growth has been reduced by acid rain. In cities acid rain erodes buildings and monuments. . . .

In the last decade, particular rivers and lakes here and there have been cleaned up to a degree by closing sources of pollution and building new sewage treatment plants. Yet in that period, nationally, there has been little or no overall improvement in the levels of the five standard pollutants that determine water quality: fecal coliform bacteria, dissolved oxygen, nitrate, phosphate, and suspended sediments. A U.S. Geological Survey report on the trends in pollution levels between 1974 and 1981 at nearly four hundred locations on major American rivers shows that there has been no improvement in water quality at more than four-fifths of the tested sites. For example, the levels of fecal coliform bacteria decreased at only 15 percent of the river stations, and increased at 5 percent. At half the locations, the bacterial count was too high to permit swimming, according to the standard recommended by the National Technical Advisory Committee on Water Quality Criteria. Levels of dissolved oxygen, suspended sediments, and phosphorus improved at 13 to 17 percent of the locations, but deteriorated at 11 to 16 percent of them. The most striking change—for the worse—was in nitrate levels: increases were observed at 30 percent of the test stations and decreases at only 7 percent. Agricultural use of nitrogen fertilizer is a main source of this pollutant; in rivers that drain cropland, the number of sampling stations that report rising nitrate levels is eight times the number reporting falling levels. Another major source is nitrogen oxides emitted into the air by vehicles and power plants and deposited in rain and snow as nitrate; this accounts for increased river nitrate levels in the Northeast, despite the relative scarcity of heavily fertilized acreage in that area. The survey also shows that there was a sharp increase in the occurrence of two toxic elements, arsenic and cadmium (a cause of lung and kidney damage), in American rivers between 1974 and 1981; but, as expected from the reduced automotive emissions, the occurrence of lead declined.

Average Trends

An overall assessment of the changes in these standard measures of water quality can be gained from the average trends. For the five standard pollutants, the frequency of improving trends averaged 13.2 percent; but the frequency of deteriorating trends averaged 14.7 percent; thus, at more than four-fifths of the test sites, overall water quality deteriorated or remained the same. In sum, the regulations mandated by the Clean Water Act, and more than $100 billion spent to meet them, have failed to improve water quality in most rivers. A few places have improved, but more have deteriorated. Moreover, the presence of at least three serious pollutants—nitrate, arsenic, and cadmium—has increased considerably. Nor is there any evidence in these data that pollution levels will improve; like the effort to clean up the air, the campaign to reduce river pollution has stalled, after reaching only a very modest level of success. . . .

Groundwater

About 50 percent of the population of the United States depends on underground sources of water—groundwater—for its drinking water. The U.S. Geological Survey and state agencies monitor the quality of groundwater by testing wells throughout the country. The results based on testing more than 100,000 wells show that in the past twenty-five years these sources are becoming increasingly polluted by nitrate and toxic chemicals. Fertilizer is chiefly responsible for the rising nitrate levels. In Nebraska a 1983 survey showed that 82 percent of the wells over the nitrate limit established by health authorities (10 milligrams per liter of nitrogen in the form of nitrate) were contaminated by fertilizer nitrogen. In California's Sacramento Valley, a very heavily farmed area, nitrate contamination of wells has been followed for a long time. In the fifty-year period following 1912, the percentage of wells with excessive nitrate (defined as 5.5 milligrams of nitrogen per liter) approximately doubled. More recently, the percentage of wells with excessive nitrate doubled again—this time in only a four-year period, between 1974 and 1978. The major source of the nitrate is nitrogen fertilizer leaching from irrigation water. A similar trend has been observed in Iowa.

Global Problems

The environmental crisis of the 1990s overwhelms that of the 1970s. From Chernobyl radiation to the Alaskan oil spill, from tropical rain forest destruction to polar ozone holes, from Alar in apples to toxins in water, the earth and all its life are in trouble. Industrial production accentuated by the global reproduction of population has severely strained Gaia's [Earth's] capacity for regeneration. Pollution and depletion are systematically linked on a global scale not previously experienced on the planet.

Carolyn Merchant, *Tikkun*, March/April 1990.

In 1984 the U.S. Geological Survey summarized the situation: "Current trends suggest that nitrate accumulations in ground water of the United States will continue to increase in the future." Clearly, we have failed to solve this environmental problem, which grows worse with time. . . .

The total toxic chemical problem is huge. According to the EPA Toxic Release Inventory, U.S. industry emits about 20 bil-

45

lion pounds of toxic chemicals annually into the environment. However, according to Congress's Office of Technology Assessment, because of underreporting and the omission of data from small establishments, this figure is very uncertain and is more likely to be about 400 billion pounds. Only about 1 percent of the chemical industry's toxic waste is actually destroyed. The chemical industry, its emissions of toxic substances largely unrestrained, has become the major threat to environmental quality.

Unfortunately, unlike standard air and water pollutants, there are no periodic estimates made of the levels of toxic pollutants in the environment; indirect evidence indicates that the trend is upward. . . .

Recently, new concerns have been raised about the impact of chemical contamination on the safety of the nation's food supply, especially for children. Since the toxic chemicals emitted into the environment occur in air, drinking water, and food, they readily enter the human body. Most of them are especially soluble in fat and therefore tend to accumulate in fatty components of the body. The EPA adipose tissue survey tested for the presence of thirty-seven toxic compounds—all of them synthetic products of the petrochemical industry. All but four of the compounds were found, generally in about two-thirds or more of the fat samples tested. Prominent among the detected substances are carcinogens such as benzene and chloroform. . . .

A Memorial to Failure

The summer of 1988 was a kind of memorial to the failure of the nation's environmental program. Smog reached unprecedented levels; on the East Coast, numerous beaches were closed by an influx of sewage debris and medical waste; the emergence of the pollution of Boston Harbor as an election issue was added evidence that a problem as old and fundamental as sewage disposal remained unsolved; everywhere in the country, communities struggled with the trash disposal problem, as landfills were closed and costs mounted; and the record-breaking heat was an alarming reminder that nothing has been done to combat the potential greenhouse effect.

In sum, the Congress has mandated massive environmental improvement; the EPA has devised elaborate, detailed means of achieving this goal; most of the prescribed measures have been carried out, at least in part; and in nearly every case, the effort has failed to even approximate the goals. In both the columns of statistics and everyday experience, there is inescapable evidence that the massive national effort to restore the quality of the environment has failed.

"The most profound consequence of the environmental crisis is the epidemic rise in the incidence of cancer."

Environmental Pollution Causes Cancer

James Morton

For most people, pollution becomes real when it affects their health and longevity. Cancer is often the greatest concern. Many health experts and research scientists contend that cancer rates have risen considerably in the last twenty years due to the environmental crisis. In the following viewpoint, author James Morton argues that the epidemic rise in cancer rates stems from manufactured chemicals. Morton writes that toxins, particularly those from petrochemicals, accumulate in human fat tissue and cause cancer. He warns that nursing mothers' milk is especially contaminated.

As you read, consider the following questions:

1. According to Morton, why are petrochemicals carcinogenic?
2. In the author's opinion, what causes petrochemical compounds to accumulate in human fat tissue?
3. Why does Morton write that nursing mothers are particularly vulnerable to toxins?

James Morton, "The Cancer Epidemic: Part 1," *Against the Current,* July/August 1990. Reprinted with permission.

In the United States the most profound consequence of the environmental crisis is the epidemic rise in the incidence of cancer. This epidemic indicates more than an ever-increasing occurrence of a fatal disease; it indicates that the body chemistry is being so disrupted by environmental toxins that our abilities to resist disease and reproduce healthy children are also failing. Cancer is for us what hunger is for the people of El Salvador, the cutting edge of the survival issue. It is *our* revolutionary issue. . . .

Petrochemicals and Cancer

Cancer is a disorder in the process of cellular reproduction, propelled to epidemic rates by the introduction into the environment of new agents which disrupt that process. Cellular reproduction is the signature process of a living creature. In a human it is the reproduction of arterial walls, blood, nerve cells, organ tissue, skin, sperm or ova, and the genetic material that will determine the physical evolution of humanity. It is also the reproduction of the body's defense against "foreign" invaders: the immune system, that "complex network of specialized organs and cells. . .which equals in complexity the intricacies of the brain and nervous system" and whose success depends on an "incredibly elaborate and dynamic regulatory-communications network. Millions and millions of cells, organized into sets and subsets, pass information back and forth like clouds of bees swarming around a hive," [according to the National Institutes of Health].

The success of the immune system or the reproduction of organ tissue relies on chemical messages which originate within the nucleus of each cell. Petrochemicals are capable of penetrating the protective membrane of the cell wall and causing a rewrite of the message by which the twin strands of DNA (basic genetic material) coiled within the cell direct its reproduction.

A petrochemical that is capable of scrambling the cellular message to cause some of the cells that reproduce the tissue of the liver, testes or ovaries to run amok and produce a cancerous tumor can also damage the genetic material that was being passed to future generations, cause sterility, miscarriages, birth defects and a weakened immune system which can itself lead to cancer. This same chemical may also influence the biochemical mechanisms that are part of thinking, making love and feeling good. An epidemic of cancer is indicative of a failure in the life process. . . .

Our Toxic World

Residents of industrial cities "live under a bubble of toxic gasses," [states Dr. Samuel Epstein, a University of Chicago cancer researcher]. Those who enjoy a more bucolic existence inhale a wide range of dioxin compounds via the incineration of municipal garbage. Even arctic wildlife is contaminated by airborne petrochemicals. A single carrot may have five different pesticide residues on it, a tomato three, and a meal of a salad, baked potato, greenbeans and meat will contain a hundred or more different petrochemicals and synthetic hormones, most of which were introduced to nature in the last twenty years.

The typical American city's water supply is contaminated by a thousand or more organic compounds. When you bathe you breathe chemicals in the water vapor and absorb them through your skin. Hundreds of billions of pounds of these chemicals are dumped into our environment each year and one way or another they move into the sea, the source of all terrestrial life.

© 1987 Joel Pett/*Lexington Herald-Leader.* Reprinted with permission.

Petrochemical compounds also accumulate throughout the human body. They can do this because they are produced from oil and thus have a carbon base and the ability to bond with other carbon-based compounds. The cellular structure of any life form has a carbon base, but because these compounds are oil soluble they have a particular affinity for an oily substance such as human fat. The highest concentrations are found in fat tissue or the part of breast milk that is richest in fat. As the National Adipose Tissue Survey shows, you can determine a person's approximate age and geographic residence by the range and volume of contaminants found in fat tissue. They are also routinely found in blood, urine and semen.

The cancer epidemic then is not a discrete process, simply one of many fatal diseases, but an unequivocal signal that the life process of humanity is failing. Every aspect of our environment becomes each day more saturated with the agents of our extinction. What we see is an unsustainable accumulation of quantitative change: too many poisons in the environment, too much poison in our flesh, too much cancer. We can anticipate a qualitative change long before simple quantity overwhelms us. The evidence and the political imperative are clear.

Modern Contaminants

Arsenic, asbestos, radiation and various heavy metals have all been causing cancer since at least the turn of the century and today they are killing a lot of people. But there is only one event, one aspect of the modern environment that is capable of propelling an epidemic of cancer: the *petrochemical transformation of the world economy* begun after the Second World War.

Chemicals that were by-products of petroleum refining began to be substituted for fertility, genetic resistance and labor in agriculture and forestry; and for wood, steel, hemp, rubber, cotton, glass, wool, natural oils and labor in manufacturing. In 1940 annual production of petrochemicals in the United States was 1 billion pounds, by the 1950s the figure was 30 billion, by 1960 it was 100 billion, and today over 400 billion pounds are produced each year.

Cancer really occurs as a series of small epidemics, most often bound in place and time to the production and use of petrochemicals. While everyone in the United States is more likely to contract cancer at a variety of sites than ten years ago, the working class bears the brunt of the cancer epidemic. The highest rates occur among folk who live around the places where organic compounds are manufactured, dumped or applied and among the workers who make them or employ them and their children.

There is a close relationship: the workers who use the chemicals the most or the people who live closest to the dump suffer the very worst. New Jersey, capital's environment of the future, sports the nation's highest cancer mortality rates, ranging from 50% above normal to 150% in the counties with densest concentration of petrochemical waste. Another geographic analysis finds excess of all sorts but particularly of the bladder, liver, and lung in the 139 counties where the chemical industry is most concentrated.

Herbicides and Cancer

The epidemic of Non-Hodgkins Lymphoma, which is showing striking increases among the general population, is 60% more likely to occur among Kansas farmers who use the dioxin tainted phenoxy herbicides. If the farmers use it for more than twenty days per year, there is a 600% excess cancer rate. And if they mix and apply it as well as frequently use it—they suffer an 800% excess of lymphoma.

Children have their own type of occupational exposure, as their parents bring the chemicals from the workplace home on their clothes, skin, and in their breath. The risk of leukemia, which provides almost a third of the cancer aggregate for white children, is $3^{1}/_{2}$ times the national average for children whose fathers worked with chlorinated solvents, $4^{1}/_{2}$ times if the fathers worked with dyes or pigments and twice as high for those whose fathers worked with spray paints while their mother was pregnant with them. In each instance the risk grew with duration and intensity of exposure to the organic compounds.

To understand the relationship in time between petrochemicals and cancer, one must bear in mind that cancer is a disease which typically has a 15-30-year gestation period. Today's cancer rates are primarily responding to the conditions of the 1960s and early 1970s. Consequently, cancer among the working class today gives an indication of what will follow in the general population as the overall chemical contamination of the environment continues to accelerate. . . .

Human Mixing Bowls

Chemical reactions are not confined to the laboratory. They occur as organic compounds mix in water systems, fields, salad bowls, smokestacks and bodies. No one understands very much about the content or consequences of these interactions—particularly when they occur within the confines of our flesh. Cancer is also a poorly understood process. However, we know that it is a complex event often involving a combination of agents over a period of time. In humanity cancer occurs within a very diverse genetic pool and among a population that is consuming a wide variety of cancer-causing agents. Thus it is difficult to pinpoint a specific agent as causing a cancer at a certain body part in the general population.

The female breast is essentially fat tissue and milk glands. In the fat of everyone in the United States can be found at the very least PCBs, DDT, Chlordane, Heptachlor, Aldrin, DDE, BHC, Pentachlorophenol, and many of the compounds of the ultra toxic dioxins including PCDFs and the most toxic of all, TCDD.

The presence of the PCBs and dioxin compounds is particularly frightening. In a survey of human milk, blood and fat in Europe and the United States, Alan Jensen found that dozens of variations of these chemicals contaminated almost everyone, but TCDD had a preference for women. The residues were unbelievably small, about 2 parts per trillion (ppt); a ppt on a plane of 183 square miles would cover the area of a quarter.

51

However, when given to a pregnant mouse at 10 ppt, TCDD damages the fetus; rats develop excess cancers at 5 ppt and toxic effects are seen in the offspring of pregnant monkeys at 2.5 ppt.

Chemical Reactions

In any part of our body fat there is a continuing series of biochemical reactions, but unlike other sites where there are heavy accumulations of fat (such as the buttocks or upper thigh) the fat of the female breast surrounds the chemically complex milk-producing organs. Thus, within the breast there are the uncontrolled chemical reactions of what easily could be hundreds of organic compounds, the most toxic known to science, many mimicking or enhancing the effects of estrogen and interacting with the normal cellular reproduction of the milk glands. The potential extent of this interaction can be measured by the list of synthetic chemical poisons in the mother's milk.

"In an overall assessment it may be wrong to look at one contaminant at a time, because these organohalogens have similar targets in the body, indicating a potential for toxicological interactions" [according to researcher Alan Jensen].

Chemicals and Cancer

Cancer death rates have been increasing about 1 percent per year, and rates are highest in areas close to petrochemical plants, steel mills and metal refineries. Many put the blame on the rapid increase in production of synthetic, organic chemicals after World War II. Cancer strikes one in four Americans, and kills one in five.

Jay Berry, *People's Daily World*, October 28, 1988.

Women who breast-feed have, by a factor of about one-half, a lower incidence of breast cancer, with longer and more frequent periods of lactation making it less likely they will have that cancer. We know that when the mother lactates she expels many of the petrochemical poisons in her system at a higher rate than the rate at which she absorbs them from the environment. In one study the levels of PCBs and DDEs (a by-product of DDT) in breast milk dropped by 20% over six months and by 40% over 18 months.

Could women who breast-feed be less likely to develop cancer because they are expelling carcinogens from their systems into the rapidly developing nervous, immune and reproductive systems of their infants? The class structure of breast cancer rates in the Seattle-Puget Sound area reinforces that contention. There is a 53% rise among low-income women (those least likely to breast-feed), a 27% rise among middle-income women and no rise among upper-income women (the most frequent breast-feeders). Also the lower the income group the more likely the individual is to work around chemical poisons, live near where they are produced and to drink contaminated water.

An Epidemic Rise

Among dioxins, insect poisons, fungus poisons, high-temperature lubricants, weed killers mixing and reacting, who can say which carcinogen in what combination triggers this terrible reaction in women's flesh. But suddenly more women in the industrialized world have begun to develop cancer of the breast, and in their breasts we find chemicals introduced over the last forty years which are known to cause cancer in monkeys, rats, mice, gerbils, hamsters, dogs, fish and humans.

What an analysis of testicular and breast cancer shows is an unequivocal epidemic rise that marches in lockstep with the introduction of petrochemicals. The reproductive cycle is in imminent danger of becoming irreparably harmed, with sperm too heavily contaminated to create a fetus and women's breasts so toxic that babies cannot survive. The poisons in the mother's womb and milk—made worse by a contaminated food and water supply—endanger our survival as a species.

If we do not stop this process that moment will come. The cancer epidemic is the most important single issue for the First World; it represents the most pressing danger in our lives and the lives of our children.

"Every single bite of food we take is laced with pesticides brewed not in the laboratory of Monsanto, but in the laboratory of nature."

Environmental Pollution Does Not Cause Cancer

Nicolas S. Martin

Nicolas S. Martin is the executive director of the Consumer Health Education Council, a consumer advocacy group based in Cincinnati, Ohio. In the following viewpoint, Martin writes that health is not deteriorating because of pesticides and toxins. He contends that nature, not industry, produces 99 percent of all toxins.

As you read, consider the following questions:

1. In the author's opinion, what role did smoking have in the increased cancer rates of asbestos workers?
2. Why does Martin believe the benefits of ethylene dibromide outweigh its risks?
3. According to the author, what are some naturally produced toxins?

Nicolas S. Martin, "Environmental Myths and Hoaxes," speech given to B'nai B'rith Hillel Foundation in Houston, Texas, January 24, 1990. Reprinted with permission.

In the intervening two decades [since Earth Day 1970] we have been pounded relentlessly with stories of man's environmental depravity. Before images of spewing waste, oil-drenched birds, deformed infants, and poisoned fields, normal people are rendered mute and helpless (though the cacaphony of activists is never stilled). None but the most callous soul could fail to be humbled and moved by the trail of environmental sin.

Well, it's atonement time, and either I have grown a very hard callus on my soul, or the evidence of guilt is insufficient, because I'm no longer touched by the pleadings of the environmental evangelists, among whose numbers I was once included. When the ecological prophet of doom says that without your tax-deductible contribution the earth will perish, I am reminded of the evangelist up in that tower—where he could talk to God better—notifying the faithful that only their *donations* could prevent his tragic demise. Or the famous *National Lampoon* cover which said: "Buy this magazine or we'll shoot this dog."

As Earth Day II rolls around, the evangelist is still alive, the dog is probably no longer with us, through no fault of poor readership, and the planet Earth is a more congenial place for humanity than ever in history. Almost without exception, the doomsayers have been wrong, their prophecies flawed, and all of us the better for it.

Unjustified Scares

Allow me to offer some specifics.

First: The asbestos scare. Sadly, before we knew of the connection between certain types of asbestos and lung cancer, many shipyard workers and those applying insulation were exposed to large concentrations of the mineral. About thirty years after exposure, somewhere between 3,300 and 12,000 people are dying from the asbestos-induced cancer mesothelioma each year in the U.S. There has been a great deal of totally justified concern over this natural environmental tragedy. Unfortunately, it has also led to one of the most ridiculous and expensive public health hysterias in history.

Initially, it must be noted that a very high percentage of mesothelioma-afflicted people were also heavy cigarette smokers, which increases the asbestos cancer risk by more than 50 times. Smoking is such a critical co-factor that the *New England Journal of Medicine* reported that "it remains uncertain whether *any* type of asbestos acting alone can cause lung cancer in non-smokers."

Due to the workers' plight, though, concern was raised about the effects of asbestos exposure on the rest of us, especially those who work in buildings insulated with asbestos. Ralph Nader, the Sierra Club, and the Audubon Society, among others, convinced Congress and President Reagan to require an asbestos inspection of all school buildings in the United States. Many cities and states followed up with their own *even more* stringent requirements for asbestos inspection and removal. The reality is that America was driven berserk by asbestos, largely due to the perpetual wailing of environmentalists, and in direct contradiction of the facts.

No Comparison

Laboratory mice have a high spontaneous incidence of pulmonary tumors, leading many scientists to question the legitimacy of relying only on mouse data. Further, there is no reason to think that if massive doses of a chemical cause tumors in lab animals, then comparatively tiny doses will necessarily have a similar effect on some humans.

Michael Fumento, *The American Spectator*, August 1990.

In a single San Francisco school $18 million (the annual cost of about 300 teacher salaries) was spent on asbestos removal and repairs, an event duplicated first at school after school, and then including offices and malls. The same governments which legally required the use of asbestos as a public health measure were now demanding its removal.

This play will run for many years. The cost of asbestos abatement at New York's World Trade Center and La Guardia Airport will run to $1 billion. The total cost for removal in California's schools will probably exceed $1 billion. The cost of removing asbestos from the country's offices is estimated to run to $200 billion.

So what are we getting for our money? The answer is, virtually nothing.

Abnormal Exposure

Besides generally being smokers, the workers who contracted cancer were regularly exposed to concentrations of the mineral *100,000 to 1 million times higher* than the amount normally present in a building insulated with asbestos. The risk of fatality to people who work in buildings insulated with asbestos has been estimated by a commission of the Canadian government in the following way: "Even a building whose air has a fiber level up to 10 times greater than that found in typical outdoor air would create a risk of fatality that was less than one-fiftieth the risk of having a fatal accident while driving to and from the building." The authors went on to state, "We deem the risk which asbestos poses to building occupants to be insignificant and therefore

56

find that asbestos in building air will almost never pose a health hazard to occupants."

The New Jersey Asbestos Policy Committee reported to the governor in the midst of all of this fiasco, "There are no documented cases of lung cancer associated with low-level asbestos exposure over a lifetime." Definitively, the World Health Organization, after exhaustive analysis, concluded: "In the general population, the risks of mesothelioma and lung cancer attributable to asbestos cannot be quantified reliably and are probably undetectably low." The great asbestos scare is a hoax, and a big one, but only one of many.

In 1984, Americans were frightened out of their wits to learn that traces of the pesticide ethylene dibromide (EDB) was found in food products. The accusation was all too familiar. It causes cancer, the activists said—in rats.

EDB was used as a fumigant for protecting grains against contamination by molds and fungi and infestation by worms and insects. The only substitutes available were either known to be more toxic or had never been tested for carcinogenicity.

The amount of EDB found in foods was 10 to 100 times less carcinogenic than the dose of the natural chemical safrole present in a typical daily amount of black pepper. The amount of EDB being ingested by the average consumer was less than one-quarter millionth as much on a body-weight basis as was fed to the rats.

The Jim Bob Effect

Nevertheless, Americans were bamboozled by what I call the Jim Bob Effect. My friend Jim Bob is an ardent environmentalist; he thinks we are doing ourselves in with all of our chemicals and technology. He wants to turn back the clock.

Recently, Jim Bob bought a loaf of bread which, soon enough, was crawling with worms. Enraged, he wrote a letter to the manufacturer demanding to know why they would foist an infested loaf off on him. "I don't like my bread with worms," he barked. The Jim Bob Effect is when someone is so far removed, so ignorant, of food production, that he can—on the one hand —demand chemical-free food, and on the other hand become addled at the sight of a worm in his "preservative-free" bread.

I've seen the Jim Bob Effect many times in health food stores. These purveyors of chemical-free goods *have* turned back the clock and are constantly caught in the throes of a war against predators. I have seen a store so infested with maggots hatching from the food that it looked like a possum two days after being squashed on the roadway. I've seen the look on a chemical-free purist's face when the granola she just popped in her mouth began to wiggle. Let me tell you, if she wasn't a victim of the Jim Bob Effect she would have begged for the fumigants and chemicals which would have prevented her distasteful experience.

But most people think we can just do without EDB and the other chemicals. They don't understand that they would have to eat 400 tons per day of EDB-laced foods to equal the amount fed the rats, and that chemicals like EDB are all that stand between us and a mouthful of maggots. So EDB was banned and the activists went on to the next chemical scare.

Cranberries and Apples

And by now the scares are abundant. In 1959, the government informed Americans that cranberries were contaminated by a cancer-causing weed killer. They neglected to mention that this chemical replaced paint thinner as the previous weed killer of choice in cranberry bogs at far lower cost and toxicity and dose. And they downplayed the real victim of the killer chemical, another poor little rat fed a dose that would choke a horse. The cranberry industry lost, in 1959 dollars, $30 million.

Déjà vu 1989. The eminent scientist Meryl Streep, TV's *60 Minutes*, and the National Resources Defense Council let fly with a report claiming that the chemical Alar, used to keep apples from maturing before reaching the stores, and to prevent internal decay, caused cancer—in mice.

Never mind that Alar helped keep a nutritious food within the price range of the economically less advantaged. Never mind that it kept apples from rotting before getting to the stores. When fed in gargantuan doses to mice it causes cancer.

There was resistance to the anti-Alar onslaught. The farmers bought TV time to plead their case. The Environmental Protection Agency determined that the amount of Alar eaten during a 70-year lifetime increased the risk of cancer by 5 in 1,000,000, an estimate many scientists consider high. They consider the risk to be zero. Forget all that. Dr. Streep wanted Alar banned and banned it was. After things quieted down, an influential biochemist estimated that the risk in a glass of apple juice from apples treated with Alar was 18 times less than the cancer risk in a peanut butter sandwich; 50 times less than the hazard of one edible mushroom; 1000 times less than the risk of one beer. But by that time nobody cared.

Toxic Nature

Something very interesting was happening in the science labs while the activists were standing in front of the cameras proclaiming the virtues of nature and the vices of man. Scientists at top universities were discovering that nature herself is teeming with toxins. Every single bite of food we take is laced with pesticides brewed not in the laboratory of Monsanto, but in the laboratory of nature.

Little by little they found things like nitrate in celery, tannin in tea, and arsenic in potato. Gradually the research accumulated until they identified tens of thousands of the natural pesticides plants generate to protect against predators. Plants most definitely are not subject to the Jim Bob Effect.

Natural Toxins

Plants produce toxins which protect them against fungi, insects, and predators such as man. Many of these natural pesticides have been discovered, and most species of plant contain a few dozen. Of the natural toxins tested in animals, one-half (25 of 50) have proved carcinogenic in MTD [maximum tolerated dose] testing of lab animals, says Bruce Ames, as compared to 58 percent for synthetic chemicals. It is probable, says Ames, that almost every plant product in the supermarket contains natural animal carcinogens. Among those already identified as such are: bananas, broccoli, brussels sprouts, cabbage, carrots, celery, cocoa, grapefruit juice, honeydew melon, mushrooms, mustard, orange juice, peaches, black pepper, raspberries, turnips—and apples, sans Alar. To worry about a substance present in apple juice in such small quantities that it can only be measured with the most advanced instruments seems fatuous indeed.

Michael Fumento, *The American Spectator,* August 1990.

By 1984 a prominent scientist who was a favorite of the environmentalists proclaimed that Americans eat 10,000 times as much of natural toxins as they do synthetic. Or to put it another way, more than 99.99 percent of all toxic chemicals ingested are natural. One of nature's carcinogens, allyl isothiocyanate, is present in cabbage at a level tens of thousands of times higher than the amount necessary to damage chromosomes, mutate cells, and produce tumors.

So, while the activists continued their love-fest with nature and their hate-fest with man, their entire paradigm was being rendered obsolete by the development of scientific research placing the real threat squarely at nature's door. In comparison, the hazard of man-made chemicals like EDB and Alar is utterly trivial.

What has the reaction of the activists been? They've done two things: They've simply ignored the facts, and they've defamed the characters of some of the finest scientists in the world.

The discovery of nature's toxins dovetails nicely with another environmental disaster hoax: The Great Dioxin Scare.

Dioxin is a group of the most enervating chemicals known to environmentalists. They have delighted in discovering it lurking in waste dumps, rice fields, drinking water, and most especially in the forests of Vietnam, in the form of the defoliant Agent

Orange. The discovery of small amounts of dioxin led to the de-population of entire neighborhoods, not due to a genuine threat, but due to fear induced by earth activists.

Another Hoax

Despite the fact that over $1 billion has been spent research-ing its effects, not a single case of chronic illness or death has ever been attributed to dioxin in the U.S. Despite an unparal-leled media outcry over dioxin concentrations in New York's Love Canal, and Times Beach, Missouri, including the govern-ment purchase of abandoned homes, no evidence was offered linking dioxin to unusual rates of sickness, birth defects, or death. On the sidelines, *Science* magazine reported: When ad-ministered orally dioxin is highly toxic, "but when bound to soil it does not pose much of a hazard." Love Canal was another en-vironmental hoax.

This was emphasized in 1987 when researchers discovered that nature's darling broccoli contained a chemical which pre-cisely mimics the toxic effects of dioxin on human cells. The twist in the tale is that the amount of this natural chemical pre-sent makes it 20 million times as toxic as the dioxin level de-clared safe by the EPA. Not one activist has spoken out in favor of banning broccoli. . . .

[Environmental hoaxes] will go on as long as we are willing to allow ourselves to be scared by activists parading as scientific ex-perts. The risks of listening to political nonsense are great. The food supply is threatened, we are goaded into disposing of tech-nologies which save lives, such as certain drugs, pesticides, and nuclear power. And worst of all, we are deceived into accepting changes in our political institutions which reduce our liberty. As famous environmentalist Paul Ehrlich puts it in calling for manda-tory sterilization: "Coercion, perhaps. But coercion in a good cause." There is no good cause for coercion of a free people.

Distinguishing Bias from Reason

When dealing with controversial issues, many people allow their feelings to dominate their powers of reason. Thus, one of the most important critical thinking skills is the ability to distinguish between statements based upon emotion or bias and conclusions based upon a rational consideration of the facts.

The following statements are taken from the viewpoints in this chapter. Consider each statement carefully. *Mark R for any statement you believe is based on reason or a rational consideration of the facts. Mark B for any statement you believe is based on bias, prejudice, or emotion. Mark I for any statement you think is impossible to judge.*

If you are doing this activity as a member of a class or group, compare your answers with those of other class or group members. You may discover that others come to different conclusions than you do. Listening to the rationale others present for their answers may give you valuable insights into distinguishing between bias and reason.

> R = a statement based upon reason
> B = a statement based upon bias
> I = a statement impossible to judge

1. We have altered natural environments so drastically and so often that Earth is becoming less hospitable.

2. Whenever mankind has cleared land to build a city or to farm, the naturalness of nature has been changed.

3. There is a growing sense that the only socially respectable attitude toward the environment is to push the panic button.

4. Since the environmental movement got its start in the United States, other leaders look to it as a leader in the area.

5. Petrochemical pollution is particularly dangerous because it bonds well to oily substances such as human fat.

6. I am no longer touched by the pleading of naysaying, doom-predicting environmental evangelists.

7. Humankind has always had problems with nature. Many of the deserts in the Middle East resulted from overgrazing and deforestation.

8. The leaders of many activist environmental groups are leftist, radical, and dedicated to blocking industrial progress and development.

9. Some environmental improvement has been made. Since 1975, the national airborne sulfur dioxide level has dropped by 25 percent.

10. Since smog can aggravate certain illnesses, the elderly and people with health problems are told to remain indoors during smog alert days.

11. It is difficult to blame only asbestos for cancer in asbestos workers when many of them were also heavy smokers.

12. The DuPont Corporation produces 40 percent of the world's CFC output. Therefore, they should help pay for its cleanup.

13. If we want a healthier world then we must rely on industry's technical expertise, entrepreneurial vigor, and their marketing genius.

14. The greenhouse effect is worsening as evidenced by the 5.5 billion tons of carbon added to the atmosphere in 1988 from fossil fuels.

15. Except in a few densely populated cities, it is ridiculous to say that America is running out of landfill space.

16. Environmental regulations like the Clean Water Act, which cost $100 billion, have failed to improve water quality.

Periodical Bibliography

The following articles have been selected to supplement the diverse views presented in this chapter.

Benjamin H. Alexander — "Why Is the Environmental Crisis Happening?" *Vital Speeches of the Day*, December 1, 1989.

Phineas Baxandall and Elizabeth Yukins — "The Environmental President: His First Year," *Mother Jones*, April/May 1990.

James Bovard — "Lester, the Sky Hasn't Fallen," *The Wall Street Journal*, June 26, 1989.

Warren T. Brookes — "The Wasteful Pursuit of Zero Risk," *Forbes*, April 30, 1990.

David Brooks — "Journalists and Others for Saving the Planet," *The Wall Street Journal*, October 5, 1989.

Vicky Cahan — "George Bush Is Acting like a Born-Again Environmentalist," *Business Week*, July 9, 1990.

Betsy Carpenter — "Living with Our Legacy," *U.S. News & World Report*, April 23, 1990.

Barry Commoner — "Ending the War Against Earth," *The Nation*, April 30, 1990.

Gregg Easterbrook — "Cleaning Up," *Newsweek*, July 24, 1989.

Evan Eisenberg — "The Call of the Wild: Nature's Four Lessons for Ecologists," *The New Republic*, April 30, 1990.

Trip Gabriel — "Coming Back to Earth: A Look at Earth Day 1990," *Rolling Stone*, February 8, 1990.

Glenn Garelik — "A New Item on the Agenda," *Time*, October 23, 1989.

David Lindorff — "A Hot Issue," *The Nation*, May 29, 1989.

Newsweek — "We Fouled Our Nest," January 22, 1990.

Peter Nulty — "Global Warming: What We Know," *Fortune*, April 9, 1990.

Kirkpatrick Sale — "The Trouble with Earth Day," *The Nation*, April 30, 1990.

Kenneth R. Sheets — "Business's Green Revolution," *U.S. News & World Report*, February 19, 1990.

George M. Woodwell — "Pollution, Erosion, Waste, Toxins," *The New York Times*, August 13, 1988.

How Should Pesticides Be Handled?

THE ENVIRONMENTAL
CRISIS

Chapter Preface

The introduction of modern pesticides revolutionized American farming. Crop yields improved, plant destruction by insects decreased, and farmers no longer had to rely on backbreaking and ineffective methods of pest and weed control. However, the American public soon learned that pesticides were killing more than insects and weeds.

In her ground-breaking 1962 book *Silent Spring*, Rachel Carson described the deadly effect of the pesticide DDT on wildlife, especially birds. Exposure to DDT caused many birds to lay eggs with weakened shells, causing the eggs to break during incubation. Hundreds of species were threatened with extinction. DDT was responsible for putting the bald eagle on the endangered species list. Due to Carson's book and a growing fear of DDT's risk to human health, the Environmental Protection Agency (EPA) in 1972 banned the use of DDT in the United States. This precedent-setting ban touched off a furor between those who wanted more pesticide restrictions and those who argued that additional bans would leave farmers defenseless in the fight against insects, crop disease, and fungus.

Agricultural leaders and environmentalists remain split over the widespread use of pesticides. Many agronomists and other scientists, as well as farmers, assert that pesticides are essential for bountiful food production. Without pesticides, they argue, grocery prices would skyrocket and consumers would have to endure poor quality produce. They maintain that an environmentally safe level of pesticide use is possible.

However, some environmental organizations and organic farmers argue that despite certain bans, too many dangerous pesticides are still in use. Public Citizen's Congress Watch, a lobbying and litigation group, maintains that while numerous pesticides are proven carcinogens, only a handful have been banned by the EPA. Many environmental groups want farmers to wean themselves from dependence on agricultural chemicals and use more organic alternatives.

The viewpoints in the following chapter discuss the risks and benefits of pesticide use.

"[Pesticides] are capable of causing birth defects, genetic mutations, sterility, and cancer."

Pesticides Must Be More Closely Regulated

Laura Weiss

Pesticide and chemical fertilizer use go hand-in-hand with modern farming techniques. Only recently have the long-term effects of some of these chemical compounds become known. A few cancer-causing pesticides, like DDT, have been banned, but most environmental organizations would like to add many more chemicals to the outlawed list. In the following viewpoint, Laura Weiss writes that the Environmental Protection Agency (EPA) has been slow in banning many harmful pesticides. Weiss, a field organizer for the special-interest group Citizen's Watch, argues that numerous cancer-causing agents need to be taken off the agricultural market.

As you read, consider the following questions:

1. Under what conditions does Weiss believe a hazardous substance can continue to be used?
2. In the author's opinion, what happens to the 2.6 billion pounds of pesticides that are used in the U.S. each year?
3. Why does Weiss consider the use of certain pesticides particularly dangerous for farm workers?

Laura Weiss, "Killer Compounds," *The Public Citizen,* January/February 1988. Copyright © 1988 Public Citizen Foundation. Reprinted with permission.

If you're like most health-conscious Americans, you pay attention to the amount of cholesterol in your diet. But when was the last time you tried to calculate the amount of captan you've eaten?

Chances are you've never even heard of captan, let alone had any idea you might be ingesting it. You won't find it listed as an ingredient of anything you buy.

Captan is a chemical pesticide, first introduced in 1951, used to control fungus. The government permits its use on 65 different types of food crops, from apples and almonds to peaches and strawberries, even though it has classified captan as a "probable human carcinogen."

In 1980, the National Cancer Institute found that captan caused tumors in mice. Based on this and subsequent scientific data indicating that captan also caused genetic mutations, the Environmental Protection Agency (EPA) decided that the chemical warranted closer scrutiny to determine whether it should be banned from use.

So later that year EPA placed captan in a special program designed to speed the process for deciding whether to restrict or prohibit the use of potentially harmful pesticides. The program, called Special Review, was intended to enable EPA to issue a decision within 18 months.

After five years of review, in 1985 EPA proposed to prohibit all uses of captan on food crops unless its manufacturers could prove that the residues remaining on food were lower than EPA had estimated or that alternative application methods could reduce the levels. Two-and-a-half years later—and more than seven years after EPA first put captan into Special Review—the agency has yet to issue a final decision. . . .

Economics vs. Health

When EPA concludes its review, it won't necessarily either declare captan safe or order its removal from the market. Under the Federal Insecticide, Fungicide and Rodenticide Act (FIFRA), EPA is required to balance the health and environmental risks of a pesticide's use against the economic benefits. This burden is placed on the agency even though chemical manufacturers are not required to provide evidence showing that their pesticide products are effective.

Even where a pesticide is found to be hazardous to human health, wildlife, or the environment, its continued use can be permitted if EPA is persuaded that there are advantages more significant than the risks. This system places heavy emphasis on economics rather than health. As EPA economists were quoted in a 1985 World Resources Institute report, "While pesticide producers, users, and consumers benefit from the use of pesti-

67

cides, . . . costs are distributed disproportionately throughout the population (in terms of acute and chronic toxic effects such as cancer)." . . .

Agents of Destruction

A pesticide is, by definition, an agent of destruction: designed to kill bugs, weeds, rodents, worms, funguses, and mold. Pesticides also have some special applications, such as to sterilize medical equipment or to regulate crop growth. Nearly 80 percent of all pesticides are used in agriculture; the rest are used for industrial and consumer purposes.

Inadequate Testing

Most pesticides in use today have not been fully safety tested. There are nearly 750 active pesticide ingredients currently on the market. The 10 chronic health effects studies required have been completed for less than 20 percent of those pesticides.

Pesticide Watch, March 1989.

Today, more than 2.6 *billion* pounds of pesticides are used annually in the United States. Long after they have served their intended purpose they can persist in the environment, seeping into groundwater, contaminating food supplies, and accumulating in the tissue of plants, animals, and people. They are capable of causing birth defects, genetic mutations, sterility, and cancer.

Many environmentalists, scientists, and farmers are convinced that we have become overdependent on pesticides. Conventional farming interests such as the Farm Bureau argue that large-scale food production is not possible without pesticides and that consumers need these chemicals to control germs, pests, and weeds. But a growing movement toward non-chemical pest control belies these claims. The U.S. Department of Agriculture estimates that 30,000 farmers are now raising crops without chemicals or are close to eliminating their use, and other experts say the numbers range from 50,000 to 100,000.

Under the federal law, originally enacted in 1947, all pesticides must be licensed, or "registered," by the government before they may be sold. The law was originally enacted to ensure that pesticide products performed as claimed; later amendments gave EPA responsibility for monitoring pesticides' health and environmental risks.

As amended, FIFRA requires a company seeking to register a pesticide to submit scientific data on the chemical's health and environmental effects. However, many pesticides have been registered without complete supporting data, or were registered prior to current scientific knowledge of their potentially adverse effects. The National Academy of Sciences estimated in 1984 that 90 percent of the registered pesticides had not been adequately tested for their health and environmental effects.

Because so many of the registration records are incomplete, in 1972 Congress directed EPA to "reregister" some 600 active ingredients that are used in about 50,000 pesticide products. Since then the agency has moved at a snail's pace in its reregistration program despite public concern about the dangers of many of the pesticides. Since 1972, the agency has reregistered only 17 active ingredients. In the course of its reexamination process, however, EPA has identified a number of pesticides that pose the greatest risks to human health or the environment; these are the ones that have been placed in Special Review.

As of 1988, 17 reviews (involving 34 active ingredients) have been ongoing for an average of about four years; for many of these, EPA is years away from issuing a final regulatory decision. Another 33 Special Reviews (involving 53 ingredients) that have ended have taken an average of about four years before either EPA issued a decision, or the manufacturer voluntarily withdrew the product from the market. EPA may continue to gather and examine data on a pesticide under the reregistration process even after a Special Review has ended, which is why many of the pesticides that have completed Special Review are still not reregistered.

"Acceptable" Cancer Levels

One of the reasons Special Reviews take longer than was originally intended is that much of the data necessary to determine the safety of a pesticide is missing and must be collected. The soil fumigant 1,3-dichloropropene (1,3-D) was registered more than two decades ago. Although the chemical was licensed for use on food crops, the manufacturer was never required to submit data showing whether or not residues remained on food until 1986, when the chemical was placed in Special Review because tests showed it caused cancer in lab animals. No action will be taken on 1,3-D until Dow Chemical Co. submits new data. In the meantime, Dow can continue to market the fumigant.

If, based on available data, EPA concludes that risks can be held to an "acceptable" level—by reducing food residue levels or imposing use restrictions, for example—then it will uphold the pesticide's registration. In evaluating cancer risk, for example, EPA has defined "acceptable" to mean that the pesticide is not likely to cause more than "one additional case of cancer in the lifetime of 1 million persons." However, EPA can be persuaded to approve a pesticide that poses a greater than acceptable risk if its manufacturers and users contend that there is no adequate substitute, that the pesticide is uniquely suitable for particular applications, or that there are other benefits from continued use.

Konopacki/*People's Weekly World.*

EPA may decide to cancel some uses of a pesticide because of unacceptably high risks, but permit other uses to continue. In October 1986, after only 10 months of Special Review deliberation, EPA issued a final decision to prohibit the use of diazinon on golf courses and sod farms based on evidence that the chemical had killed birds from 23 different species. Diazinon is apparently so toxic to birds that large numbers have fallen dead on the greens soon after coming into contact with the chemical.

Dangerous Alternatives

Common sense would suggest that if diazinon kills birds when it is sprayed on golf courses, it kills birds when sprayed on apple orchards or corn fields. But EPA has not proposed to cancel any of the food crop uses of the chemical because, as Jay Ellenberger, chief of the Regulatory Management Section of EPA's Special

Review Branch, explains, without the "smoking gun" of bird carcasses from diazinon-sprayed crop fields, the agency probably couldn't uphold its case on appeal. Apparently EPA does not have any such evidence nor the resources to get it. Meanwhile, diazinon manufacturers are appealing EPA's partial ban.

As part of its risk/benefit analysis, EPA considers the alternatives available. However, the alternatives to a dangerous chemical may be no less hazardous. Three of the five effective chemical replacements for benomyl, a potentially hazardous fungicide evaluated under Special Review, are or have also been in Special Review. Non-chemical alternatives receive only minor consideration by EPA, even though many farmers are moving away from chemical-based agricultural techniques. The agency only has five staff members devoted to non-chemical pest control methods, and as a result the Special Review staff receives limited information about non-chemical alternatives.

Another flaw in EPA's risk/benefit analyses is that the agency does not have to evaluate whether the pesticide under review is effective and provides the benefits intended. This is because a 1978 amendment, successfully sought by agribusiness interests, permits EPA to waive that data requirement.

Farm Workers

In many cases, farm workers who apply pesticides, work in sprayed fields, and handle freshly sprayed crops face much greater exposure risks than does the general population. The Occupational Safety and Health Administration does not have jurisdiction over farm worker exposure to pesticides; however, EPA may impose "use restrictions" intended to protect workers. For example, EPA may require that workers wear protective clothing when applying a type of chemical, that no one be permitted to enter a sprayed area within a certain time period, or that the manufacturer print warnings and instructions for safe use on the pesticide container labels.

In a 1982 reversal of a preliminary decision to cancel the carcinogenic herbicide diallate, EPA concluded that the risk to applicators did "not appear to be unreasonable, given the benefits" of continued diallate use as long as specific use restrictions are imposed: that applicators wear protective clothing and only certified applicators use the product. Five years earlier, EPA had recommended cancelling diallate because of the cancer risk to workers who mix or apply the compound. Several scientific studies had shown that the herbicide caused tumors and gene mutations in lab animals, and might affect the nervous system.

EPA's reversal was based on new data submitted by diallate's manufacturer, Monsanto, and on the agency's finding that cancellation of diallate would cost the sugar beet industry (which consumes 60 percent of the diallate used in the U.S.) $4 million of its $500 million annual income.

It is a disputed point whether the new use restrictions for diallate will protect farm workers from the pesticide's hazards. All too frequently, says Cesar Chavez, president of the United Farm Workers Union, use restrictions are not enforced, are deliberately sidestepped by farm management, or are disregarded by farm workers ignorant of the risks. Chavez adds that label requirements are generally ineffective because "the majority of farm workers either do not speak English or they can't understand the instructions on the label because it's too technical.". . .

Protecting Profits

"A bill that started out decades ago to protect farmers against ineffective pesticides now protects little other than the profits of the pesticide manufacturers," notes Laura Rhodes, staff attorney with Congress Watch. "The health and environmental problems caused by dangerous pesticides are insidious and slow-building. They are not as visible as automobile or industrial accidents caused by corporate negligence, but they are just as harmful.

"We cannot permit the 'silent' deaths and devastation to continue," Rhodes adds. FIFRA reforms sought by Public Citizen would repair many of the failures in the Special Review process as well as in other aspects of federal pesticide law.

"The majority of the established pesticides have no adverse effect on people, animals, or the environment."

Pesticides Need Not Be More Closely Regulated

Bert L. Bohmont

Bert L. Bohmont is a professor and coordinator of pesticide programs in the college of agricultural sciences at Colorado State University in Fort Collins. In the following viewpoint, Bohmont writes that pesticides are essential for modern agricultural production. He notes that the benefits of pesticide use in producing more abundant, blemish-free crops outweigh the hazards that might be posed to humans. Bohmont argues that environmentalists, ignorant of the facts, have exaggerated the dangers of pesticide use.

As you read, consider the following questions:

1. Why does Bohmont say that pesticides are responsible for the well-being of American consumers?
2. In the author's opinion, how does public demand for umblemished produce affect pesticide use?
3. According to Bohmont, why is the actual amount of pesticides released into the atmosphere so small?

Bert L. Bohmont, *The Standard Pesticide User's Guide,* © 1990, pp. 1-5, 8, 10. Reprinted by permission of Prentice Hall, Englewood Cliffs, New Jersey.

History records that agricultural chemicals have been used since ancient times; the ancient Romans are known to have used burning sulfur to control insects. They were also known to have used salt to keep the weeds under control. The ninth-century Chinese used arsenic mixed with water to control insects. Early in the 1800s, pyrethrin and rotenone were discovered to be useful as insecticides for the control of many different insect species. Paris green, a mixture of copper and arsenic, was discovered in 1865 and subsequently used to control the Colorado potato beetle. In 1882, a fungicide known as Bordeaux mixture, made from a mixture of lime and copper sulfate, was discovered to be useful as a fungicide for the control of downy mildew in grapes. Mercury dust was developed in 1890 as a seed treatment, and subsequently, in 1915, liquid mercury was developed as a seed treatment to protect seeds from fungus diseases.

The first synthetic, organic insecticides and herbicides were discovered and produced in the early 1900s; this production of synthetic pesticides preceded the subsequent discovery and production of hundreds of synthetic, organic pesticides, starting in the 1940s. Chlorinated hydrocarbons came into commercial production in the 1940s, and organic phosphates began to be commercially produced during the 1950s. In the late 1950s, carbamates were developed and included insecticides, herbicides, and fungicides. The 1960s saw a trend toward specific and specialized pesticides, which included systemic materials and the trend toward "prescription" types of pesticides. Many of these new families of pesticides are so biologically active that they are applied at rates of grams or ounces per acre. These include the pyrethroids, sulfonylureas, and imidazolinones. Most of the newer compounds offer greater safety to the user and the environment. Presently, there are over 600 active pesticide chemicals being formulated into over 30,000 commercial preparations. Approximately 200 of the 600 basic active chemicals represent 90% of the agricultural uses in the United States.

Improving Human Life

Pesticides are used by people as intentional applications to the environment to improve environmental quality for humans, domesticated animals, and plants. Despite the fears and real problems they create, pesticides clearly are responsible for part of the physical well-being enjoyed by most people in the United States and the western world. They also contribute significantly to the existing standards of living in other nations. In the United States, consumers spend less of their income on food (about 12%) than other people anywhere. The chief reason is more efficient food production, and chemicals have made an important contribution in this area. In 1850, each U.S. farmer produced enough food and fiber for himself and three other persons; over 100 years later (1960) he was able to produce enough food and fiber for himself and 24 other people; himself and 45 other people in 1970; and in 1990 he is able to produce enough for himself and 78 other people. World population was estimated at 4.25 billion people in 1980 and is expected to increase to over 5 billion by 1990 and to over 6 billion people by the year 2000. There will be great pressure on the farmers of the world to increase agricultural production to feed and clothe this extra population.

Starving the Planet

I live in this world with everyone else. I want my family protected and healthy, with a clean environment, and with an abundant food supply! If we want to starve our planet, increase the incidence of disease, and spend over 50% of each dollar we earn on groceries (instead of the present 15%) then it would be justified to eliminate pesticides. I do not want my kids growing up in that world!

J.F. Petta, *Chico Enterprise-Record,* February 26, 1989.

World food supply is inadequate to satisfy the hunger of the total population. As much as one-half of the world's population is undernourished. The situation is worse in underdeveloped countries where it is estimated that as much as three-fourths of the inhabitants are undernourished.

In spite of pest control programs, U.S. agriculture still loses possibly one-third of its potential crop production to various pests. Without modern pest control, including the use of pesticides, this annual loss in the United States would probably double. If that happened, it is possible that (1) farm costs and prices would increase considerably, (2) the average consumer family would spend much more on food, (3) the number of people who work on farms would have to be increased, (4) farm exports would be reduced, and (5) a vast increase in intensive cultivated acreage would be required. It has been estimated that 418 million less acres are required to grow food and fiber than might otherwise be required. This is said to be due to modern technology, which includes the use of pesticides.

Pests and People

In most parts of the world today, pest control of some kind is essential because crops, livestock, and people live, as always, in a potentially hostile environment. Pests compete for our food supply, and they can be disease carriers as well as nuisances. Humans coexist with more than 1 million kinds of insects and other arthropods, many of which are pests. Fungi cause more than 1500 plant diseases, and there are more than 1000 species of harmful nematodes. Humans must also combat hundreds of weed species in order to grow the crops that are needed to feed our nation. Rodents and other vertebrate pests can also cause problems of major proportion. Many of these pest-enemies of humans have caused damage for centuries. . . .

Some good examples of specific increases in yields resulting from the use of pesticides in the United States are corn, 25%; potatoes, 35%; onions, 140%; cotton, 100%; alfalfa seed, 160%; and milk production, 15%.

Modern farm technology has created artificial environments that can worsen some pest problems and cause others. Large acreages, planted efficiently and economically with a single crop (monoculture), encourage certain insects and plant diseases. Advanced food production technology, therefore, actually increases the need for pest control. Pesticides are used not only to produce more food, but also food that is virtually free of damage from insects, diseases, and weeds. In the United States, pesticides are often used because of public demand, supported by government regulations, for uncontaminated and unblemished food.

Environmental Concerns

In the past, pest problems have often been solved without fully appreciating the treatments and effects on other plants and animals or on the environment. Some of these effects have been unfortunate. Today, scientists almost unanimously agree that the first rule in pest control is to recognize the whole problem. The agricultural environment is a complex web of interactions involving (1) many kinds of pests; (2) relationships between pests and their natural enemies; (3) relationships among all these and other factors, such as weather, soil, water, plant varieties, cultural practices, wildlife, and people.

Pesticides are designed simply to destroy pests. They are applied to an environment that includes pests, crops, people, and other living things, as well as air, soil, and water. It is generally accepted that pesticides that are specific to the pest to be controlled are very desirable, and some are available. However, these products can be very expensive because of their limited range of applications.

Unquestionably, pesticides will continue to be of enormous benefit to humans. They have helped to produce food and protect health. Synthetic chemicals have been the front line of defense against destructive insects, weeds, plant diseases, and rodents. Through pest control, we have modified our environment to meet esthetic and recreational demands. However, in solving some environmental problems, pesticides have created others of undetermined magnitude. The unintended consequences of the long-term use of certain pesticides have been injury or death to some life forms. Much of the information on the effects of pesticides comes from the study of birds, fish, and the marine invertebrates, such as crabs, shrimps, and scallops. It is clear that different species respond in different ways to the same concentration of a pesticide. Reproduction is inhibited in some and not in others. Eggs of some birds become thin and break, while others do not.

A Modern Dilemma

Residues of some persistent pesticides apparently are "biologically concentrated." This means that they may become more concentrated in organisms higher up in a food chain. When this happens in an aquatic environment, animals that are at the top of the chain, usually fish-eating birds, may consume enough to suffer reproductive failure or other serious damage. Research has shown that some pesticides decompose completely into harmless substances fairly soon after they are exposed to air, water, sunlight, high temperature, or bacteria. Many others also may do so, but scientific confirmation of that fact is not yet available. When residues remain in or on plants or in soil or water, they usually are in very small amounts (a few parts per million or less). However, even such small amounts of some pesticides, or their breakdown products, which also may be harmful, sometimes persist for a long time.

An Essential Role

We should maintain perspective about the essential role of pesticides in promoting health and maintaining an adequate food supply. . . .

A diminished use of pesticides leaves our food supply vulnerable to infestation and other attack by insects, a condition which poses real threats to human health, through reduced food supply and contamination by naturally occurring chemical agents like aflatoxins and by insect contamination with bacterial and other infectious agents.

Elizabeth M. Whelan, *Columbus Ledger-Enquirer,* April 6, 1989.

Pesticides, like automobiles, can create environmental problems, but in today's world it is difficult to get along without them. Those concerned about pesticides and pest control face a dilemma. On the one hand, modern techniques of food production and control of disease-carrying insects requires pesticides; on the other hand, many pesticides can be a hazard to living things other than pests, sometimes including people.

No clear evidence exists on the long-term effects on humans of the accumulation of pesticides through the food chain, but the problem has been relatively unstudied. Limited studies with human volunteers have shown that persistent pesticides, at the normal levels found in human tissues at the present time, are not associated with any disease. However, further research is required before results are conclusive about present effects, and little information exists about the longer-term effects. Meanwhile, decisions must be made on the basis of extrapolation from results on experimental animals. Extrapolation is always risky, and the judgments on the chronic effects of pesticides on people are highly controversial.

No Adverse Effect

Public concern about the possible dangers of pesticides has manifested legal actions initiated by conservation groups. Pesticides, like virtually every chemical, may have physiological effects on other organisms living in the environment, including people. The majority of the established pesticides have no adverse effect on people, animals, or the environment in general as long as they are used only in the amounts sufficient to control pest organisms. Pest control is never a simple matter of applying a pesticide that removes only the pest species. For one thing, the pest population is seldom completely or permanently eliminated. Almost always there are at least a few survivors to re-create the problem later. Also, the pesticide often affects other living things besides the target species and may contaminate the environment.

There have been and continue to be unfortunate and generally inexcusable accidents where workers become grossly exposed due to improper and inadequate industrial hygiene or carelessness in handling and use. Children sometimes eat, touch, or inhale improperly stored pesticides. Consumers have been inadvertently poisoned by pesticides spilled carelessly in the transportation of pesticides in conjunction with food products. These cases are, however, no indictment of the pesticide itself or the methods employed to establish its efficacy and safety. They are solely due to the irresponsibility of the user.

Pesticides are very rarely used in the form of a pure or technically pure compound, but rather are formulated to make them easy to apply. Formulations may be in the form of dust or granules, which usually contain 5% to 10% of active ingredients, or wettable powders or emulsifiable concentrates, which usually contain 40% to 80% active ingredients. It is important to remember that the formulations that are used as sprays are further diluted with water, oil, or other solvents to concentrations of usually only 1% or less before application. The amount of active ingredient, therefore, that is eventually released to the environment is generally extremely small.

Few responsible people today fail to recognize the need for pesticides and the importance of striving to live with them. Several national scientific committees in recent years have stressed the need for pesticides now and in the foreseeable future. These same committees also recommended more responsible use and further investigation into long-term side effects on the environment. It is generally agreed among scientists that there is little, if any, chance that chemical pesticides can be abandoned until such time as alternative control measures are perfected. . . .

Fear and Misunderstanding

The general public, most of whom are far removed from daily food production, have a poor understanding of pesticides. This is partly due to lack of understanding of chemical uses and agricultural production practices, but it is also due to fear and misunderstanding brought about through publicity of accidents and misuses involving pesticides. The perception of widespread hazards associated with presumed long-term accumulations of pesticides in people, other organisms, or the environment often appears to stem from lack of knowledge of the processes of metabolism, elimination, and degradation that largely preclude such perceived problems. . . .

Motor vehicles of all kinds kill approximately 50,000 people annually; 3000 die while swimming and 1000 people die annually in bicycle accidents. Approximately 30 people die each year from pesticides, which includes the tragic accidental ingestions mostly by children.

Individuals using pesticides and those concerned about pesticide use must seek all the facts and become better informed about the benefits as well as the risks of using these technological tools.

"As NutriClean tests more and more produce, the end result should be a move toward cleaner food."

Rigorous Produce Testing Protects Consumers from Pesticides

Geeta Dardick

The United States Department of Agriculture (USDA) routinely checks grocery store produce for dangerous levels of pesticides and other toxins. However, some scientists do not believe the USDA standards are strict enough. Instead, they advocate private testing, as provided by companies like NutriClean, who use stricter guidelines, to ensure that foods are safe. In the following viewpoint, Geeta Dardick, a free-lance writer who has written widely on environmental and health issues, maintains that companies like NutriClean are providing a valuable service. Dardick believes that commercial testing of produce not only guarantees pesticide-free food, but forces farmers to use fewer chemicals during crop preparation.

As you read, consider the following questions:

1. What does Dardick think is the most serious concern for grocery shoppers?
2. Why does the author believe the agricultural community resists commercial produce testing?
3. What standards must fruit and vegetables meet to be considered pesticide-free, according to the author?

Geeta Dardick, "The NutriClean Option," *East West,* July 1989. Reprinted with permission.

As dietary consciousness is raised across all segments of American society, food shoppers are making more and more of their selections in the produce department of their favorite supermarket. But even though we know that fresh, whole fruits and vegetables are nutritionally good for us, we must now, ironically, ask, Are those fragrant cantaloupes and plump strawberries *safe*, or are they full of pesticides? What dangerous residues lurk on that spotless spinach? What hidden chemical threat is in those perfect potatoes? Is there Alar in the apples?

Buying fresh produce at conventional supermarkets can be an unnerving experience. In a 1987 study of consumer attitudes, the Food Marketing Institute found that 78 percent of all grocery shoppers ranked pesticide residues as their most serious concern. If that same study were done today, the percentages would undoubtedly be closer to 100 percent. In February 1989, millions of consumers learned about a Natural Resources Defense Council (NRDC) study showing that pesticide residues on produce may significantly increase the incidence of cancer among children over the course of their lifetimes. So now even the most jaundiced couch potato believes that a saunter along the produce aisle resembles a march down the plank.

A Comforting Sign

"Should I stay or should I go?" The words of the Clash's song run through my mind as I pace back and forth in front of a handsome display of fresh corn at the Raley's supermarket in Grass Valley, California. The sight of the fat ears makes me salivate. My organic homegrown crop won't be ready for seven more weeks . Still, I reason, it would be safer to leave these commercial ears behind. They might have been sprayed with large quantities of pesticides.

And then I see the comforting sign, posted next to the corn: "CERTIFIED, CONTAINS NO DETECTED PESTICIDE RESIDUES." A beacon in the darkness. I toss twelve ears into my basket.

Today, at a growing number of supermarkets around the country, shoppers are noting similar small signs perched over a variety of fresh products. "NutriClean laboratory tests reveal NO detectable pesticide residues." A new marketing trend has begun that appeals to consumers who are worried about pesticides in our food supply.

To date [mid-1989], Raley's chain in Northern California and Nevada, Ralph's in Los Angeles, Fred Meyer's in the Pacific Northwest, Farmer Jack's in Michigan, Farm Fresh in Virginia, Stop and Shop in Boston, and a host of other smaller chains and single markets have signed on with NutriClean, a company that helps supermarkets develop comprehensive policies to address the issue of pesticides. Although the total number of food chains involved with NutriClean currently numbers only ten, they represent some 1,000 out of the 17,000 food stores in the nation, and NutriClean's clout within certain geographic areas is considerable. And with megastars like Meryl Streep now publicizing on popular TV shows like Donahue the issue of pesticide contamination, it's a good bet that the number of supermarkets signing on with NutriClean will double or even triple.

The growing popularity of pesticide-testing programs such as NutriClean's, however, does not mean that they have no critics. Agribusiness growers contend that such a small fraction of foods have dangerously high pesticide residues that NutriClean-type services are misleading and a waste of supermarkets' (and thus consumers') money. On the other end of the farming spectrum, organic growers worry that an over-emphasis on detecting pesticide residues at the market will distract from the more important issues of soil-building and growing crops without any pesticides instead of merely low levels. How companies such as NutriClean address such concerns may ultimately decide their impact on our food choices.

NutriClean was founded in 1984 by Stan Rhodes, a chemist who spent eight years in the natural foods business. The company has already quadrupled in sales every year since its inception. According to Rhodes, NutriClean has two long-term goals for the supermarkets making up his clientele: to reduce the amount of pesticides used by growers by 50 percent in the next five years, and to reduce the amount of pesticide residues on the food by 99 percent during that same period. These goals do not endear Rhodes to members of the conventional, pesticide-oriented agricultural community. "The industry hates me," says Rhodes. "They say we are trying to make money on a problem that doesn't exist."

The NutriClean program has two main aspects: food certification and dock screening. The dozen ears of corn I bought were labeled residue-free under the certification program. To become certified, the farmer who grew the corn paid a fee and signed a legal agreement with NutriClean disclosing every chemical used on the corn. Next NutriClean designed an individual testing program to determine if the corn was residue-free at harvest. Then the crop was inspected in the field to gather samples, plus additional data on any variables (like water runoff from a neighboring crop) that could affect the residues remaining in the corn. In the lab, the samples (not the husks) were ground up in a blender and tested for the listed pesticides. Once it passed lab scrutiny as residue-free, the crop was kept separate from other (perhaps contaminated) produce during shipping and storage, until it received the NutriClean certification label in the supermarket. (If the corn hadn't passed its tests as 100 percent residue-free, it would still be sold to participating supermarkets, but without the desirable safety label.)

Strict Standards

As of mid-1989, NutriClean has approximately forty certified shippers on line, who supply produce to participating retailers. In February 1989, Kerry Hodges, vice president in charge of purchasing for the 135-store Ralph's chain, said that shoppers could find NutriClean certified broccoli, cauliflower, yams, sweet potatoes, carrots, and avocados at his stores. This might sound like an exciting assortment of vegetables, until you realize that this represents only six out of two hundred produce items for sale at Ralph's.

According to NutriClean, one of the reasons there aren't very many certified products available yet (there are always more in summer than in winter) is that it is hard for most commercial farmers to meet their standards for no detected pesticide residues. Explains Linda Brown, director of corporate communications for NutriClean, "Our 'no detected residue' standard is very strict. Federal and state regulations are all over the map, but in general laws allow for outrageous amounts of pesticides on foods. We have a grape grower with 2,000 acres who underwent an 83 percent decrease in pesticide use to become certified. Now he's working with NutriClean to help other growers learn how to do the same thing."

To attract more growers into NutriClean's certification program, Stan Rhodes conducts growers' meetings, where he tries to convince commercial farmers that the time has come for them to start reducing their pesticide use so they can sell certified products. "I've become part preacher," says Rhodes. "I tell the growers that if they want to stay in business, they better get on the stick and use less pesticides, because life will pass them by.". . .

Reducing Pesticide Use

"It's hard for growers to convert overnight from heavy pesticide use," says Rhodes.

"They need to go slow enough to feel comfortable. The idea is to let the marketplace keep the pressure on them."

As major supermarkets sign on with NutriClean, the pressure on farmers increases. Gilbert Borman, spokesperson for Farmer Jack's, the largest supermarket chain in southeastern Michigan and a NutriClean participant since September 1988, had a meeting with Michigan growers to introduce them to the concept of NutriClean. "We told them that this is where we are directing our produce business and asked them to join us," says Borman. "A lot of them expressed concern whether this meant they couldn't sell to us anymore. Others said that they wanted to be certified too."

Because many consumers fear that produce with illegally high pesticide levels is getting through government checkpoints, NutriClean also provides participating supermarkets with a dock screening program, which supplements federal and state tests by randomly checking for pesticide residues after the produce arrives at the markets' warehouses. In dock screening, NutriClean typically focuses on the nine produce items known to contain 90 percent of all carcinogenic residues: apples, corn, tomatoes, potatoes, peaches, carrots, lettuce, grapes, and oranges. They do random checks to make sure that these fruits and vegetables don't contain illegally high residues of some twelve to fifteen chemicals known to cause the most danger to human health. At Raley's, dock testing of Mexican tomatoes and Chilean grapes will soon be expanded to include over one hundred additional pesticides. Also, additional imported products will be added to the test list to satisfy consumer worries about their safety. . . .

Raley's uses NutriClean to test its organic produce for residues, just to make sure that it is really safe. Because consumer response has been so positive, these organic products sell out rapidly. "All else being equal, organic is the ultimate," says Raley's Frank McMinn. "Especially if it has been tested for verification."

A Move Toward Cleaner Food

The possibility that NutriClean is pushing American agribusiness to look more carefully at organic principles pleases some long-time advocates of sustainable agriculture. Bob Cantisano, an agricultural supplier who has spent the past ten years advising farmers across the country on how to cut down on pesticide use, says that some supermarket chains like Safeway and Lucky are now buying organic products just to compete with Raley's and NutriClean. "NutriClean broke open the door and created competition," says Cantisano. "In that way it has been very good for organic growers.". . .

As NutriClean tests more and more produce, the end result should be a move toward cleaner food, which will certainly bring a sigh of relief from consumers anxious for less pesticides on their produce. Stan Rhodes claims he has started a revolution, and he may be correct. In 1990 he will have ten times the residue-free grapes that he had in 1989, and if he keeps that kind of increase going, in a few years he may have put pressure on the food industry that they simply cannot ignore.

Rhodes admits that it will take a lot of innovation to convert some crops to residue-free, because of the need to ship perishable foods to distant markets. "Those fungicides that are used are no good for anybody," says Rhodes. "We advocate that more food be grown locally, and we are also working on new ways to get food to the East Coast."

Surprisingly, Rhodes also has nothing nice to say about organic products that may be grown with natural pesticides like rotenone or pyrethrum. "They are still poisonous," he maintains. "The organic industry will have to clean up its act to get into the NutriClean system.". . .

The Coming Change

Chris Kilham, vice president of marketing for Bread and Circus, a supermarket chain that sells only natural products, believes that NutriClean will eventually have a tremendous effect on the entire food industry. "NutriClean is like a thorn in the side of agriculture," says Kilham. "The company will be helpful in increasing public awareness of chemical issues, and this is what will ultimately lead to a change in our agricultural system."

"Independent, commercial pesticide residue testing programs may promote fear, [and] perpetuate misinformation."

Rigorous Produce Testing Does Not Protect Consumers from Pesticides

Carl K. Winter

Carl K. Winter, researcher at the University of California at Riverside, studies the effect of toxic substances on the environment. In the following viewpoint, Winter writes that commercial testing programs, such as NutriClean, are simply money-making ventures that play off the public's concern over pesticide residue on fruits and vegetables. He contends that government tests are more than adequate to safeguard consumers. Winter states that commercial testing programs obscure the important issues regarding produce.

As you read, consider the following questions:

1. Who does Winter believe ultimately pays for independent testing?
2. In the author's opinion, how much pesticide residue does the average American have in his or her system?
3. Why does Winter write that the lack of pesticides may actually increase toxins in food?

Carl K. Winter, "Independent Testing of Foods for Pesticide Residues," *Environmental Toxicology Newsletter*, February 1989. Reprinted with permission.

The recent increase in consumer concern regarding pesticides in the food supply has led to the birth of a new phenomenon in the food industry—independent testing of foods for pesticide residues and certification of foods as being "clean" or "residue-free" following analysis.

Independent testing of foods has proven to be a widely publicized and highly controversial item. Consumer advocates and environmentalists have supported these new programs, citing that such programs offer consumers additional choice and protection from the potential hazards of pesticide residues. On the other hand, the majority of agricultural producers, governmental agencies, and University scientists have opposed these programs on the grounds that independent testing programs are marketing gimmicks that prey upon consumer concerns by promoting fear and misinformation. Opponents of the programs maintain that the programs are unnecessary due to the insignificant risk posed by pesticides in the food chain and serve to undermine the much more comprehensive pesticide testing programs by State and Federal agencies that are already in existence.

The most active independent certification service in this controversy is an Oakland, California operation called NutriClean. This firm has engaged in contracts with a number of California produce growers and with major California retailers such as Raley's in Northern California and Ralph's and Irvine Ranch Farmers Market in Southern California. A couple of smaller retailers in the Bay Area are also using the service. NutriClean also currently does business with retailers and growers in the Pacific Northwest, Michigan, and Virginia. . . .

A Money-making Venture

On the surface, it might appear that the NutriClean programs are providing a valuable service to concerned consumers. A 1987 consumer attitude survey indicated that over three-fourths of consumers view pesticide residues in foods as a serious matter of concern. This is reflected in the success of NutriClean's program at the retail level. One Raley's executive indicated that the response to the program was unprecedented and that Raley's was having difficulties keeping the NutriClean-certified products on the shelves. Although the majority of the scientific community considers the risks from pesticide residues in foods to be insignificant, what can be the harm in providing additional testing of residues for consumers who are unaware of the relative risks or are skeptical of the views expressed by scientists and governmental agencies?

From a purely economic standpoint, it should be pointed out that NutriClean is in business to make money. Retailers and growers involved in the NutriClean program are footing the bill to participate in the service. The cost of chemical analysis is significant. A single, routine analysis may cost several hundred dollars and specific tests for chemicals that are difficult to detect may increase these initial costs dramatically. The costs of the retailers and growers for their participation in the Nutri-Clean program must be recovered; most often, consumers are ultimately required to pay for this service in the form of increased food prices.

A Difficult Task

[Food analyzation] programs are faced with an enormous number of pesticide/food combinations to test, and the difficulty of the task is compounded by a lack of information on what pesticides actually have been used on specific crops (especially for imports). Analyzing for all pesticides on all types of food products is currently impossible because of limitations in testing methods as well as time and resource constraints. Although the number of pesticide/food combinations to address can be narrowed by focusing on the potentially moderate to high health hazard combinations, current analytical methods are not adequate to identify and quantify all residues of these pesticide/food combinations within available resources.

U.S. Congress, Office of Technology Assessment, *Pesticide Residues in Food,* 1988.

The presence of the NutriClean program and the subsequent amount of media and consumer attention it has received have fostered the development of several important and inappropriate implications.

Safe Produce

The first implication is that the foods certified to be free of residues are safer than foods which have not been certified. It is somewhat ironic that the same foods certified at Raley's are also sold to other retailers who do not advertise that the foods are free of residues. Additionally, the majority of food items tested by government agencies using far more comprehensive testing have also been shown not to contain detectable levels of pesticides. As an example, results from the California Department of Food and Agriculture's (CDFA) routine marketplace sampling program, which analyzed over 7,000 food samples for residues of over 100 different pesticides from more than 200 types of foods in 1987, showed that no residues were detected in 80 percent of the samples.

Our preoccupation to desire fruits and vegetables that are free of pesticide residues also erroneously implies that any detectable level of a pesticide residue represents a health hazard. This violates the fundamental principle of toxicology that states that the risk associated with a chemical depends both upon the toxicity of the chemical as well as the amount of exposure to the chemical. Scientific evidence has shown that foods containing small amounts of pesticide residues do not appear to pose risks significantly greater than foods from which residues have not been detected. This is particularly important when one considers that our analytical capabilities allow for the detection of residues at extremely low levels. Routinely, pesticides can be detected in foods at levels below one part per million, which is roughly equivalent to about one ounce of a material in more than thirty tons. Residue findings involving tens of thousands of analyses over the past decade have indicated that typical human exposure to pesticide residues in foods is at levels about one hundred thousand times below the levels which have caused even minimal toxic effects in laboratory animals.

Government Testing

The creation and acceptance of the NutriClean program has also led to the implication that State and Federal residue testing programs are inadequate. In actuality, the governmental programs are far more comprehensive than NutriClean's program. In 1987 alone, CDFA analyzed over 13,000 food samples for pesticide residues. From 1982 to 1986, the U.S. Food and Drug Administration's (FDA) Los Angeles District Laboratory analyzed nearly 20,000 samples. While NutriClean's program routinely analyzes for only a handful of different pesticides, CDFA's program routinely screens for over 100 and FDA's program screens for over 200. Other existing CDFA and FDA residue analysis programs are capable of the detection of several other pesticides that cannot be analyzed using the routine screening procedures.

Consumer concerns about pesticide residues in their foods, which appear to be heightened through the existence of firms such as NutriClean, have led many consumers to change their purchasing habits. A survey indicated that 18 percent of consumers are now taking additional steps to minimize their exposure to pesticide residues by taking actions such as buying more organically-grown produce (at a greater cost) or purchasing only produce that has been grown in season. It has been proposed that both approaches could theoretically *increase* the health risks of consumers. Consumption of organic produce may increase human exposure to naturally-occurring toxins since many of these chemicals are produced in greater amounts when plants are subjected to stress from insects, weeds, and fungi. In many cases, the use of pesticides, or other cultural or biological processes, may reduce plant stress and subsequently decrease levels of natural toxins. Reliance on produce that has been grown in season may serve to decrease total consumption of fruits and vegetables. Scientific evidence has indicated that consumption of such foods may reduce the risk of some human cancers.

Mistaken Priorities

The greatest problem with our emphasis on the insignificant risks from pesticide residues in foods is that it clouds our ability to focus upon much more important concerns. In the area of food safety, there are significant areas of concern which are largely ignored. In terms of food safety priorities, the FDA considers pesticide residues in foods as only its fifth priority, and far less of a concern than 1) microbial contamination of foods (deaths occur every year from microbial contamination), 2) nutritional imbalance and malnutrition, 3) environmental contaminants, such as lead and mercury, and 4) naturally-occurring toxins. In the area of pesticides, a far greater potential for human health effects exists for pesticide applicators and for field workers. In both cases, numerous poisoning cases are reported in California each year. As a result of the widespread concern regarding pesticide residues, fueled by operations such as NutriClean, the public is desiring additional governmental testing of pesticide residues, which would appear to be a poor use of the taxpayers' dollars. The money would be much better spent on the more serious food safety and pesticide safety concerns.

A Consumer Disservice

In summary, while the NutriClean program would appear to be a reasonable and legitimate service provided to responsible food retailers and to concerned citizens, it may ultimately serve to the detriment of the consumer. Independent, commercial pesticide residue testing programs may promote fear, perpetuate misinformation, and increase the public's distrust of effective regulatory programs. It also hurts consumers in the pocketbook and influences the allocation of valuable and finite government resources to insignificant issues while neglecting more important ones.

"The potential benefits of alternative agriculture are too attractive to continue to lie fallow."

Low-Input Farming Will Reduce the Use of Pesticides

Donella H. Meadows

Low-input farming means using natural predators, crop rotation, and tillage to combat harmful insects. It also means preventing soil erosion and using natural fertilizers rather than applying liquid nitrogen. This is considered the organic approach to farming. In the following viewpoint, Donella H. Meadows, an adjunct professor of environmental and policy studies at Dartmouth College in Hanover, New Hampshire, writes that low-input farming is necessary to ensure bountiful harvests into the next century. Meadows believes that current agricultural practices, especially the heavy use of pesticides and chemical fertilizers, are ruining the environment.

As you read, consider the following questions:

1. Why does Meadows believe current farming practices are ruining America's agricultural future?
2. What examples of low-input farming techniques does the author provide?
3. In Meadows's opinion, why are chemical companies opposed to low-input farming?

Donella H. Meadows, "Ecology and Agriculture: A Marriage That Must Be Made on Earth," *Los Angeles Times*, November 19, 1989. Reprinted with permission.

Once it was the O-word—organic farming—an idea associated with kooks and branded by chemical companies as a sure route to starvation.

Now it goes by many names—sustainable agriculture, alternative agriculture, low-input, regenerative, ecological agriculture. To the surprise of nearly everyone, those are now buzzwords in Washington. . . . We may be on our way toward kinder, gentler farming.

In September 1989, the National Research Council concluded a four-year study of America's organic agriculture. In summary, Committee Chairman John Pesek of Iowa State University said: "Our committee is convinced that such methods do work, that they would produce an ample food supply if widely adopted, and that our nation's environmental problems and health concerns due to pesticide residues would be reduced. The potential benefits of alternative agriculture are too attractive to continue to lie fallow."

Agricultural and environmental experts assembled a month later in Salina, Kan., to celebrate what geneticist Wes Jackson, co-director of Salina's Land Institute and convener of the meeting, called the marriage—or maybe the engagement, or at least the courtship—of ecology and agriculture.

The Bleak Future

Prof. David Pimentel of the College of Agriculture at Cornell University opened the ceremonies with a zinging testimony on why this marriage is badly needed. American agriculture may look successful, he said, but it can't last. Not economically, not environmentally. It is unsustainable.

Preventable soil erosion costs the nation $44 billion a year in fertilizers carried off fields, in decreased crop production and in eroded soil piling up behind dams, silting up canals and polluting waters. To put that number in perspective, the food and fiber sectors account for about $700 billion a year of the U.S. gross national product. Of that amount, roughly $30 billion is farmers' net income, which is supplemented with another $25 billion in government price supports.

Soil loss from erosion is, on average, 16 times the rate of soil formation. Half the topsoil in Iowa has disappeared in just 150 years of farming. About 100 million acres of U.S. cropland have been so severely degraded that they have been abandoned.

The only reason this soil loss has not yet shown up as enormous drops in yield is that farmers have been able to disguise it with purchased fertilizers made from fossil fuels. They are substituting oil for soil, a non-renewable resource for a renewable one, a practice that can last only as long as oil is cheap.

Between 1945 and 1975, the nation blacktopped an area of

prime agricultural land the size of Ohio and Pennsylvania combined. As land has been lost to pavement, it has been gained from wetlands. Half the nation's wetlands have been drained for agricultural use, with an immeasurable loss in wildlife, ground water recharge and flood control.

Wasteful Methods

The government spends $4 billion a year subsidizing irrigation, causing farmers to waste artificially cheap water. Irrigation districts are, on average, mining aquifers 25% faster than the ground waters are being recharged. In the Texas Gulf area, the overdraft is 77%.

Livestock in the United States eat 10 times more grain than the human population. Their manure contains five times more soil nutrients than farmers buy in fertilizer, but only a fifth of that nutrient is used effectively. The rest is a massive pollution problem.

The Benefits

Well managed alternative farms use less synthetic chemical fertilizers, pesticides, and antibiotics without necessarily decreasing—and in some cases, increasing—per-acre crop yields and the productivity of livestock systems. Wider adoption of proven alternative systems would result in even greater economic benefits to farmers and environmental gains for the nation.

National Research Council, *Alternative Agriculture,* September 7, 1989.

Farmers spray a billion pounds of poison on the land each year to kill pests. They lose 37% of crops to pests, anyway. The loss rate is slowly increasing, though pesticide use is also increasing. Why? Because pesticides allow farmers—for awhile—to plant huge swaths of a single crop, a standing attraction to pests. Because pesticides wipe out pest-eating predators. Because 25% to 50% of air-sprayed pesticide doesn't hit the intended field, and 98% doesn't hit the pest. Because the more pesticides are used, the more pests evolve to become resistant to them.

One price we pay for the pesticide habit is 45,000 human poisonings a year. Those are only diagnosed and reported incidents of acute poisonings—not the cancers that may come years later. Another price is $1.2 billion for monitoring wells, inadequately, for pesticide residues. (The pesticides themselves cost $4.1 billion a year.) The cost of poisons working through ecosystems—affecting birds, fish and the microbial populations of soils—is uncountable.

Pimentel calculates that pesticide use in this country could be reduced by 50% with *no decrease* in yield, and with a food-price increase of only 0.6%.

A Working Partnership

Our unsustainable, unecological agriculture cannot—and should not—continue. The good news, reported by many speakers at the celebration in Salina, is that it doesn't have to. Where ecology and agriculture have gotten together, the partnership works. Quietly, with little help from science or government, thousands of American farmers have been pioneering a new form of modern, high-yield agriculture using industry much less and the nutrient-cycling, pest-controlling principles of nature much more.

About 5% of American farms are now "low-input" (but not low-output)—in total, about 100,000 farms, in all parts of the country, of all sizes, raising all types of crops. The National Research Council study profiles 11 of them, including a 720-acre mixed farm in Ohio, a 1,280-acre vineyard in California, a 284,000-acre cattle ranch in Colorado. They use no commercial fertilizers and few or no manufactured pesticides; they build and protect their soils; they keep down weeds with cultivation and cleverness. They fight pests with natural enemies and by breaking up monocultures and rotating crops. They do not drench their animals with drugs or hormones.

Their yields are comparable to those of their high-input neighbors. Their production costs are much lower; their selling prices are often, because of an "organic premium," higher. They are doing right well.

The relationship between ecology and agriculture has come as far as it has against strong parental opposition, not only from chemical companies, but also, most of the time, from government and agriculture schools.

Except at the edges of a few enlightened experiment stations, like the University of Nebraska, and at private facilities, like the Rodale Research Center, there has been, until recently, little serious research on alternative agriculture. A network of 280 low-input farmers calling themselves Practical Farmers of Iowa did its own experimenting and teaching, until it finally got an extension agent at Iowa State. In Nebraska, 359 alternative farmers created their own on-farm demonstration system. Each farm is open to visitors, with a sign labeling it and a special mailbox stuffed with one-page sheets written by the farmer describing what cover crops are used, how erosion is reduced, how soil fertility is restored, pests are kept in balance, weeds are controlled.

Even in the face of disapproval and ridicule, with no help and no official blessing, the romance between ecology and agriculture has been thriving. Garth Youngberg of the Institute for Alternative Agriculture contrasted where organic farming is now, compared with 10 years ago [in 1979].

The number of farms under low-input practices has roughly tripled. In 1979, only three states had legislation stipulating rules for certifying organic produce. Now [in 1989,] 20 states do, and many more are working on it. Most land-grant universities are now instituting research on low-input management. Major grocery chains, in response to consumer pressure, are finally providing a significant market for foods raised without troublesome chemicals.

For the last three years [1987-1989], the U.S. Department of Agriculture has provided funding for Low-Input Sustainable Agriculture research, at the level in 1988 of $4.5 million. Rumors are that the 1990 farm bill will increase that to $6 million, maybe even to $10 million.

You can see that as amazing progress, or you can see it, as some of the speakers in Salina did, as only a vapor in the bucket. Of the 800 research proposals received by the sustainable-agriculture research program in 1988 and 1989, only 74 could be funded. Even at $10 million, the program would be barely visible in the government's $600-million budget for agricultural research.

Corporate Opposition

But it's visible enough to upset the chemical companies. Some industry spokesmen are labeling alternative agriculture as "unilateral disarmament." Others, however, are acknowledging the problems of high-chemical agriculture and coming up with their own Washington buzzwords, "Best Management Practices." That means using plenty of chemicals, but using them less wastefully—not spraying until pests actually appear, for instance, and doing soil tests instead of automatically pouring on a nitrogen-rich fertilizer.

Marriage is, above all, a state of mind, a commitment. The agricultural Establishment in Washington may already be committed—to industry, money and power. But there's hope that the next farm bill will provide some help to those 100,000 or more farmers out on the land who are committed to the health of the soils, the waters, the plants, the animals, the farmer—and the consumer.

"The current movement to support low-input systems is based more upon emotion and philosophy than on science and experience."

Low-Input Farming Will Reduce Crop Yields

Harold Reetz, Paul Fixen, and Larry Murphy

Harold Reetz is the Westcentral director of the Potash and Phosphate Institute. Paul Fixen serves as the Institute's Northcentral director and Larry Murphy as its vice president. The Institute, which is based in Atlanta, Georgia, is an organization of chemical and fertilizer companies dedicated to educating Americans on the benefits of their products. In the following viewpoint, the authors argue that low-input farming cannot maintain the current high level of agricultural productivity necessary to feed the U.S. and the world. They argue that chemical fertilizers and pesticides are essential for success in modern farming.

As you read, consider the following questions:

1. What evidence do the authors present that modern farming techniques are successful?
2. Why do the authors argue that low-input farming cannot be used by mainstream farmers?

Harold Reetz, Paul Fixen, and Larry Murphy, "LISA—The Industry Perspective," a paper presented at the Fortieth Annual Far West Regional Fertilizer Conference, July 23-25, 1989. Reprinted with permission.

U.S. agriculture has developed the most productive and efficient food and fiber production system in the world. This has been achieved by focusing the attention of farmers, agribusiness, and university research and extension programs on the goals of improving yields and profitability and efficiently utilizing the land, climate, labor, and financial resources. The need to protect the productive capacity of the agricultural industry forces all involved to be concerned about protecting the natural resources upon which it depends. The success of U.S. agriculture has made it a model for other countries as they search for improvements in productivity and profitability. Agriculture throughout the world is a major contributor to economic stability.

Progressive crop management systems in the U.S. are the result of research, extension, agribusiness, and farmers working together to develop, adapt, and apply new and improved technology and production practices. Site-specific management is becoming increasingly important to ensure sustained profitability and maintain responsible stewardship of natural resources. Research, extension, and industry specialists, in cooperation with farmers, are working to develop lists of recommended best management practices (BMPs) for individual crop-soil-climate-management systems. These will provide farmers with management guidelines for making their crop production decisions to help maintain productivity and protect environmental quality.

Plentiful Food

The chief benefactor of our high-technology, high efficiency, specialized agricultural production system is the ultimate food and fiber consumer. Relative to other parts of the world, U.S. consumers spend a very small portion of their disposable income on food. And this is accomplished with less than 2% of the U.S. population working on farms. Our efficient agriculture has made it possible for more of the population to move away from direct involvement in production of food.

Fewer people involved in production agriculture means fewer people understand production agriculture. Policies and regulations pertaining to agriculture set by legislatures and by regulatory officials are increasingly influenced by well-intentioned, well-educated, but misinformed special interest groups. These groups are motivated by increased public awareness and concern about food quality, quality of water resources, and other environmental issues.

In the course of these comments, the term "conventional" agriculture is not meant to include any and all farming methods. Rather, the term implies a modern production system using all available technologies and inputs effectively and efficiently for highest productivity and lowest production costs per unit.

Interest in low-input agriculture was generated in the mid-1980s as a result of increasing public concern about severe financial stresses in farming and agribusiness, increasing sensitivity to environmental issues, and concerns over erosion under intensive row-crop management systems in highly erodible areas. Many people associated these concerns with capital-intensive farming systems and concluded that a return to less intensive management with a reduction in use of purchased inputs—especially pesticides and fertilizers—would lead to a solution of the problems and a more economically viable and environmentally acceptable agriculture.

A Damaging Phobia

Organic farming is fine for one- or two- or even 10-acre plots, but for commercial, low-labor farming, we couldn't provide the food for this country's needs. The phobia about food chemicals could easily be disastrous to our entire food production industry.

Alvin Young, *The Washington Times*, April 12, 1990.

Legislation mandating USDA [U.S. Dept. of Agriculture] support for low-input systems was developed during the mid-1980s and enacted by Congress in 1988 under the Agricultural Productivity Act. The acronym LISA, for *Low-Input, Sustainable Agriculture*, was adopted to serve as the focus of this program, with stated objectives of preserving the family farm, conserving natural resources, and improving environmental quality. LISA was developed in concert with individuals and groups supporting the general concepts of organic farming and employing the terms alternative agriculture, regenerative agriculture, and appropriate technology. A primary goal of LISA advocates was to reduce use of commercial fertilizers and chemical pesticides. . . .

LISA has become a rallying point for individuals and groups with a wide range of interests and goals, such that it is not clear what the ultimate objective of LISA might be. Supporters are generally well-educated, dedicated people who are firmly committed to developing a sustainable farming system. Unfortunately, they have some serious misconceptions about agriculture and its economic and technological basis.

Perspectives

There is a popular misconception that reducing the use of agricultural chemicals and fertilizers would automatically reduce the contamination of water resources, [insure] safer food supplies, and improve sustainability of U.S. agriculture. Unfortunately, the current movement to support low-input systems is based more upon emotion and philosophy than on science and experience. It is supported on small-scale demonstrations that cannot necessarily be extrapolated to mainstream agriculture.

Farmers don't want to buy pesticides and fertilizers. When they purchase these inputs, they are actually seeking control of pests and increased yields for increased profitability. They know from research and experience that they will be able to produce more of a higher quality product and do it more efficiently by using these inputs. They know that the long-term sustainability and productivity of their farming business depends upon the profitability these inputs can help provide.

Sound fertility management utilizes available livestock manures and crop rotations wherever practical, taking appropriate nutrient credits for these materials, then using commercial fertilizers to balance the crop needs for realistic yield goals.

Sound pest management includes a combination of mechanical, cultural, and biological practices with chemical systems in an overall integrated pest management system. But pest management is essential to maintaining production and quality. Food products damaged or contaminated by insects and diseases pose a more serious health risk to consumers than they face from crop protection chemical residues. But, using chemicals in a safe and responsible manner is essential for environmental protection.

LISA's Shortcomings

Research and extension support for low-input systems is important for the farmers who want that information, but it is very unlikely that the mainstream U.S. agriculture will be able to meet the demands for food and fiber through the adoption of such systems. Sustainability of a management system is directly tied to its profitability. In the evolution of today's progressive management systems, practices now being promoted by low-input advocates have sorted out as being inefficient and not competitive for most producers. Hired labor has given way to increased used of pesticides and larger field equipment because labor-intensive systems were not able to compete and because of more desirable employment opportunities for the farm labor supply.

Unfortunately there is nothing very "newsworthy" about progressive management systems. It is much easier for critics to get media attention. "Official agriculture", university research and extension specialists, and industry agronomists, are forced to spend valuable time and resources reacting to claims made against modern systems. This detracts from their ability to refine and implement improvement on these systems. It would be much more wise and productive to use this expertise and limited financial resources to channel efforts into further improvements in progressive production systems to make them even more efficient and environmentally sound.

A Step Back

Americans have every right to be grateful to Mother Nature for the most bountiful food supply in human history for only 13.5 cents out of every income dollar.

But some of that gratitude should be reserved for the most advanced agricultural technology in the world, which over the last 50 years has revolutionized the productivity of our food chain.

Sadly, the Luddite leaders of Earth Day seem determined to destroy that technology by forcing the banning of all agricultural chemicals and pesticides—or at least drastically limiting their usage through something called "Low-Input Sustainable Agriculture" (LISA), recently endorsed by the National Research Council.

Fifty years ago, when we practiced that kind of farming, we paid 26 cents of every dollar for our food, and it took nearly 20 percent of our population to feed us. Today, it takes only 2 percent, as U.S. agri-technology has confounded the hunger mongers worldwide.

Warren Brookes, *The Washington Times*, April 12, 1990.

Progressive crop production systems in place today are based upon a long history of research, development, demonstration, and implementation that has sorted out the best practices for a given situation. These systems are constantly evolving, incorporating results of new research and adding new technology. As attention focuses on site-specific recommendations, more intensive management and more efficient and environmentally sound use of inputs will result while productivity and profitability are maintained.

The Drawbacks

The LISA program has some positive points but there are many shortcomings that must be considered. Low-input systems in the short-term may be more profitable, but they deplete resources. To the extent that they utilize excess resources (such as unused labor, livestock waste, municipal sludge, etc.) they can be sustainable for the long-term. But extra labor is not common on today's farms, less than 10% of U.S. nitrogen needs can be met with livestock manures, and only a few farmers have access to municipal wastes. These organic nutrient sources are more difficult to manage and pose a greater potential for contamination of groundwater and surface water supplies.

From a soil fertility perspective, eliminating inputs of required nutrients is not a sustainable practice. When crops are removed from the field, nutrients are taken out of the system and must be replaced to maintain long-term productivity. It may take several years for the impact of the nutrient removal to be fully identified. But it will often take several more years to correct the problem and restore productivity. . . .

Profitability and Protection

Industry response to the low-input, sustainable agriculture discussion will continue to focus on the real aspect of keeping agricultural producers in business, profitability. But, with the essentiality of profitability, that discussion will also continue to emphasize concerns for protection of the soil and the environment in general.

Because agricultural issues have the attention of the public, now is the time to place emphasis on the essential role of agriculture in society, both in the U.S. and in the world. The positive aspects of progressive agricultural production must be emphasized as well as the source of much of that information, Land Grant University research and extension. Similarly, the important roles of manufactured inputs in that food production system must be noted. Forceful confrontation with detractors will likely be less effective in influencing attitudes than calm, logical and factual discussion of the issues.

Distinguishing Between Fact and Opinion

This activity is designed to help develop the basic critical thinking skill of distinguishing between fact and opinion. Consider the following statement as an example: "Chemical pesticide and fertilizer use has saved American farmers millions of hours in work while substantially increasing crop yields." This statement is a fact with which no one could disagree. But consider another statement about pesticides. "Pesticide residues on food pose no risk to consumers." This statement expresses an opinion with which anyone who opposes widespread pesticide use would disagree.

When investigating controversial issues it is important that one be able to distinguish between statements of fact and statements of opinion. It is also important to recognize that not all statements of fact are true. They may appear to be true, but some are based on inaccurate or false information. For this activity, however, we are concerned with understanding the difference between those statements which appear to be factual and those which appear to be based primarily on opinion.

Most of the following statements are taken from the viewpoints in this chapter. Consider each statement carefully. *Mark O for any statement you believe is an opinion or interpretation of facts. Mark F for any statement you believe is a fact. Mark I for any statement you believe is impossible to judge.*

If you are doing this activity as a member of a class or group, compare your answers with those of other class or group members. Be able to defend your answers. You may discover that others have come to different conclusions than you have. Listening to the reasons others present for their answers may give you valuable insights into distinguishing between fact and opinion.

> *O = opinion*
> *F = fact*
> *I = impossible to judge*

103

1. The current EPA system of regulating dangerous chemicals puts more emphasis on economics than it does on health.

2. Many environmentalists, scientists, and farmers are convinced that we have become overdependent on pesticides.

3. The U.S. Department of Agriculture estimates that thirty thousand farmers now raise crops without chemicals.

4. In 1980, the National Cancer Institute found that the pesticide Captan caused tumors in mice.

5. Americans could improve their health and reduce the risk of cancer by eating less fat and more fiber, rather than worrying about pesticide residues.

6. In 1983 the EPA banned the pesticide ethylene dibromide.

7. Currently, more than 2.6 billion pounds of pesticides are used annually in the United States.

8. The public's initially strong acceptance of pesticides changed when Rachel Carson published her antipesticide book, *Silent Spring.*

9. America's food is free from pesticide residues.

10. The Food Marketing Institute discovered that 78 percent of all grocery shoppers ranked pesticide residues as their most serious concern.

11. In general, current laws allow for outrageous amounts of pesticides on food.

12. Apples, corn, tomatoes, potatoes, peaches, carrots, lettuce, grapes, and oranges contain 90 percent of all carcinogenic residues.

13. Services like NutriClean will ultimately lead to a complete change in the American agricultural system.

14. Farmers should oppose commercial testing of produce because it promotes fear.

15. The California Department of Food and Agriculture analyzed over seven thousand food samples for residues of over one hundred different pesticides in 1987.

16. Government studies show that typical human exposure to pesticide residues is 100,000 times below the levels that cause any effects in lab animals.

17. The emphasis on the insignificant risks from pesticide residues clouds our ability to focus on more important environmental issues.

18. Modern American agriculture cannot last. It is neither economically nor environmentally sustainable.

19. Preventable soil erosion costs the nation $44 billion a year in fertilizers carried off fields.

Periodical Bibliography

The following articles have been selected to supplement the diverse views presented in this chapter.

Larry L. Armstrong — "The Nifty Nematode and Those Bug-eating Bugs," *Business Week*, November 6, 1989.

Sharon S. Begley — "Dangers in the Veggie Patch," *Newsweek*, January 30, 1989.

Douglas H. Bosco — "Food Irradiation," *USA Today*, January 1988.

Arthur S. Brisbane — "Making Money the Old-Fashioned Way," *The Washington Post National Weekly Edition*, October 30-November 5, 1989.

Consumer Reports — "Too Much Fuss About Pesticides?" October 1989.

Naomi J. Freundlich — "Why the Great Grape Scare Missed the Point," *Business Week*, April 3, 1989.

Susan Gilbert — "America Tackles the Pesticide Crisis," *The New York Times Magazine*, October 8, 1989.

Howard H. Kohn — "Fields of Dreams: Old Farming Is New Again," *Rolling Stone*, October 5, 1989.

Warren E. Leary — "The Debate About the Carcinogens That Man Didn't Make," *The New York Times*, March 5, 1989.

Dale A. Miller — "The American Paradox," *Vital Speeches of the Day*, December 15, 1989.

Madeleine Nash — "It's Ugly, but It Works," *Time*, May 21, 1990.

Richard Rhodes — "Organic Farms: Agriwisdom," *The New York Times*, November 24, 1989.

Jim Schwab — "The Attraction Is Chemical," *The Nation*, October 16, 1989.

Sue Shellenbarger — "A Movement to Farm Without Chemicals Makes Surprising Gains," *The Wall Street Journal*, May 11, 1989.

Joanne J. Silberner — "Protecting Against One Bad Apple," *U.S. News & World Report*, March 27, 1989.

Cheryl Stubbendieck — "Man-made Chemicals Are Less Hazardous than Believed," *The New York Times*, March 5, 1989.

Anastasia A. Toufexis — "Dining with the Invisible Danger," *Time*, March 27, 1989.

3

CHAPTER

How Can the Garbage Problem Be Reduced?

THE ENVIRONMENTAL
CRISIS

Chapter Preface

The freighter *Pelicano* set sail from Philadelphia in September 1986 laden with fourteen thousand tons of toxic incinerator ash. For over two years the ship plied the seas seeking a port that would accept its lethal cargo. Finally, after illegally dumping four thousand pounds of the ash on a beach in Haiti, the captain claimed the rest of the cargo was accepted by an unspecified country.

The *Pelicano*'s sad journey is indicative of the growing refuse problem facing the United States. According to a study reported in *Time*, each American generates over fifteen hundred pounds of garbage annually. In the past, waste was generally buried in landfills, but now many landfills are full. To compound the problem, hundreds of citizen groups have organized to block efforts to build new landfills due to a concern over toxic landfill leakage and the threat of groundwater contamination. Waste management experts, politicians, public interest groups, and environmentalists agree that new solutions to waste disposal must be found.

In this chapter, the authors present their solutions to the growing problem of handling America's garbage.

"Burning wastes has a long list of positive environmental benefits, in addition to solving landfill problems. "

Incinerating Waste Can Help Reduce Garbage

Harold M. Draper

Harold M. Draper is a waste management analyst for the Tennessee Valley Authority, an independent U.S. government agency responsible for the development of the Tennessee River Basin. In the following viewpoint, Draper asserts that burning city garbage in power plants is less harmful than burying garbage in landfills. He contends that it is possible to produce energy from waste which offsets disposal costs and reduces the total volume of garbage by 75 percent. While he also supports recycling, Draper argues that recycling can only be partially effective.

As you read, consider the following questions:

1. Why does Draper discount the notion that citizens must choose between burning and recycling?
2. According to the author, how does waste-to-energy ash compare to landfill leachate?
3. Why is Draper not concerned about the dioxin emitted from waste-to-energy facilities?

Harold M. Draper, "Waste-to-Energy Controversy: Background," unpublished paper, 1990. Reprinted with permission.

108

W aste management is a controversial area in most parts of the U.S. As in all controversial policy areas, there is much misleading information being disseminated.

A bad public perception of waste-to-energy is being promoted by local grassroots groups in many cities. These groups stress that garbage incinerators are expensive and pose environmental and health hazards. They sometimes say that incinerators are "too subject to breakdowns and explosions," and are a high-tech rather than simple low-tech solution. Furthermore, money for an incinerator will go to a multi-national corporation whereas recycling and composting will foster local industries. Organic vegetable gardening in cooperatives using compost from solid waste is part of what is being promoted. Usually, the argument against waste-to-energy is framed so that the alternatives are either recycling or waste-to-energy, with no possibility of compromise.

Misleading Arguments

There are other arguments presented against waste-to-energy, but the above are the major ones. I believe that all of them are either wrong, misleading, or at best, only half true. The misinformation begins with the language used, "garbage incinerator," and continues when "recycling" is used to include every kind of product imaginable except energy.

The correct term should be "waste-to-energy" or "municipal waste combustion." The word incinerator implies a 1950s style plant with no energy recovery and no pollution control. Old incinerators are not much better than if you burned garbage in your fireplace or wood stove. In contrast, a modern waste-to-energy facility has controlled combustion with extensive emission monitoring. Modern waste-to-energy has no relation to old incinerators.

Here are some inaccurate statements to watch for:

We either recycle or we burn.

Response: This is the wrong question. The correct statement is that we can either landfill or do something else. This "recycle or burn" statement assumes that recycling and burning are at odds with each other. In fact, recycling is totally compatible with burning. Waste-to-energy is a part of "integrated solid waste management" as promoted by EPA [Environmental Protection Agency]. It makes no sense to burn an aluminum can, or glass, or steel. The types of high grade papers that can be recycled are a small portion of all the paper in the waste. Removing recyclables from the waste will make a better fuel, by raising the BTU [British thermal unit] content of the waste. Keeping metals out will reduce the wear and tear on machinery. Finally, energy is a useful product and should be considered a form of recycling.

We can easily recycle 25 percent (or 50 percent or 90 percent) of the waste stream far cheaper than we can burn it.

Response: There is really no way to answer this question because no one has ever done it at these levels on a large scale. Since markets for recyclables are not well developed, recycling at these levels would involve heavy subsidies. These might be higher than waste-to-energy costs. Waste-to-energy offers the opportunity to stabilize waste disposal costs for 20 years or more, and revenues from energy sales can help to reduce tipping fees. If energy prices rise in the 1990s, waste-to-energy would appear to be a more attractive solution.

An Effective Tool

Municipal waste combustion has been and continues to be a primary strategy for environmentally sound solid waste management in Europe and Japan. It is a technology that has continued to develop with each new facility employing the latest design features for environmental controls, energy recovery, and materials recycling. It is a technology that represents a demonstrated tool for local governments who are responsible for the management and disposal of municipal solid waste.

Hunter F. Taylor, a paper presented at the International Conference on Municipal Waste Combustion, April 1989.

When the word "recycling" is used here, it usually means more than just making a new aluminum can out of an old one. It means taking the garbage and making it into another product, such as compost. Again, if composting is a form of recycling, then energy production should be considered recycling.

Recycling Misconceptions

Instead of comparing the costs of recycling with burning, a more appropriate comparison would be to compare the cost of landfilling with that of recycling/waste-to-energy. For a state like Florida, burning is cheaper than a landfill, from an environmental as well as an economic standpoint. This is why Florida leads the nation in waste-to-energy capacity. For other areas, I do not know which is cheaper. This would be influenced by the availability of good clay soil and cheap land. However, if all the environmental and economic benefits are factored in, waste-to-energy should compare favorably with landfilling and recycling.

Until new manufacturing plants are built to use recycled materials, and new markets developed, recycling and composting will not result in a significant decrease in the amount of waste landfilled. A decision to recycle is a decision to landfill the majority of the waste for the next 20 years or more. A decision to build a waste-to-energy facility is a decision to reduce the volume of wastes going to a landfill by up to 90 percent, depending on the composition of the waste and how much bypasses the combustion process.

The current craze in state governments to mandate recycling (Florida in 1988 and Louisiana in 1989 are examples) will result in market gluts of materials. Many Florida counties currently pay dealers to take newsprint off their hands, as opposed to receiving money for them. When the extra costs of collection and handling are taken into account, curbside recycling can be very expensive—as much as $150 to $200 per ton. We should be careful about producing a product for which there is no market. Current examples are newsprint and compost.

If a decision is made to promote recycling for a large portion of the waste stream, other technologies for energy recovery should also be studied. These include methane production from waste, ethanol production, and pyrolysis. All of these are technically feasible, although not demonstrated economically, and probably hold out more hope than massive recycling and composting of truly reducing the waste stream. Again, recycling is totally compatible with these technologies. Methane production even produces compost.

Non-hazardous Ash

The ash is a hazardous waste.

Response: This is a deliberate effort at confusion. There are many unhealthy components of household municipal solid waste, but Congress has chosen to regulate this as non-hazardous under the Resource Conservation and Recovery Act (RCRA). There is nothing in the ash that was not in the garbage before it was burned. Although there are several bills in Congress that address ash management, Congress currently has not specified under which section of RCRA it wishes to regulate municipal waste combustion ash. If regulated under the same subtitle of the law as municipal solid waste (subtitle D), ash will by definition be non-hazardous. If placed under the hazardous waste subtitle, it will by definition be hazardous.

Since ash is not now on EPA's list as hazardous or non-hazardous, it can be tested according to an EPA test. If it fails the test, it is hazardous. When the test is performed on ash from a waste-to-energy facility, the ash passes almost all of the time. When it fails, it is because of lead and cadmium leachate. When compared to landfill leachate, ash leachate has much lower concentrations of almost all metals, as well as 20 times less chemical oxygen demand. So landfilling ash is much better than landfilling unburned waste.

In addition, ash can be treated so that it will pass the EPA test all the time. There are several companies selling these processes. In response to all the misinformation, a new market has opened up for these companies.

Waste-to-energy creates a new environmental problem.

Response: The assumptions here are that landfills are completely safe and that recycling is totally benign. Both assumptions are wrong. Strict landfill regulations on leachate control, lining, monitoring, and methane control exist and are proposed because groundwater pollution is a major national problem, and landfill gases are explosive.

Environmental problems with recycling exist, but are rarely publicized. Any manufacturing plant, whether producing a material from virgin feedstocks or recovered feedstocks, will have some impact. Newspaper recycling results in sludges which fail hazardous waste tests, for example. Composting also has environmental impacts. If there are heavy metals in the municipal waste, there will be heavy metals in the compost. This compost should not be used on food crops, and I suspect should not be spread over any other lands, either. The solution to pollution is not dilution by spreading composted garbage everywhere. In waste management debates, it is very important to separate yard waste composting from municipal waste composting. Yard waste composting should be promoted; municipal waste composting should be undertaken very cautiously, if at all.

Contributors to acid rain are sulfur dioxide and nitrogen oxides. As a fuel, municipal waste contains much less sulfur than coal, and this should be a benefit in controlling sulfur dioxide emissions. Waste-to-energy facilities remove 50 to 70 percent of the sulfur dioxide that is created in combustion. Nitrogen oxides can be reduced by combustion control measures, but will result from all combustion.

Safe Emissions

Ozone problems are primarily caused by hydrocarbons interacting with nitrogen oxides. Ozone control strategies are focused on hydrocarbon emissions, and the primary sources of these are motor vehicles, petroleum refining, and dry cleaning. A good way to reduce ozone formation is through the use of alternative fuels such as ethanol. For waste-to-energy facilities, it is possible to achieve nearly complete (99 percent) removal of volatile organic compounds involved in ozone formation.

Unlike coal, oil, and natural gas combustion, waste-to-energy is not a net contributor to the greenhouse effect. Most of the wastes (75 percent) are from biomass such as paper, yard wastes, food wastes, and wood. Assuming as many trees are grown as are burned, there is no net release of carbon dioxide. To the extent that fossil fuels are displaced, there is a net benefit in reducing the greenhouse effect.

An important point is that any new power plant will have better emissions controls than an older fossil fuel plant, since technology has improved and regulations are tougher.

Finally, it should be pointed out that 99.9 percent of everything emitted from the stack of a waste-to-energy facility is a non-pollutant. These are molecular nitrogen, oxygen, carbon dioxide, and water. It is ironic that all the attention is focused on the 0.1 percent of all emissions, and that dioxins are only 0.0000000001 percent of all the emissions.

The Misled Public

Asking the public to choose between burning and recycling suggests there are two means of solid waste disposal available to the local government and it's an either/or situation. One is high tech, threatening, and expensive, the other low tech, nonthreatening and seemingly inexpensive. It is easy to predict which the public would choose. Unfortunately, the public has been misled and the effectiveness of local government officials trying to solve the problem has been compromised.

Hunter F. Taylor, a paper presented at the International Conference on Municipal Waste Combustion, April 1989.

Clearly, burning wastes has a long list of positive environmental benefits, in addition to solving landfill problems. Recycling is good and should be required; it is just not the sole solution to all our waste management problems. If we have good markets, we should recycle, compost, and recover energy. . . .

A Desirable Coalition

If your goal is to reduce waste volumes going to the landfill, recycling will not eliminate the need for burning. If you have plenty of landfill space, then you can probably afford to put off a study of waste combustion options. To raise us to EPA's goal of 25 percent recycling will take more than mandates by legislatures. It will take large federal subsidies and preferences. To get us higher than 25 percent, fundamental changes in our economic system and way of life may be needed. Waste-to-energy, whether mass burn or RDF [refuse-derived fuel], can stabilize waste disposal costs and extend landfill life significantly. Together with recycling, composting, and waste reduction, it is a necessary and desirable part of municipal solid waste management.

"Incinerators perpetuate landfills and all of the problems associated with them—contamination of water supplies and loss of resources."

Incinerating Waste Cannot Help Reduce Garbage

Judy Christup

Opponents of burning municipal wastes in power plants argue that these plants simply create landfills in the sky. Instead of burning garbage, these critics advocate recycling, composting, source reduction, product redesign, and other non-hazardous methods of dealing with waste. In the following viewpoint, Judy Christup, an associate editor of *Greenpeace*, a magazine produced by the well-known environmental organization, writes that waste-to-energy plants are serious polluters. Christup argues that incinerating garbage spews toxins into the air while the residual ash creates groundwater contamination. She maintains that burning wastes is a temporary measure that will not solve the garbage crisis.

As you read, consider the following questions:

1. What toxic metals does the author believe are present in waste-to-energy plant ash?
2. Why does Christup think dioxin is so dangerous?
3. How does the author say European waste-to-energy plants differ from their American counterparts?

Judy Christup, "Rising from the Ashes: Our Trash Shouldn't Burn," *Greenpeace*, May/June 1988. Reprinted with permission.

A drab yellow Department of Public Works dumptruck pulls into a rusting sheet-metal alcove at the incinerator in northeast Washington, D.C. The driver positions the truck bed under a grimy chute and with a clattering roar, the truck fills with dense dark ash and charred twisted metals. Pausing only a moment, he pulls his truck out, the container full yet uncovered, and heads for the on-ramp to I-295 East.

Our Toyota follows, bumping along the pitted interstate. The windshield darkens as the ash blows off the load. A circuitous route leads us to our final destination—a dumpsite in a ravine off Martin Luther King Avenue, in southeast Washington, behind the mission-style brick buildings belonging to Saint Elizabeth's psychiatric care hospital. The ash-filled canyon creates an eerie tableau. Crumpled bedsprings jut from the cooled embers while a noxious liquid, glimmering like a futuristic rainbow, trickles from a drainage pipe.

Saint Elizabeth's, called Saint E's by local residents, is one of the oldest and largest federal psychiatric hospitals in the United States. Dumping this waste in the patients' backyard is serious business—incinerator ash contains a host of dangerous toxic chemicals. But a certain irony is unmistakable. A nation neck-deep in garbage, garbage that is rich in recoverable resources, is rushing to burn its refuse. The burning precludes recovery, releases toxic wastes into the air and leaves a poisonous pile of black ash, which is buried in the ground—certainly a form of madness, by any standards.

Running Out of Time

America's cities are drowning in garbage. With landfills in the U.S. closing at a rate of ten per week, the days of town dumps are clearly numbered. According to David Morris and Neil Seldman of the Institute for Local Self-Reliance, more than half the cities in the U.S. will exhaust their current landfills by 1990. More than 2,000 have closed [since 1983] for environmental reasons, and another 700, for lack of space.

With the landfill clock ticking away, town and city councils are under pressure to make quick decisions about waste management. With little or no guidance from federal and state governments, they are forced to deal with their garbage crises alone. Well, not actually alone. Large corporations and high-priced consultants gladly offer their services, presenting what appears to be an out-of-sight, out-of-mind solution: mass-burn incineration.

Richard Denison of the Environmental Defense Fund (EDF) describes the usual scenario: "You have a local solid waste manager, a city government employee, with a garbage problem. An incinerator company or consulting firm waltzes in and says,

'Give us money, get municipal bonds issued, and we'll take care of your problem.' It's one-stop shopping." Hearing the hard-sell, most local solid waste managers don't even think about the residual ash.

Recycling's Advantages

Incineration and recycling divert garbage from the landfill, but recycling has many more advantages. It produces no air pollution and no ash. It reduces the need to harvest or mine new materials such as trees, iron ore, aluminum and oil, consequently reducing environmental impacts associated with processing those materials. Recycling aluminum uses only 5 percent of the energy needed to mine aluminum and recycling paper uses 25 to 75 percent the energy of tree harvesting.

Mary Beth Pfeiffer, *American Legion Magazine*, January 1990.

And there's the rub. Both the ash and the smoke from the incinerator stack are poisonous. Fly ash, gleaned from the stacks by filters, is the most harmful; according to EDF's compilation of data from dozens of U.S. incinerators, all fly ash samples exceeded the Environmental Protection Agency (EPA) hazardous waste limits for cadmium or lead. Bottom ash, the burned remains of the garbage, exceeded EPA's lead limits in four of ten samples, and roughly half the samples of combined fly and bottom ash were over the limit.

The EPA's November '87 report on four municipal incinerators supports EDF's findings—dangerously high levels of lead, cadmium, and other metals were found in the ash from all four incinerators. According to EDF's Richard Denison, "The EPA report corroborates what we've seen around the country but underestimates the problem. It's representative of one set of incinerators out there—the older ones." Ironically, ash from state-of-the-art plants is even more hazardous, because the modern facilities have more efficient air pollution control devices. Toxics scrubbed out of the stacks end up in the ash.

Toxic Ash and Landfills

So why would any city in its right mind want to deal with the stuff? Jim Vallette, Greenpeace toxics campaigner, explains, "Right now most municipalities aren't worrying about ash. The EPA hasn't technically classified incinerator ash as hazardous waste, so they can landfill it as though it were household garbage."

But the city landfill is where the worries begin, not where they end. Ash is spread by wind and water. Dioxins and toxic metals in the ash accumulate up the food chain and are readily absorbed and retained in the tissues of living organisms. Bound to soil particles, their persistence in the environment increases significantly. As rain water trickles through buried ash, dioxins, heavy metals, and other toxic substances are carried along. They work their way down to the aquifers and streams, polluting local water supplies.

"It's ironic," says Jim Vallette. "The reason cities started building incinerators in the first place is because town dumps are filling up and polluting water supplies. Now they're dumping the same toxics that were in their garbage to start with, plus a whole new set created in the furnaces. The difference is that some of those toxics are more concentrated and more soluble in water than they were in their original state."

What comes out of the stacks is just as frightening. Besides dioxins and furans, incinerators emit roughly 27 different metals, over 200 organic chemicals and a variety of acidic gases. An average 1,600 ton-a-day incinerator blows out 0.06 pounds of dioxins and furans, 510 pounds of hydrocarbons, 5,000 pounds of lead, 361 pounds of cadmium, 2,244 pounds of chromium, 20 pounds of mercury, and 13,250 pounds of zinc every day.

The toxic effluent receiving the most attention is dioxin. According to Dr. Barry Commoner, it is actually created inside the smokestack after the gases leave the combustion chamber. His findings were confirmed by Canadian scientists, who reported in the *Journal of Chromatography and Science* that fly ash acts as a catalyst in the formation of dioxin.

Dioxins in Humans

EPA's National Human Adipose Tissue Survey demonstrated that seven out of ten samples of human fat tested in recent years contain the most toxic of dioxins: 2, 3, 7, 8-tetrachlorodibenzo-p-dioxin. According to the Center for the Biology of Natural Systems (CBNS), the fatty tissues of citizens in several parts of the U.S. contain average dioxin levels of 6.4 parts per trillion. CBNS says that this dosage is sufficient to cause an "unacceptable" increase in cancers in the exposed population, especially breast-fed children. If all 220 of the incinerators proposed across the U.S. are built, dioxin emissions would bring many segments of the U.S. population beyond this already "unacceptable" level.

In a report released in the fall of 1987, the EPA estimated that the health threat from breathing incinerator pollution will be minimal—four to sixty more cases of cancer nationwide each year. But the agency considered only inhaled airborne pollutants, ignoring the other pathways into the human body: skin, food and water. "There hasn't been enough work on exposure to dioxins through the food chain, where the impact is much

117

greater," says Dr. Paul Connett, assistant professor of chemistry at St. Lawrence University. Connett, who is national coordinator of Work on Waste U.S.A., says, "The brunt of risk analysis is being done by highly-paid consultants who are very conscious of the desired outcome by those footing the bill. Nobody knows what the cancer rate is going to be. These risk analyses can be off by a factor of a thousand."

Technologies do exist to limit the release of metals and acid gases into the atmosphere, but they are not systematically used, and they do nothing to reduce dioxin formation. Only a handful of the 110 incinerators operating in the U.S.—in Framingham, Massachusetts; Marion County, Oregon; Clairmont, New Hampshire; Biddeford, Maine; and Commerce, California—employ acid gas scrubbing procedures. The scrubbers in the Oregon facility, for instance, have reduced hydrogen chloride emissions to 10 parts per million (ppm). In contrast, the Peekskill, New York, incinerator emits 500 to 600 ppm of hydrogen chloride, a level which *Technology Review* magazine calls "typical of scrubberless plants throughout the U.S."

State-of-the-art pollution controls will not be required on current or new plants for some time. The EPA plans to impose technology-base limits. . . on existing incinerator emissions beginning in 1993. Until the EPA writes emission guidelines, states and localities are on their own.

Tax-exempt Burners

Despite the health and environmental issues, the rush to burn is being hastened by incentives provided by Congress, the EPA and the Department of Commerce. From the late 1970s through 1986, incinerator investors could take advantage of energy tax credits, the investment tax credit and accelerated depreciation rules. Since 1986, the trend is away from private ownership and toward government-owned waste-to-energy plants, which are leased to private firms that operate them. Public ownership means that tax exempt bonds can be used for financing. And the 1978 Public Utilities Regulatory Policies Act requires utilities to buy power from waste-to-energy incinerators at a price set by each state, guaranteeing another source of income.

EPA policy historically has tilted toward an incineration regime by not dealing with the garbage crisis. After President Reagan took office in 1981, nearly all of the money devoted to garbage disposal was diverted to hazardous waste enforcement—a hot issue at the time. But even after Superfund was implemented to help clean up hazardous dumps, resources were not directed back to garbage disposal.

Garbage and other "non-hazardous" waste programs were systematically starved—their budgets cut from $29 million in 1979 to $16 million in 1981, and their staff nearly halved, from 128 to

74. Then in 1982, 73 of the 74 employees were either reassigned or laid off, and funding plummeted to $322,000. A particularly useful EPA grants program—one that provided money to states developing long-range garbage disposal plans—was discontinued.

There are now ten EPA staff members working on garbage programs. [As of May 1988] EPA had neither issued new regulations for municipal landfills (ordered by Congress in 1984) nor formulated guidelines regarding incinerator ash disposal. In the absence of such requirements, waste handlers are free to fill in the blanks for themselves.

Inside Incinerators

What this institutional bias has brought us is the modern mass-burn incinerator—technologically sophisticated, shiny and sleek and, unlike the Washington incinerator, difficult to approach without security clearance. All of the action is inside, in a vast storage room, where a crane operator is sealed off from the garbage by a plexiglass window. With the slide of a lever, the gigantic steel crane is activated, lifting tons of trash with each bite, and forcing it down the gullet of the combustion chamber.

The trash is engulfed by scorching 40-foot flames, while the supporting grate shakes and mixes it to allow even burning. Actual incineration time is just a second or two at 2,000 degrees Fahrenheit. Forced air is injected above the fire to maintain temperatures in excess of 1,500 degrees, in an attempt to destroy some of the toxic gases. The burning trash heats water in the boiler to produce steam. The steam drives a turbine to generate electricity.

When approaching city and town councils, waste-to-energy corporations often cite the success of mass-burn technology in Europe. But trash incinerators in places like West Germany start from a different premise. Garbage is reduced at the source by discouraging excess packaging; glass, metals, paper and combustibles are extracted and collected for recycling. Only the remainder is burned.

U.S. incineration is approached in a more direct fashion —throw it all into the fire. In fact, many incinerator contracts require municipalities to produce a certain amount of garbage. If the quota is not met, garbage must be imported from other sources. This "burn everything" mentality wreaks havoc in the guts of incinerators and in the lungs of people breathing the heavy metals and toxic chemicals in incinerator-contaminated air.

European-style mass-burn incinerators used in America have suffered frequent breakdowns and repairs. Our trash (high in plastics and metals) produces strong acidic gases that corrode incinerator interiors, especially when it is burned at the temperatures required to produce enough steam for electricity generators. Most European plants don't generate electricity, although

119

many use the steam to heat proximate buildings. According to a *Newsday* survey, half of all mass-burn plants operating in the U.S. have had unscheduled shutdowns, and three others have closed permanently.

No Time-tested Experience

The marketers of these facilities are as new to the business as their clients. Wheelabrator Environmental Systems, Ogden Martin, American REF-FUEL, Combustion Engineering, Foster Wheeler, Westinghouse Electric, Waste Management Inc., Consumat, and Thermo Electron are earning millions selling incineration technology, yet four of them have never built an incinerator plant of any kind. Ogden Martin Systems, one of the more experienced waste-to-energy corporations, is under contract to build 14 incinerators at a cost of $2.3 billion, yet it has only three plants in operation [as of May 1988], none more than two years old.

Money and Air Pollution

Incineration is not a viable alternative for every community. . . . Incinerators require much initial capital and usually take from three to five years to construct. The community must have a need for the supply of energy produced by the incinerator and must weigh the impact of the incinerator on the environment.

Air pollution persists as the major concern for incinerator technologies. Gases emerging from the stack of an incinerator contain particles and unburned, volatile compounds such as hydrochloric acid, nitrous oxides, dioxins and furans.

Philip R. O'Leary, Patrick W. Walsh, and Robert K. Ham, *Scientific American,* December 1988.

Still, waste-to-energy plants have been welcomed in more than forty states, the bulk of which are mass-burn facilities. More than 111 incinerators burn about 5 percent of the nation's garbage, and over 220 are planned or under construction. By the mid-1990s there could be 300 incinerators burning up to 25 percent of the municipal waste stream. According to Cynthia Pollock of the Worldwatch Institute, "Mass-burn plants appeal to city administrators because they require no change in waste collection patterns, their management can be turned over to a private owner if desired, low cost financing mechanisms are available and there is a guaranteed market for the energy produced."

Ultimately, this enormous investment of time, money and expertise, with its accompanying environmental and public health costs, is doing little more than reduce the volume of the nation's wastes. And even this small gain is disputed. Not all garbage in the waste stream is incinerated, and raw garbage compacts in a landfill. Given the practical realities, a well-operated incinerator will reduce the amount of landfill space required by about 60 percent. This means that landfill space will be extended by two-and-a-half times: five years of landfill space is extended to about thirteen. And the technology that provides this "service", the modern incinerator, has a lifetime of about 20 years and a cost of $50-$400 million.

Perpetuating the Problem

The mind-set associated with incineration is that we can deal with the whole trash stream with one method, and we can if we want to "waste" our land, air, water, health and money. Incinerators perpetuate landfills and all of the problems associated with them—contamination of water supplies and loss of resources. Other choices are far cheaper and safer and can still achieve a 60 percent volume reduction in our waste stream. A combination of recycling and composting, source reduction, education, reuse and product redesign are affordable, environmentally benign solutions to our garbage problems.

Neil Seldman of the Institute for Local Self-Reliance says that 30 to 40 percent of municipal waste can be separated at the source into compost material, cans, glass, and paper. Another 30 to 40 percent can be recovered at special processing plants. The final 20 to 40 percent can be landfilled—this is equal to the volume of ash produced by a modern incinerator.

"It's a plastic bag crisis, not a waste crisis," says Dr. Connett. "The solution is to go down and see what's in our plastic bags. The paper, cardboard, cans, glass, and food are all resources until they're mixed up and put into a plastic bag. Then they're waste. Using high-tech burning machines is simply perfecting the destruction of our natural resources. We need to recycle in a way we've never done before. People are ready for it, but they're not being given the leadership. When given a chance, people recycle. We've got to recycle as if there's a war on. And there is a war on—a war against waste."

> *"The overall volume of garbage that must be sent to landfills and waste-to-energy plants will grow steadily."*

New Landfills Can Solve the Garbage Crisis

National Solid Wastes Management Association

The National Solid Wastes Management Association (NSWMA) is a special-interest group that conducts public-opinion polls and presents position papers on how America's waste should be handled. In the following viewpoint, the Association contends that exaggerated media accounts of waste problems have unnecessarily turned public opinion against landfills. NSWMA believes that no level of recycling or incineration will completely erase the need for landfills.

As you read, consider the following questions:

1. What does the NSWMA mean by the term "integrated waste management"?
2. According to the NSWMA, how did the public's attitude toward groundwater pollution affect its thoughts on environmental regulation?
3. What misconceptions does the NSWMA think Americans have about recycling?

National Solid Wastes Management Association, "Public Attitudes Toward Garbage Disposal," a special report, May 4, 1989. Reprinted with permission.

Since 1988's crescendo of bad news about medical waste, public concern about garbage disposal has eased. American voters now place "ensuring adequate garbage disposal" third on a list of major problems facing local officials—behind improving public education and providing affordable housing. This marks a significant shift in opinion since July and August 1988, when waste disposal ranked second only to education. But it closely mirrors the results of a similar poll in May 1988.

We live in a throw-away society. According to the U.S. Environmental Protection Agency, every American produces around 3.6 pounds of garbage a day—over 80 percent more than in 1960. All together, we discard nearly 160 million tons per year, enough to bury 2,700 football fields in a layer ten stories high.

Meanwhile, our country's disposal capacity continues to decline. In 1978, approximately 14,000 solid waste landfills operated in the U.S.; today, 70 percent of these have closed. Faced with intensified concern about groundwater contamination, local officials have rarely approved construction of new or expanded facilities. As a result, only five states—California, Maine, New York, Texas and Wisconsin—now encompass 40 percent of the nation's landfills. Here are a few other examples:

• In the Chicago metropolitan region, five landfills have closed since 1987. Using a "best case" scenario, Illinois officials estimate that the remaining 29 sites will reach their capacity by 1995.

• In 1980, 150 facilities were operating in Indiana; 83 remain open today. By 1992, this number will drop again—to 53—leaving half of the state's rubbish without adequate disposal.

• Officials at the Connecticut Department of Environmental Protection have calculated that most of the state's landfills can operate for only two more years. Already 88 of the state's 169 cities and towns must ship their rubbish to other jurisdictions for disposal.

• Finally, four states—Florida, Massachusetts, New Hampshire and New Jersey—will close virtually all active landfills within ten years.

Integrated Waste Management

To manage the country's rising quantities of garbage safely and effectively, most specialists now agree that public officials should adopt an "integrated waste management system" which emphasizes four components: source reduction (eliminating unnecessary discards before they enter the waste stream), recycling, resource recovery (building waste-to-energy plants that reduce the volume of trash by up to 90 percent) and landfills. EPA estimates that around 11 percent of our waste is being recycled; with enhanced public participation and other efforts, this figure may reach 20 or 25 percent.

How has the public reacted to this approach? As disposal capacity shrinks, uneasiness about the "garbage crisis" has increased dramatically. But recognition of the country's rubbish dilemma has not yet been translated into greater acceptance of waste-to-energy plants or additional landfills. Our polling shows why: whereas most Americans now realize that they have created a problem, they remain unwilling to take the steps which will be needed to solve it. Clearly, siting new waste management facilities has become a major public policy issue throughout the country.

More Space Needed

It has been argued that we can recycle waste and reduce waste at the source to such an extent that our need for disposal facilities will disappear. But this is pie in the sky. The Environmental Protection Agency estimates that by the year 2000, 55% of municipal wastes will still have to be landfilled. That's down from 77.5% now, but that still means finding a place for an estimated 107 million tons of waste. Ten years ago landfill disposal commonly cost $5 to $10 a ton. Today, fees of $50 a ton are common and $140 is not unknown.

William D. Ruckelshaus, *The Wall Street Journal*, September 5, 1989.

To understand these trends, it is important to consider how public concern about the environment has risen. Until 1987, nearly 40 percent of American adults believed that environmental quality in the country was improving, while only one-third felt that increased pollution was a major cause for alarm. Since then, however, such attitudes have shifted dramatically. As the country prepared for presidential elections in 1988, renewed fears about environmental degradation once again occupied the national agenda.

Public Concerns

How did these concerns arise? Throughout the 1970s, public attention was largely directed toward reducing air pollution and industrial discharges into lakes, rivers and streams. From 1983 to 1988, however, the number of people who listed air emissions by industry as "the single most important environmental problem in the country today" dropped from 22 percent to 14 percent; surface water pollution by business and industry remained steady at about 11 percent. Meanwhile, hazardous waste—and its unseen threat to our drinking water—moved to the top of the list: around 20 percent of the general public now believe that toxic waste disposal represents the greatest danger to environmental quality.

Reflecting this shift, public attention has begun to focus on groundwater. In 1981, only 7 percent of American voters believed that "most underground sources of water" had been contaminated with chemicals or other pollutants. By 1986, this figure had risen to 11 percent; since then, it has reached 22 percent. At the same time, between 1981 and 1988, the total number of people who feel that groundwater pollution has become a serious problem exploded—from 28 percent to 54 percent.

One major outcome of these trends involves renewed support for stricter environmental regulation. Most Americans believe that more government intervention and oversight—not less—will address the country's most urgent problems. They also believe that increased regulation will not inhibit economic growth or threaten jobs. Essentially, they demand a national agenda which will assure both greater prosperity and environmental protection.

Garbage Disposal

Garbage disposal remains a prominent issue in most parts of the country. Despite intense publicity about drugs and drug-related crime, for example, most respondents place "assuring adequate disposal capacity" ahead of expanded police protection on their list of local priorities. But concern about garbage has also subsided to a degree since August 1988, when daily news stories about medical waste riveted public attention.

One significant outcome of this inquiry is reflected in the difference between "opinion leaders" and the public at large. Whereas 15 percent of American voters believe that solid waste disposal ranks first among local issues, only half as many opinion leaders (public officials, business executives, journalists, public interest activists and academics) share such views. In contrast, decision makers are more worried than other people about improving public education. These differences have not changed appreciably since February 1988.

What should we do with our garbage? At present, around 75 percent of the country's residential and commercial waste is deposited in landfills. By 1992, when many large cities run out of landfill space, 70 percent will still require such disposal. Yet few Americans seem inclined to accept new facilities. In May 1988, for example, only 30 percent favored building additional landfills in their communities, while 62 percent were opposed. Six months later, the number of outright opponents remained unchanged—65 percent—but support had dropped to 20 percent.

Support is greater when waste-to-energy plants are involved. Nearly 40 percent of American adults favor building such plants, while 48 percent oppose them. Among opinion leaders, the outcome is even more dramatic: almost 60 percent believe that such plants offer a viable solution to their community's disposal needs.

The explanation for such differences lies squarely in varying perceptions of environmental risk. Among adult Americans, 40 percent believe that ash residues from waste-to-energy plants pose a serious threat to underground water resources, and 56 percent are concerned about air emissions. Fewer than 40 percent are convinced that existing air pollution control technologies provide adequate safeguards against dioxins and other pollutants. In contrast, opinion leaders tend to feel that such technology is effective (59 percent) and are less worried about air and groundwater contamination.

The Recycling Myth

According to EPA, Americans recycle around 11 percent of their waste—a total of 17 million tons per year. Recycling involves several stages: collecting and separating reusable products, preparing them for manufacturing (so-called "intermediate processing"), using them as raw materials to produce new goods and returning them to commerce. Most recycling focuses on three or four common materials: aluminum, glass, cardboard and newspaper. As communities across the country adopt recycling programs, EPA estimates that as much as 25 percent of our waste may ultimately be reclaimed.

Public support for recycling remains overwhelming. In February, 1988, 70 percent of American adults agreed that "recycling can solve much of the solid waste disposal problem." In July and August, 84 percent said that "we could make a substantial reduction in the amount of solid waste if the nation made a major commitment to recycling.". . .

A Necessary Part

The uncertainties of incinerator technology highlight the need for resource conservation and recycling. But even after the municipal waste has been reduced, collected, recycled and incinerated, at least 20 percent remains to be disposed of in landfills. Landfills are therefore a necessary part of all integrated waste-management systems.

Philip O'Leary, Patrick W. Walsh, and Robert K. Ham, *Scientific American,* December 1988.

These figures raise an important question. Large pluralities of American voters apparently believe that by recycling somewhere between 25 and 50 percent of our waste, the country's garbage problem would be solved. Naturally, recycling represents a major element of our national waste management strategy. But it must be combined with other approaches. [By the year 2000,] for example, EPA estimates that we will throw away around 190 million tons of garbage per year. Even if we recycle half of that amount (more than Japan and West Germany, the world's best recyclers), we will still need disposal capacity for 95 million tons. And that disposal capacity may not be available.

As local officials face the mounting problem of garbage disposal, how will they address public opposition to new facilities? One frequent proposal involves appointing state or regional "siting boards" that would have the authority to resolve difficult political questions. When asked whether they would support or oppose this approach, one-third of American voters responded that they favored such boards; among opinion leaders, this figure rose to 50 percent. Perhaps more important, only 11 percent of those who opposed the idea said that they would seek legislative restrictions against new facilities.

Most Americans recognize that garbage disposal has become a significant problem while largely rejecting the need for new disposal facilities. Yet the success of integrated waste management systems depends in large measure upon assuring adequate disposal capacity. Even with a major expansion of recycling and waste reduction, the overall volume of garbage that must be sent to landfills and waste-to-energy plants will grow steadily into the next century. Unless new facilities can be built to meet this demand, public officials will face a continuing "garbage crisis" and escalating disposal costs.

"As landfill costs continue to rise because of space constraints and stricter environmental regulations. . .the appeal of recycling will inevitably grow."

Recycling Can Solve the Garbage Crisis

Cynthia Pollock-Shea

As landfill sites near large cities begin to close, the cost of dealing with garbage has nearly quadrupled. The dwindling waste dumps will become more expensive, argue many environmentalists, unless Americans get serious about recycling. In the following viewpoint, Cynthia Pollock-Shea writes that recycling can significantly reduce the volume of waste bound for landfills. In addition, Pollock-Shea writes that garbage is a veritable gold mine of recyclable materials. She argues that recycling conserves resources like water, energy, trees, bauxite, and tin. Pollock-Shea is a senior researcher at the Worldwatch Institute, a resource center for global issues in Washington, D.C.

As you read, consider the following questions:

1. How much air pollution does Pollock-Shea believe is decreased by recycling aluminum?
2. How much of America's refuse does the author say is buried?
3. In Pollock-Shea's opinion, what are the economic incentives for recycling?

Cynthia Pollock-Shea, "Recycling Urban Wastes: Solving the Garbage Glut." Reprinted, with permission, from *USA Today* magazine, July 1988. Copyright 1988 by the Society for the Advancement of Education.

Residents of New York City collectively discard 24,000 tons of materials each day. The amalgam, considered trash by most of its contributors, contains valuable metals, reusable glass containers, recyclable paper and plastic, and food wastes high in nutrient value. It also contains hazardous wastes—mercury from batteries, cadmium from fluorescent lights, and toxic chemicals from cleaning solvents, paints, and wood preservatives. New Yorkers hold the world record for producing the most garbage per capita, although growing volumes of refuse, as well as a scarcity of disposal sites, plague cities everywhere. Municipal governments worldwide are struggling to find the best methods for managing their residents' wastes. In industrial countries, the premium placed on space and environmental quality is restricting the use of traditional landfills. Increasingly, refuse is either hauled long distances to a sanitary landfill, burned in incinerators designed to recover energy, or separated to retrieve valuable materials for recycling.

Urban Mines

Most products available to consumers are intended for a one-night stand. They are purchased, utilized, and discarded with little regard for their remaining value. The energy, materials, and environmental losses associated with this consumption pattern are staggering. David Morris of the Washington-based Institute for Local Self Reliance explains: "A city the size of San Francisco disposes of more aluminum than is produced by a small bauxite mine, more copper than a medium copper mine and more paper than a good sized timber stand. San Francisco is a mine. The question is how to mine it most effectively and how to get the maximum value from the collected materials."

Recycling offers communities everywhere the opportunity to trim their waste disposal needs, and thereby reduce disposal costs, while simultaneously combating global environmental problems. Recycling metals, paper, glass, plastics, and organic wastes lessens the demand for energy and materials. Producing aluminum from scrap instead of bauxite cuts energy usage and air pollution by 95%. Making paper from discards instead of virgin timber not only saves valuable forests, it reduces the energy used by almost 75% and requires less than half as much water. Cutting fossil fuel consumption is one of the most effective actions people can take to slow the buildup of carbon dioxide that is warming the Earth's atmosphere, and recycling must be part of this effort to delay climate change. . . .

Some 90% of the refuse in the U.S. is still buried, but many U.S. landfills rapidly are filling up, and fears of groundwater contamination make landfills unwelcome neighbors. From January, 1984, until August, 1985, Chicago enforced a moratorium on the development of new landfills until better systems for monitoring and controlling leachate and methane gas migration were devised. . . .

© Matt Wuerker. Reprinted with permission.

Disposal space is becoming a coveted and more strictly regulated commodity, and prices are beginning to rise accordingly. Philadelphia, a metropolitan area of 6,000,000 people, no longer has access to a local landfill and has sometimes shipped its waste as far away as Ohio and southern Virginia. Since 1980, Philadelphia's disposal costs have risen from $20 to $90 per ton. Even when cities are able to gain access to new, environmentally sound landfills, the sites usually are remote. Disposal costs increase by 50 cents to $1.00 for every mile each ton of garbage is transported. Yet, landfill fees still are artificially low in many areas. Until city managers and waste producers are forced to pay the higher costs of diminished capacity and stricter operating and closure requirements, they will not pursue other strategies.

Maurice Hinchey, chairman of New York's legislative commission on solid waste management, believes that "the most critical defect in our present waste economy is the gross underpricing of our disposal capacity. Since landfill charges are set so low, private haulers and municipal waste collection agencies alike have little incentive to sort and salvage recyclable materials from the refuse or to invest in their own materials recovery system." He reasons that, since "there is no access capacity left in the system, the cost of remaining capacity should rise as each new ton of waste is deposited.". . .

Reusable Materials

Wastes available for recycling theoretically include all consumer discards. In practice, it is necessary to distinguish between quantity and quality. Although some analysts assert that more than half the consumer waste stream can be economically recycled, achieving such high rates requires careful refuse handling. Paper rapidly loses its value when mixed with other trash, particularly organic food waste. Some consumer disposables, such as refillable glass bottles, only require a thorough washing before reuse. They are about 50% heavier than their nonrefillable counterparts and are designed for up to 30 roundtrips. Aluminum, nonrefillable glass, and steel require more elaborate processing, but can be recycled almost indefinitely. Recycling these products yields an enormous energy and material savings.

Aluminum is the most energy-intensive commodity in common use, and in some areas of the world, energy is a greater share of its production costs than the raw materials. Recycling aluminum requires only five percent as much energy as producing it and each can recycled saves the energy equivalent of a half can of gasoline. For every ton of crushed glass used in the manufacturing process, some 1.2 tons of silica and other raw materials are saved. Every 10% of post-consumer glass introduced into a furnace results in energy savings of two-five percent. The recent adoption of stricter air pollution standards in Japan, Sweden, the U.S., and West Germany has led to an increase in the demand for crushed glass by glass producers because its use reduces emissions. Many different grades of paper products are recycled, ranging from the highest quality computer and office paper to corrugated cardboard, newspaper, and mixed miscellaneous sheets. Recycling programs spare millions of hectares of trees, conserve water and energy, and reduce air and water pollution. Additional savings are reaped—a mill designed to use waste paper instead of virgin pulp is 50-80% cheaper. In the U.S., some 200 mills use only reclaimed paper. Developing countries that rely on waste paper can reserve scarce water for drinking supplies and keep down foreign debts, since mills using waste paper require less imported equipment.

Recycling commonly used materials like aluminum, paper, and glass is on the upswing in many industrial countries. In the past 10 years, Austria has tripled and Japan more than doubled their aluminum recycling rates. Glass recycling increased by more than 50% from 1981 to 1985 in Austria, Britain, and West Germany. Paper recovery also has increased substantially over the years, but appears to have reached a plateau in many countries. Only Austria, Sweden, and Switzerland boosted their paper recovery rates by more than 20% during the 1980's.

Despite these over-all gains, recycling rates could be improved considerably. Only the Netherlands collects more than half its aluminum, paper, or glass for recycling. The Organization for Economic Co-operation and Development estimates that over 90% of waste glass could be made available for recovery. Recycling half the paper used in the world today would meet almost 75% of new paper demand and preserve 8,000,000 hectares of forestland, an area equal to six percent of Europe's forests.

Processes for cleaning plastics are not well developed and the industry presently is not able to turn a used PET (polyethylene terephthalate) soda bottle into a new PET bottle. Containers turned in for recycling are sometimes shredded and stuffed into seat cushions or used as insulation in sleeping bags and jackets. There is also an emerging market for "plastic lumber" in low-maintenance fences and pier supports. However, in New York State, 66% of the plastic soft drink containers returned under the deposit system were buried in 1985 because of poor scrap markets.

The Bottom Line

The economics of recycling depend largely on the alternatives available, the markets for the recovered products, and the costs of operating the recycling program. Recycling has been hampered by the belief that it should make money, but it is a cost-effective "disposal" option when it requires fewer government subsidies than landfilling or incineration. Lower taxes, energy savings, and a cleaner environment are the real bottom lines. As landfill costs continue to rise because of space constraints and stricter environmental regulations, and as the high capital costs of incinerators and their pollution control technologies sap city budgets, the appeal of recycling will inevitably grow.

"Single-use diapers should not be going to landfills. "

Using Cloth Diapers Can Reduce Garbage

Francesca Lyman

Waste management experts say that disposable diapers take up 2 percent of the space in modern landfills. While that amount seems small, environmentalists point out that 2 percent is a large amount for any single item. In the following viewpoint, Francesca Lyman argues that using cloth diapers instead of disposables reduces waste and protects the environment. She writes that the plastic backing and pads of disposables do not decompose for centuries and that biodegradable diapers are little better. Lyman is an environmental writer and author of the book *The Greenhouse Trap.*

As you read, consider the following questions:

1. Why does Lyman oppose biodegradable diapers?
2. Which type of diaper does the author believe makes the most economic sense? Why?
3. What does Lyman mean by writing that disposables are not "fully costed"?

Francesca Lyman, "Diaper Hype." Reprinted with permission from the January/February 1990 issue of *Garbage* magazine. Subscriptions available for $21/year from *Garbage* magazine, PO Box 56519, Boulder, CO 80322-6519.

Eskimo mommies wrapped their babies' bottoms in peat moss. Plains Indian tribes used animal skins. In old Europe women knit wool flannel pants. And only one generation ago, we spent our infancies clad in cotton cloth.

Then came the throwaway diaper, born in the late 1950s, which promised to free women from motherhood's most drudging chore. By the '70s, the disposable had cornered the market. So greatly did it change mothers' routines that the disposable diaper was featured several years ago in a Smithsonian Institution exhibit of American products and services that have "revolutionized our lives," alongside the Pill, antibiotics, smoke detectors, and shopping malls. Some observers of modern culture regard the advent of disposable diapers as a primary reason more women have been able to work outside the home. On the other hand, the disposable diaper, which will lie around for centuries, has become *the* symbol of the garbage crisis we're leaving for our children. There's no doubt that the popularity of single-use diapers has soared during the past 30 years. By one industry estimate, when Pampers were introduced in 1961, disposable diapers accounted for less than one percent of all diaper changes; they now account for nearly 85 percent. Once considered an occasional luxury item, the disposable diaper is sold as an indispensable household article. Their handiness has made them into a $3.5 billion business; and a New York marketing consultant has called disposables the most dynamic new product category in consumer marketing history.

A Serious Problem

As miraculous as they may seem, however, disposable diapers, we now know, are becoming an increasingly serious garbage problem. Carl Lehrburger, solid-waste expert and author of a study for the National Association of Diaper Services, *Diapers in the Waste Stream,* bluntly concluded, "Single-use diapers should not be going to landfills." According to industry estimates, there are some 16 billion disposable diapers, made of woven cellulose and polyethylene plastic backings, buried in landfills each year. By weight, they represent about 12,300 tons of waste a day.

Diapers are by no means the only landfill problem—they represent, in fact, less than two percent of the total amount of waste in landfills. (Although that figure may sound small, environmentalists argue that it's a large percentage for any one single item.) What's significant is that this one item could be easily reduced without the organized effort of, say, newspaper or beverage-container recycling.

Since throwaway diapers made their debut, diaper companies have been battling to find the most sophisticated diaper design possible. Plasticized diapers have evolved from unwieldy pads that often shredded when pinned into the high-tech products they are today, with fitted waistbands, reclosable adhesive flaps, and cartoon-character imprints. Now, with landfills closing and protests mounting, we find ourselves in a new era of diaper wars, as manufacturers attempt to put a pro-ecology face on their products.

Choking on Disposables

The desire for a disappearing diaper has precipitated a revolution in American diapering practices. Over a few decades, cloth diapers, rubber pants and duck-headed diaper pins have been all but replaced by Pampers, Huggies and other single-use throwaway diapers.

Of course, throwing diapers away didn't make them disappear. The 18 billion disposable diapers Americans throw away each year—enough to fill an Islip-style garbage barge every six hours —are choking up the nation's rapidly filling landfills and increasing the need for other disposal options like incinerators.

Jeanne Wirka, *Environmental Action,* March/April 1989.

Touting its product as the "biodegradable, nonchemical" alternative, RMED International Corporation of Tulsa, Oklahoma, started marketing TenderCare diapers [in 1988] by mail order and through health food stores. During [1989] the company has seen its business double. RMED claims that the plastic backing on its diapers contains a cornstarch derivative that will help the product break down into water and carbon dioxide in two to five years. "We're changing the world, one diaper at a time," reads their slogan.

Trashing the Biodegradables

But this semi-biodegradable diaper, along with a few others like it, has taken some trashing—with good reason. Environmentalists as well as the biggest disposable diaper makers, Procter & Gamble and Kimberly-Clark, say claims made by manufacturers of biodegradables are unsubstantiated because crowded landfills lack the water and oxygen necessary for degradation to occur at such a rate. Jeanne Wirka, a solid-waste expert at the Environmental Action Foundation in Washington, D.C., contends "there's no evidence that the diapers can decompose any more quickly than conventional throwaways." Also, biodegradable disposables consume as much paper and plastic as do the major brands. (According to one study, 1,000,265,000 tons of wood pulp from trees and 75,000 metric tons of plastic are used every year to make disposable diapers in the United States alone.) So it would seem that these new products won't reduce the volume of solid waste. (And of course, they do nothing to get fecal matter out of the landfill and into the sewage treatment facilities where it belongs.)

In the meantime, Procter & Gamble, which sells $1.65 billion worth of disposables per year, has underwritten a small pilot program to see if the paper pulp, plastic, and chemicals in their disposables can be recycled. In so doing, says their public relations division, they will be "redefining the concept of disposable" by turning the material into a resource.

Procter & Gamble has teamed up with the Rabanco Corporation, a Seattle recycling company, to pick up disposable diapers at curbside from as many as 1,000 families, deliver the collected diapers to the recycling center, separate the plastic from the paper pulp and sanitize its components, and finally take the reclaimed materials from the recycled diapers to produce products such as plastic flowerpots, drywall backing, and computer paper.

Recycling is certainly a laudable goal. But the economics of separating out component parts of plasticized diapers and finding markets for the paper, plastic, and even absorbent chemicals may kill the idea. There are doubtless, consumers who support the experiment. Still, the cost of collecting, separating, and recycling plasticized diapers would most likely fall on the taxpayer, because Procter & Gamble's financial support may end with the pilot project. Mr. Lehrburger estimates that the cost of recycling plasticized diapers would be much higher than the cost of the diaper.

A better alternative than recycling, Mr. Lehrburger says, would be to have companies develop a sewer-safe flushable diaper. Interestingly enough, it's only been a few years since Procter & Gamble discontinued a Pampers that was partially flushable. Consumers were instructed to separate the absorbant paper liner, which could be flushed, and discard only the plastic backsheet. The company now says that's not the way to go. "There are markets for recycling the materials," says a spokesman, "rather than flushing them away." [Ed. note: Flushable diapers aren't compatible with the water-conserving, ultra-low-flush toilets that may be standard in the future.]

The Alternatives

Composting diapers is another option being considered by Procter & Gamble. The corporation is working with a composting company in St. Cloud, Minnesota, to turn diaper parts into humus. Eighty-seven percent of the diaper is comprised of cellulose, and is compostable. Composting may be a workable option but, as Mr. Lehrburger reminds us, "What we really need are the composting facilities to do it."

The *obvious* alternative to disposables of any sort? Cotton diapers, those soft squares of cloth that used to be held together with Donald Duck pins, can be used again and again and pose no garbage problem. They're also the most economically sound alternative—for both individual parents *and* for society as a whole. With single-use diapers costing about 22¢ a piece (according to Mr. Lehrburger), biodegradables 26¢ to 39¢ a piece, cloth diapers 13¢ a piece when washed at home and 15¢ when laundered at a service, cotton ends up being the bargain. As Carl Lehrburger warns us, "We have been sold on the idea of disposability without full recognition of the social costs associated with convenience." He says that disposing of "disposables" costs us more than $300 million each year.

So cotton diapers, far less resource-intensive than disposables, make good sense. But there's still reluctance among new parents to convert to cloth. *Eighty-five percent of parents use disposable diapers all the time. Ninety-seven percent of them use disposables part-time.* Thanks to disposables' hightech moisture retention, and thanks to powerful marketing campaigns by manufacturers of disposables, cloth is often considered to be less effective, less sanitary, and less convenient for the diaper changer. "The reason disposables are so popular is their superior performance," says Tina Barry, a spokesperson for Kimberly-Clark. "They're more convenient, so there are a lot of parents out there who are reluctant to stop using them.". . .

Making Social Sense

Many agree that encouraging the use of cloth diapers over disposables makes sense socially—it saves landfill space, cuts down on litter, keeps human waste out of the garbage, and saves trees and petrochemical-based plastics. But day-care centers and hospitals almost universally use disposables. Some day-care centers even *require* that disposables be used, according to a June 1989 study by Environmental Action and the National Center for Policy Alternatives.

Jack Shiffert of the National Association of Diaper Services adds that day-care centers are often unenthusiastic about switching to cloth because it means extra responsibility for them. "Most day-care centers require that parents bring a box of Pampers with them," says Shiffert, "while those who switch have to set up a system and then bill parents for it."

"Many facilities," says Laurene Ellmers, director of the Elmtree day-care center in Boulder, "are under the misconception that they ought to use disposables—they think they're more sanitary." Actually, she says, regulations only require that centers have a clean supply of diapers on hand and that they ensure proper disposal of them.

[In 1988,] Elmtree, along with 11 other Boulder-area day-care

137

centers and one hospital, switched to cloth, a move spurred by Citizens for Cloth Diapers. The results, says Ms. Ellmers, have been very successful. As day-care centers have converted, so have the parents. The reverse, Ms. Ellmers speculates, may be happening. "As parents' awareness increases, they will demand cloth of their day-care centers."

The Disposable Mentality

Not only are disposable diapers a large and growing portion of the waste stream, but more importantly, they're a perfect illustration of what's wrong with the mentality that disposable is better.

Erica Guttman, *Environmental Action,* March/April 1989.

Day-care centers that have switched say that it takes no longer to change a cloth diaper than a disposable diaper. Ellmers say that, while they had to add a diaper fee to their charge, they now no longer have the headache of keeping track of everybody's "own stack of disposables."

The National Association of Diaper Services is currently trying to enlist hospitals. General Hospital in Lancaster, Pennsylvania, a 566-bed facility that switched from disposables to cloth, reported that the change would bring them a 15 percent yearly savings.

An Outright Ban?

Whoever thought that shopping for baby diapers could be so complex? Most parents shop for the best buy and hardly consider such equations as post-processing cost. Linda Shearer, a former banker, now spends her time on basic home economics. "If you pardon my jargon, part of my reason for switching to disposables was that they weren't 'fully costed.' It doesn't include air and water pollution, litter, and garbage."

Given the landfill and other problems with so-called disposables diapers, *does it make sense to ban them altogether?* Some states think so. Nebraska became the first state to ban the sale of all diapers that aren't biodegradable by the year 1993 (a development which many attribute to the presence there of Archer Daniels Midland, the maker of the cornstarch-laden "degradable" plastic). Another bill has been introduced in New Jersey, a state widely known for its garbage-containment problems, banning the sale of hundreds of "disposable," plastic, non-reusable items.

As environmentalists have pointed out, encouraging biodegradables is not really a solution to the solid-waste crisis. Colin Isaacs, director of the Pollution Probe Foundation, wrote an editorial in Canada's *Probe Post* arguing that biodegradables are just "the latest gimmick with which to calm the consumer and befuddle the politician."

It's unlikely that most states will pass sweeping bans on disposables. However, as Jeanne Wirka and Jeffrey Tryens of the National Center for Policy Alternatives claim, regulating and restricting throw-aways could discourage consumers from using them except for travel and special occasions, and encourage people to use cotton as a regular method. One disincentive would be to require labels on packages of throwaway diapers detailing their hidden hazards. New York State introduced legislation to require such labels. The Connecticut Assembly considered legislation to require manufacturers to place labels saying that soiled diapers contained viruses and microbes that could transmit diseases. Another approach is to tax makers of disposables and give tax credits to makers of reusables.

Crunch Time

With garbage mounting, it's coming down to crunch time for landfills. Ultimately—and that's only a few years away for some states—it will reach the point where people can't get their garbage taken away. Then the misnomer "disposable" will finally become what some have always thought of it as—the non-disposable.

But if we wait that long for the tide to change, the tide will begin to move in on us—and our children. And future raiders of the lost ark who will sift through our civilization's remains won't find houses of dead kings, ancient treasures made of silver and gold, statues, and sacred objects. Instead they will find dirty diapers.

"To call disposable diapers an environmental problem is to slide into this ambiguous and random alarmism. "

Using Cloth Diapers Cannot Reduce Garbage

Robert J. Samuelson

The following viewpoint is taken from two separate columns written four weeks apart. In it, Robert J. Samuelson, a columnist for *Newsweek,* writes that cloth diapers create as much pollution as do disposable diapers. Samuelson disputes the notion that disposables cause landfill problems and argues that cloth diapers take more energy to produce, deliver, and clean. He calls for better information on environmental issues so the true problems can be solved.

As you read, consider the following questions:

1. According to Samuelson, how much of the nation's garbage consists of disposable diapers?
2. Why does the author claim that neither diaper is environmentally superior?
3. In Samuelson's opinion, do disposable diapers pose a health threat? Why or why not?

Johnny wears disposable diapers, and that's not an environmental disaster. By Johnny, I mean John Samuelson, who joined his sister Ruth (5) and brother Michael (3) [in January 1990]. I also mean most of the other 9 million American babies under 30 months who wear disposable diapers. I do not feel guilty that my wife and I use them, and the idea that we are destroying the planet for our children is mostly nonsense.

Disposable diapers are an instructive metaphor for the exaggerations of modern environmentalism. We all should want to be good environmentalists, but just what that means in practice isn't always easy to say. The tendency these days is to call many different problems "environmental," as if the label—all by itself—implies an impending catastrophe whose solution is a moral imperative. "Environmentalism" thus becomes a loose collection of diverse concerns, with few distinctions made about whether some problems are more serious than others.

No Threatening Crisis

To call disposable diapers an environmental problem is to slide into this ambiguous and random alarmism. Disposable diapers are about garbage; that's ordinary garbage, not hazardous waste. Getting rid of our garbage is a problem and, in some places, a serious one. Mainly, it involves handling the trash at an acceptable cost. But this is not a crisis that threatens the earth's future, and even if it were, disposable diapers wouldn't matter much. The 15.8 billion used annually constitute less than 2 percent of all garbage.

These complexities are being lost in rising rhetoric. Disposable diapers have come to symbolize growing wastefulness, because most people still remember the era of reusable, cloth diapers. Although Procter & Gamble first test-marketed Pampers in 1961, the product didn't go national until 1970. (P&G says that disposables now account for 90 percent of diapers, up from 65 percent in 1980 and 25 percent in 1970.) Vermont Governor Madeleine Kunin has proposed banning disposables, though her legislature probably won't go along. And *Forbes* magazine lambasted them on its cover: "Can We Have a Cleaner Environment and Pampers Too?"

In fact, the symbolism is misleading. Our garbage problem is not primarily the result of our becoming an increasingly throwaway society. The Environmental Protection Agency estimates that the average American generates (after recycling) 3.3 pounds of garbage a day, only slightly higher than in 1970. The truth is that almost everything you probably believe about garbage is wrong, as archeologist William Rathje, head of The Garbage Project at the University of Arizona, argues in [the] December [1989] *The Atlantic Monthly*.

You think plastics are the problem? Guess again. They account for about 8 percent of the garbage. Metals? They're about 9 percent. By contrast, paper represents 37 percent and yard waste 20 percent of garbage. Nor is today's problem especially bad historically. "Our society is filled with. . .reminders of waste," Rathje writes. "What we forget is everything that is no longer there to see. . .the 1,200 pounds per year of coal ash that every American generated at home at the turn of the century. . .[and] the hundreds of thousands of dead horses that once had to be disposed of by American cities every year."

Landfill Space

The problem today stems from shifting societal standards. Landfills now absorb more than three quarters of all garbage, and in a country as vast as ours, there's plenty of room for new ones. The trouble is that fewer communities want them, and tighter regulations are raising their costs. Between 1985 and 1988, average tipping fees—the cost of dumping a ton of garbage in a landfill—jumped from $12 to $27, reports the National Solid Wastes Management Association. Our task is to make landfills acceptable or find alternatives, from garbage prevention to recycling to incineration.

Find Another Symbol

Unlike many other alleged labor-saving inventions for child and home care, disposable diapers have substantially eased one aspect of child care. Ask the people who do it, women. And diapers constitute only about 2 percent of the entire solid waste stream, less than unnecessary plastic packaging. Until child care is equally shared by men and women—and all the recent surveys reveal that men do not share child care and housework equally with women, even though women make up nearly half the labor force—then environmentalists should target another component of the waste stream to symbolize the problem of waste.

H. Patricia Hynes, *Earth Right,* 1990.

I have no quarrel with parents who prefer cloth diapers, as a rising minority apparently do. The National Association of Diaper Services reports its members' business is up about 40 percent. "I've never seen such a dramatic turnaround," says Jack Mogavero, president of General Health Care Corporation, the largest diaper service. (Environmentalism isn't the only reason. New diaper covers with Velcro closures make cloth diapers easier to use.) But parents are deluding themselves if they think using cloth diapers is somehow saving the environment.

Suppose everyone switched to cloth diapers tomorrow. All those diapers (43 million a day, at current rates) have to be washed in hot water, which requires energy and generates pollution. For families using diaper services, the diapers have to be picked up and delivered by trucks that burn fuel, create fumes and worsen traffic congestion. By contrast, most disposables are purchased in shopping trips that would be made anyway. The extra effects of higher energy consumption would be modest, but so is the impact of disposables on garbage.

A Lesser Evil

The point is not to show that one diaper is environmentally superior to the other. It is simply to emphasize that comparisons are iffy. Each diaper does some damage, but how are we to judge relative dangers? Are air pollution and the threat to global warming more serious problems than garbage disposal? Environmental debates tend to slide by these messy choices.

My own hunch is that garbage is a lesser ill. To some extent, the problem—higher costs—is also the solution. As disposal costs rise, recycling becomes more attractive and economically viable. Carefully crafted, recycling laws aid the process by lowering collection costs. In 1988, about 31 percent of all paper was collected and reused. By 1995, the paper industry estimates, that could rise to 40 percent. There will be more efforts to cope with yard waste through mass composting rather than using landfills.

Personally, I'm doing my part within the bounds of common sense. I brought a coffee mug into the office. This will cut my use of polystyrene cups by somewhere between 300 to 600 a year. I want the best possible world for my new son, who has a beguiling smile and a calming stare. Relax, Dad, he says. Being a worrier, I can't. I already have lots of concerns for his future. But the way we diaper is not among them. . . .

No Easy Choice

The debate over disposable diapers is important by itself but it also teaches a larger lesson. Environmentalism isn't a simple morality play. It's not just Good Guys versus Bad, as in: only lazy parents (indifferent to the planet) use disposables, while caring parents (concerned about the earth's future) use cloth. If you doubt me on disposables, listen to Allen Hershkowitz, a scientist at the Natural Resources Defense Council, a major environmental group.

"We simply can't say that disposables are terrible and reusable diapers are great for the environment, or vice versa," he writes. "Whatever the choice, there are environmental costs." One study found, for example, that disposables create about 90 times as much garbage as cloth but that cloth diapers use about three times as much energy (reflecting all the washing, pickups and deliveries) and cause nine times as much air pollution.

Every environmental problem is not a tragedy. The greenhouse effect, if the worst fears were realized, could have a devastating impact. But garbage isn't this sort of problem. It's like traffic congestion: although we'd be better off without it, it doesn't threaten our future. The letters reacting to my column reflect widespread ignorance, because the facts are either wrong or out of context.

Misconceptions

Consider some misconceptions.

We produce so much garbage that the country will be covered with landfills.

This horrific vision of coast-to-coast landfills is absurd. When was the last time you saw a landfill? In truth, they don't take up much space. Edward Repa of the National Solid Wastes Management Association estimates that a typical 10-acre landfill could handle the garbage of a city of 100,000 for 10 years. Once filled, dumps are usually landscaped so they're not eyesores. Recall also that there are 640 acres in a square mile and nearly 3 million square miles in the 48 states.

Recyclable Diapers

Diaper makers around the world are experimenting with better products. Procter and Gamble is working with a company in St. Cloud, Minnesota, to compost 2 to 3 tons of Pampers and Luvs diapers a day. Mixed with sewer sludge, the diapers move through 120-foot-long drums, 12 feet in diameter, which rotate 24 times an hour. Essentially, all this procedure does is hasten the biological process. The remnants are screened and cured for weeks before being sold as fertilizer.

Will Steger and Jon Bowermaster, *Saving the Earth*, 1990.

Plastics represent a huge part of our garbage.

It's true that plastics' share of landfills is greater by volume than weight. But one reader's claim that they occupy 30 percent of landfills (by volume)—rather than the 8 percent (by weight) I cited—is an exaggeration. The congressional Office of Technology Assessment puts plastics' share (by volume) at 12 to 13 percent. By weight or volume, paper and yard waste still take up more than half of landfills.

Diapers in landfills contain feces and may threaten public health by contaminating ground water.

There's no evidence that this problem exists. Dean Cliver, a water-safety expert at the University of Wisconsin, calls it a "red herring." Hershkowitz agrees. One government study found that medical wastes in landfills (which would be more dangerous than diapers) pose almost no risk. Bacteria and viruses tend to die in landfills. Some older landfills have polluted ground water, but experts worry most about contaminants from heavy metals (lead, mercury) and chemical solvents. New landfills are designed to prevent ground-water pollution by being lined with both plastics and impermeable clays. Drainage pipes at the bottom of the landfill catch any water so it can be recovered and treated.

No Obvious Good or Bad Way

We do have a garbage problem. Between 1970 and 1986, population and economic growth increased total trash by 31 percent. But the problem is mainly economic and political. Fewer localities accept landfills, and tougher environmental controls raise operating costs. Ditto for incinerators. The problem is worst in the Northeast, with lots of garbage and dense development. Higher costs are inevitable: garbage will be trucked further, and some communities will (in effect) be bribed into taking landfills. Rising costs will spur recycling and efforts to prevent garbage.

All this is desirable, as long as we keep our perspective. Reducing garbage isn't life's only aim. For our first two children, my wife and I used both cloth and disposable diapers. My wife ditched the cloth diapers after noticing that our second child had less diaper rash with disposables. Studies confirm her observation: the absorbent in disposables draws moisture from the skin and reduces rash.

What my critics really resent is that I've denied their moral superiority. Using cloth diapers is an environmental badge, and I've said the badge isn't worth much. Their response is to accuse me of rationalizing my bad behavior. I opt for convenience and minimize the social costs of my waste because, after all, what difference would one family make? Wrong. The problem here is that there's no obvious good or bad way.

"The primary solution to the world's mounting garbage problem is 'source reduction.'"

Garbage Must Be Reduced at Its Source

Will Steger and Jon Bowermaster

Will Steger is a former science teacher turned adventurer and environmentalist who has led dogsled expeditions to the North Pole and across Antarctica. Jon Bowermaster is an editor and journalist who has written about the environment for *The New York Times Magazine* and *Outside.* In the following viewpoint, Steger and Bowermaster write that consumers must reduce garbage by buying items that do not require frequent replacement or excessive packaging. They claim that while recycling is helpful, the best solution to the garbage crisis is for individuals to change their lifestyles.

As you read, consider the following questions:

1. What type of design changes would the authors like to see in consumer goods?
2. According to Steger and Bowermaster, why are landfills dangerous?
3. What drawbacks do the authors see to recycling?

Perhaps no pollutant is argued about more vociferously among environmentalists, politicians, and the man on the street than garbage—not the simple litter that lies in gutters and gathers along roadsides, but bulky, plastic-bagged and dumpster variety trash that accumulates on the edges of town, in piles bigger than most city halls. What we throw away may be the closest we come to our pollution of Earth. We never really touch the acid in acid rain, or spot those dangerous CFCs [chlorofluorocarbons]. Garbage, on the other hand, you can easily touch, see, and smell. This growing accumulation of rubbish depresses land values, increases truck traffic, and ruins health, aesthetics, and the necessities of life—the air we breathe and water we drink.

Debate about trash, especially what to do with it, fills small-town newspapers and provokes long-running arguments in coffee houses and meeting rooms around the world. The talk focuses on the fact that we're running out of room. Every day, the people of the United States churn out more than 432,000 tons of garbage. Over 80 percent of it is carted to landfills and covered with a patina of clay. It is bad enough that we so casually send dead refrigerators, old tires, plastic bottles, commercial junk, mounds of food scraps, and household trash to the local dump; what's worse is that this burgeoning mass is accompanied by an increasing load of hazardous chemical waste.

Not in My Backyard

Around the globe this torrent of waste—toxic and non-toxic—has run smack up against the NIMBY mindset. "Not In My Back Yard" is a shout heard around the world. Proposals for new landfills arouse stiff local opposition and fights drag on for years. Shipping trash across state lines and international boundaries has become a lucrative business for some, but the mood in communities at the receiving end is increasingly inhospitable.

Our garbage problem worsens because most consumer goods are designed, in the words of the Worldwatch Institute's Cynthia Pollock, "for a one-night stand." They are bought, used, and tossed with little regard for their lasting potential. America's biggest misconception was that the limits on dumping were endless—a naivete that encouraged history's biggest throwaway society.

We should have known that the immense and growing bulk of refuse would spell trouble sooner or later. But as with so many of our environmental problems, we chose an "out of sight, out of mind" attitude toward garbage. Now that the crisis is here and starkly evident, states and localities, rightfully concerned about water and air contamination, methane gas leaks, and sheer ugliness, have begun to close up the dumps.

Now, more than half of the landfills in the United States boast

"Closed" signs. In West Germany, 35,000 to 50,000 landfill sites have been declared potentially dangerous because they threaten groundwater supplies. Few developing nations have the instinct, motivation, or expertise to make solid waste disposal a priority; as a result, trash heaps are developing faster than industries in some nations.

© Wicks/Rothco. Reprinted with permission.

The symbolic turning point in our changing attitudes toward the world's dumps is the garbage barge *Mobro 4000*—and its 3,186 tons of garbage—which became an international joke, then dilemma, in 1987. Its cargo, initially rejected by an overflowing landfill in Islip, New York, floated up and down the Atlantic for nearly six months, seeking a home. It was systematically rejected by North Carolina, Florida, Alabama, Mississippi, Louisiana, Mexico, the Bahamas, and Belize. Finally, after a 6,000-mile voyage, the *Mobro*'s garbage found a resting spot—after being reduced to 400 tons of ash in a New York City incinerator—in the same landfill that first rejected it. The plight of the *Mobro* snapped the world to attention. Its message was clear: We are running out of places to put our garbage.

That message is now being sounded emphatically around the globe, from the wealthiest nations to the poorest. In California the problem is nearly epidemic. The state produces roughly 8.5 pounds of waste per person every day. State Assemblywoman Delaine Eastin describes her fellow Californians as possessed of a "TWABAL" mentality. "There Will Always Be a Landfill" is their idée fixe, she claims. As the state's population continues to grow by 600,000 people a year, California is running out of room, for people and garbage. All of Los Angeles' landfills are expected to close by the mid-1990s. Chief executive of the state's Waste Management Board, George T. Eowan, voices the concerns of many when he warns that Californians can't pick and choose among alternative solutions. "We've got to do everything," he says. . . .

Trashing the Globe

Perhaps the most ominous vision of the world's garbage future sits on New York's Staten Island. The 3,000-acre Fresh Kills landfill is without doubt the most significant monument to our seeming disregard for the trashing of the globe.

The 40-year-old dump is listed in the *Guinness Book of World Records* as the largest anywhere. Its height and volume challenge the pyramid of Khufu, the grandest of the great pyramids of Egypt, as well as most of the best-known urban landmarks of the world. When it closes sometime soon after the turn of next century, it will have risen to more than 500 feet tall, and will rival the Great Wall of China as the largest man-made structure in the world.

The landfill, built on a swampy lowland, became a dump in 1948. Three years later a report to the mayor concluded that "the Fresh Kills landfill project cannot fail to affect constructively a wide area around it. It is at once practical and idealistic." Today it contains an estimated 100 million tons of oozing, leaking garbage. (When 17 garbologists dug into it recently, they came up with everything from ham to newspapers that looked as fresh as on the day they were discarded.) Fresh Kills will soon be the tallest "mountain" on the Atlantic coast between Florida and northern Maine. When it closes, the city plans to turn it into a grass-covered park. Its peak will be reached by a curving two-lane paved road and will be served by power lines.

Perhaps the most dangerous factor in the growth of the world's landfills is their contamination of nearby drinking water. Toxic chemicals bound up in the garbage we throw away every day eventually leach from landfills into nearby aquifers, streams, and lakes. This deadly cocktail moves slowly through surface water or down through the soil into groundwater, which is the source of drinking water in most communities. Fresh Kills alone leaks more than one million gallons of such toxic "juice" directly into nearby waterways every day.

Dead Fish

Examples of such contamination abound and some are horrific in scope. In a small Florida town near Miami, a 291-acre lake is flanked by a now-inactive landfill, which was open for less than 20 years and accepted mostly construction site waste. Today, if a healthy fish is thrown into the water, it dies in less than 30 seconds. Poisons clog the region's aquifers and foul its air. Cleanup is estimated to cost more than $100 million. In 1984, a landfill in Old Bridge, New Jersey, simply collapsed under the weight of its non-precious collection. Waves of mud rushed down a slope, knocking down supporting structures and allowing contaminated water to escape into nearby waterways.

One alternative to landfilling, incineration, has been argued about by communities around the world. For the good it promises—reducing the bulk weight of garbage by 75 percent—its potentially dangerous effects have prevented such plants from blossoming like dandelions. The process sounds good, but the air emissions of sulfur and nitrogen oxide, hydrochloric acid, heavy metals and dioxins from burn plants are as dangerous as the leaking landfills they replace. The toxic ash residue often requires a separate home (although in Los Angeles toxic ash is mixed with mainstream waste), and must be transported and dumped in hazardous-waste landfills, which are often in another county or state.

The Solution

The primary solution to the world's mounting garbage problem is "source reduction." Its definition is simple: The less we create, the less we have to throw away. Reducing the amount of waste generated by placing limits on packaging or restricting the use of disposable products should be at the top of every nation's, community's, and individual's list of environmentally wise "things to do." For example, a community might ban the use of polystyrene (as did Suffolk County, New York, and Berkeley, California), or taxes might be levied on excess packaging or frequently purchased disposable products, which has been proposed in a handful of state legislatures and city councils.

Next, we must begin to reuse as many products as possible, from bags to boxes, and anything else that may have a life other than in the dump. Third, recycling must be emphasized at home, work, and in every neighborhood. It is no longer a chore for hippies only. Instead, what is gradually emerging across the country is a broad recycling structure initiated by government, private enterprise, and new technology. Various urban governments are designing new systems for separating the variety of recyclables. States, localities, and private companies are building or contracting for such systems. Mandatory recycling laws are being passed in communities worldwide. Solid waste management is finally in a state of transition. . . .

Reduce Garbage

If the garbage problem is ever to subside, manufacturers of consumer products must cooperate. Reducing packaging and disposables should be an intrinsic part of every manufacturing and sales effort. Unfortunately, far too often, industry pays lip service to solid waste problems by offering things like biodegradable disposable diapers and plastic bags that may never decompose in tightly packed landfills.

Manufacturers and retailers understandably prefer plastic over glass because it is lightweight, cheaper, microwavable, durable, and more resilient. Consumers like it because it's secure, strong, and waterproof. Environmentalists hate it because it's hard to recycle. Less than two percent of all plastic is currently recycled. The packaging industry, the largest user of plastics in the world, produces 40 percent of all plastic waste.

Reducing packaging and encouraging recycling appears to be inching up on the agendas of most major corporations (in many instances, just a step ahead of legislation that would require them to be responsible for disposal of their products). A Gallup poll commissioned by the Glass Packaging Institute showed that more than 50 percent of Americans would change their purchasing habits to buy food and beverage containers that recycle. London's *Financial Times* reports similar trends in Britain. Some McDonald's franchises ask their customers to separate garbage before throwing it away. Procter and Gamble is using containers made of 20 to 100 percent recycled plastic for a number of its products. The Scotch Corporation, a chemical manufacturer in Dallas, has introduced plastic pouches of concentrated household cleaners that consumers can mix with water and use to refill empty spray bottles.

Ruffies and Good Sense are plastic bag brands that are photodegradable. Anheuser-Busch now uses only photodegradable plastic yokes to hold six-packs together. Varta, a West German manufacturer, makes batteries that contain no air-polluting cadmium or mercury.

Smart manufacturers are capitalizing on the nascent signs of a swing towards more recycling, by including "Recycled Goods" or "No CFCs" on product labels. The best labeling approach, and one already in use in Germany, Canada, and elsewhere, is a kind of universal code that guarantees a product is environmentally benign or recommended. Dorothy MacKenzie, director of product development at a New York and London-based consulting firm, has studied such movements in Europe and North America and is convinced they will proliferate. "Just as the 1980s saw a proliferation of 'lite' products designed to meet growing consumer health awareness, the 1990s will be the decade of 'green' products designed, packaged, and marketed with a strong environmental perspective," she told a reporter.

The Real Solution

Recycling efforts and biodegradability are not the promised panaceas. The real solution: reduced consumption. . . .

A true ecologist or eco-feminist would never use a disposable plastic product. They would remember back to a time when the world worked fairly well without these conveniences. People ate and drank off real dishes and simply washed them. According to Donella Meadows of Dartmouth College: "It's easier to deal with a flood by turning it off at its source than by inventing better mopping technologies."

Holly Jensen, *The Christian Science Monitor,* March 6, 1990.

The symbol used in Canada boasts three intertwined doves. Surveys show that Canadians are prepared to pay more for environmentally friendly products that carry this symbol. Standards require that the products be nontoxic, derived from renewable resources, recyclable and/or biodegradable, and sold in packaging that meets criteria established by a 14-member products advisory board.

In Japan, environmentally approved products carry a logo called an Ecomark. The West German mark is called the Blue Angel, and has been awarded to 2,000 consumer products over the past 10 years. In Sweden, newspaper ads boast 100-percent recycled goods from paper to toothpaste containers, all without excessive packaging. In the United States, supermarket chains including A&P, Winn-Dixie, Kroger, and Safeway sell products with a "Recycled" label (three arrows following each other around a circle). A loose coalition of industry and environmental groups is pushing for one international logo, which would be recognized worldwide as the sign of an environmentally sound product.

Garbage has long been one of the world's greatest bargains

—easy to accumulate, just as easy to get rid of. Now we're paying the price for past negligence. If we are to stem the sweeping tide of trash, we must adopt integrated, organized, solid-waste management. It doesn't sound very sexy, but it's a must.

Experts believe that we should ultimately be able to reduce at least 10 percent and recycle more than 50 percent of consumer waste, given proper technology, careful handling, and lots of cooperation. Recycling processes have their own flaws—glass making, paper pulping and bleaching, and steel, aluminum, and copper smelting all produce toxic emissions and residues that must be disposed of. Water pollution from these industries is also a concern, as are the currently limited markets for recycled goods. Still, reduction and recycling should be the goal, and both should be promoted over incineration.

"What we need to do is get rid of the garbage, not just move it through one more machine," says Thomas Webster, research associate at the Center for Biology of Natural Systems at Queens College in New York. "To get high levels of recycling you have to work hard. You need legislative strategies and you need political will. But once you have the systems in place, you've solved the problem."

The world's future economic stability depends on how we use three things: energy, raw materials, and money. Governments now spend far too much collecting and disposing of garbage. Billions more are spent on the environmental damage caused by out-of-control consumption. Making the transition to a sustainable, recycling society will result in both better economies and healthier environments.

A Conserving Society

People are not without power. By reducing the amount of waste they produce and recycling a large share of their discards, individuals can have an effect. But consumers cannot effect change without the support of government and industry. The degree to which people and nations work together to conserve raw materials and resources will determine the rate at which the global environment is altered.

The challenge does not lie so much with more "technical fixes" but with our approach to the world around us. "There will always be another landfill" cannot be the words we live by, because we are simply running out of room. The time for the shift from throwaway society to conserving society has arrived.

a critical thinking activity

Recognizing Deceptive Arguments

People who feel strongly about an issue use many techniques to persuade others to agree with them. Some of these techniques appeal to the intellect, some to the emotions. Many of them distract the reader or listener from the real issues.

Below are listed a few common examples of argumentation tactics. Most of them can be used either to advance an argument in an honest, reasonable way or to deceive or distract from the real issues. When evaluating an argument, it is important for a reader to recognize the distracting, or deceptive, appeals being used. Here are a few common ones:

a. *bandwagon*—the idea that "everybody" does this or believes this

b. *scare tactics*—the threat that if you don't do this or don't believe this, something terrible will happen

c. *strawperson*—distorting or exaggerating an opponent's ideas to make one's own seem stronger

d. *personal attack*—criticizing an opponent *personally* instead of rationally debating his or her ideas

e. *testimonial*—quoting or paraphrasing an authority or celebrity to support one's own viewpoint

f. *deductive reasoning*—the idea that since a and b are true, c is also true

g. *slanters*—to persuade through inflammatory and exaggerated language instead of reason

h. *generalizations*—using statistics or facts to generalize about a population, place, or idea

The following activity will help to sharpen your skills in recognizing deceptive reasoning. Most of the statements below are taken from the viewpoints in this chapter. *Beside each one, mark the letter of the type of deceptive appeal being used. More than one type of tactic may be applicable. If you believe the statement is not any of the listed appeals, write N.*

1. The notion that garbage can be completely eliminated through the use of waste-to-energy plants is blatantly ridiculous.

2. Parents who use disposable diapers are irresponsible, short-sighted, and totally oblivious to the growing waste crisis.

3. All competent scientists and waste-management experts support the idea of reducing waste at its source.

4. Since waste-to-energy plants emit dioxin, and dioxin causes cancer, one could say that waste-to-energy plants cause cancer.

5. People who oppose landfills think some magical solution, like shipping waste into deep space, will solve the garbage problem.

6. If more than one-half of the American public does not start recycling soon, the country will be overwhelmed by disease-causing refuse.

7. President Bush said that everyone must do his or her part to solve the garbage crisis; that includes using cloth diapers and saying no to excessive packaging at fast-food restaurants.

8. Environmentalists who protest every new solution to the garbage problem have their heads in the sand when it comes to modern technology.

9. According to the National Solid Wastes Management Association, less than one-third of Americans support creating more landfills. Therefore, landfills should not be considered an alternative.

10. Unlike the concerned citizens of Germany and Japan, Americans are ignorant, wasteful, and lazy when it comes to cleaning up the environment.

11. Several leading waste-management experts, including Hunter Taylor, maintain that recycling is not the complete answer to reducing garbage.

12. Since plastic constitutes a large part of our non-biodegradable garbage, it is logical that if consumers stopped buying plastic we would solve the waste problem.

13. The toxic liquids and gases that seep from landfills threaten to poison most of America's drinkable groundwater.

14. Diapers are but a tiny part of the garbage problem. To focus the discussion on such a trivial issue as diaper usage displays a grievous lack of understanding about the waste crisis.

15. The leading opponents of waste incinerators are failed scientists who are incapable of creating anything constructive, so they attack others' ideas.

Periodical Bibliography

The following articles have been selected to supplement the diverse views presented in this chapter.

Brian Ahlberg	"Garbage Burners Losing Steam," *Utne Reader*, September/October 1989.
William P. Barrett	"Scrapman," *Forbes*, October 30, 1989.
William Booth	"Sometimes a Little Degradation Is Desirable," *The Washington Post National Weekly Edition*, April 14-20, 1989.
Brian Bremner	"Recycling: The Newest Wrinkle in Waste Management's Bag," *Business Week*, March 5, 1990.
George J. Church	"Garbage, Garbage, Everywhere," *Time*, September 5, 1988.
James Cook	"Garbage into Gold," *Forbes,* January 22, 1990.
William J. Cook	"A Lot of Rubbish," *U.S. News & World Report,* December 25, 1989-January 1, 1990.
Tim W. Ferguson	"Where the Greens Risk Soiling Themselves," *The Wall Street Journal*, April 17, 1990.
Dan Grossman and Seth Shulman	"Down in the Dumps," *Discover*, April 1990.
Jodi L. Jacobson	"Recycling Our Most Prolific By-Product," *USA Today*, July 1989.
Mary Morse	"Degradable Plastics?" *Utne Reader*, May/June 1989.
Faye Rice	"Where Will We Put All That Garbage?" *Fortune*, April 11, 1988.
William J. Ruckelshaus	"The Politics of Waste Disposal," *The Wall Street Journal*, September 5, 1989.
Thomas A. Sancton	"What on Earth Are We Doing?" *Time*, January 2, 1989.
Eric Schmitt	"Creating New Habits for the Common Good," *The New York Times*, April 27, 1989.
Ruth Simon	"Yes, in My Backyard," *Forbes*, September 3, 1990.
William K. Stevens	"Degradable Plastics Show Promise in Fight Against Trash," *The New York Times*, April 11, 1989.

4 CHAPTER

How Should America Dispose of Toxic Waste?

THE ENVIRONMENTAL
CRISIS

Chapter Preface

Toxic waste is a by-product of humanity's ingenious efforts to improve the quality of life. People rarely think of the toxic waste problem as they take photographs, pick up their dry cleaning, throw away a used battery, spray backyard insects, or clean a toilet. Nevertheless, these activities are rooted in manufacturing processes that produce tons of chemical wastes each year.

Unfortunately, human ingenuity has not been as successful at finding methods to dispose of toxic wastes as it has been at developing new products. Landfills leak, incinerators emit air pollutants, ocean dumping contaminates the sea, and recycling cannot completely reuse waste. Many people have grown to accept these current, deficient methods of waste disposal because they fear alternatives would cripple the American economy with excessive regulation of products on which Americans have grown dependent. Using imperfect methods to dispose of toxic wastes is a lot easier than learning to live without countless modern conveniences like cleansers, degreasers, photographs, and decaffeinated coffee, these people argue.

Many environmentalists, however, think the human imagination needs more incentive to create new ways of eliminating toxic wastes at their source—the manufacturing process. Environmentalists contend that while companies are rewarded by consumers for coming up with new products, they are not sufficiently punished for generating waste. The government should severely curtail the amount of toxic waste private companies can generate, they say, and assess heavy fines to violators. Companies would then have a financial incentive to work on the waste problem.

Is it possible to have the many products Americans have learned to love *and* a clean environment? The authors in this chapter debate this question.

"Incineration should be seen as a vital component of the total solution to our waste problem."

Toxic Waste Should Be Incinerated

B.M. Thompson

The following viewpoint is excerpted from a speech presented by B.M. Thompson, the executive vice president for Phillips Petroleum Company. In it, Thompson advocates incineration as part of an overall strategy to reduce and dispose of toxic waste. He argues that burning waste can turn leaking toxic waste barrels into manageable piles of ash. Thompson maintains that the public must be educated about incineration's benefits so they will understand and accept the risks.

As you read, consider the following questions:

1. What does Thompson say are the two main by-products of toxic waste incineration?
2. According to the author, how hot must incinerators be to vaporize toxic waste? What residues are left?
3. In Thompson's opinion, why must society be willing to accept certain risks?

B.M. Thompson, "Good Riddance," speech delivered to the Coalition for Responsible Waste Incineration, Crystal City, Virginia, May 24, 1989.

The hazardous waste problem is not isolated to a handful of industries and a few hundred locations.

It's integrated into everything we make, consume and throw away, in every community.

Nearly everyone makes some hazardous wastes, from big chemical companies to the family dry cleaning business down the street.

But industry is the largest producer of hazardous wastes.

In 1987 alone, U.S. industry generated 275 million tons of hazardous waste, nearly twice the amount of solid waste collected from American curbsides that year.

Most of these hazardous wastes were the by-products of important consumer goods like plastics, paints and solvents.

But unlike the consumers who buy these goods, the industries that make them can't just set their used motor oil and empty paint cans out on the curb and wait for the trash man to pick them up.

Furthermore, because of the lifestyle we've grown accustomed to, hazardous wastes will continue to be generated whether we dispose of them properly or not.

And that job is getting tougher by the minute.

No Cheap Solutions

The EPA [Environmental Protection Agency] is phasing out land farms—those broad expanses of land where hazardous wastes are mixed with soil and gradually decomposed.

What's more, getting permits for storage sites and incinerators is no cinch, especially when you consider the growing number of local groups protesting hazardous disposal methods.

So far I've painted a bleak portrait of our nation's waste problem.

And I've tried to show that while hazardous waste is only part of the picture, it's an integrated part that touches all of our lives.

Therefore, solutions to the hazardous waste problem must be incorporated into our nation's total system of waste disposal.

There's no doubt in my mind that the U.S. garbage crisis is manageable.

But there are no simple—or cheap—solutions. . . .

Incineration

That's where incineration comes into the picture.

Basically, incineration involves burning wastes at such high temperatures that they're broken down into simple elements that occur naturally—like carbon dioxide and water.

Incineration should not be seen as a cure-all that renders source reduction, recycling or other treatment methods obsolete.

But incineration should be seen as a vital component of the total solution to our waste problem—and a permanent component at that.

Incineration destroys virtually 100 percent of many wastes.

Efficient Destruction

Incineration:
Potentially the safest method of destroying many of the more toxic of today's hazardous wastes—particularly such substances as organic solvents, chlorinated hydrocarbons and oily wastes. . . .

Effective incineration requires sophisticated equipment, including such anti-pollution devices as scrubbers, and depends critically on good management. Properly operated, the most modern high-temperature incinerators have "destruction efficiencies" of 99.99999 per cent.

Edward Goldsmith and Nicholas Hildyard, *The Earth Report*, 1988.

In effect, it speeds up nature's own process of decomposition.

And for some man-made materials, in fact, incineration is the only way to destroy them.

Let me offer an illustration:

Say this banquet hall were filled with drums full of a hazardous waste, like paint thinner.

Incineration could reduce this roomful of liquid waste to a cupful of ash.

Now, that cupful of ash might still be hazardous.

And if so, it would have to be carefully handled and stored.

But isn't it safer, easier and more sensible to store a cupful of hazardous ash than several hundred drums full of hazardous liquid? . . .

Credibility

Those of us involved in hazardous waste incineration realize that hazardous waste is a latent public issue.

That is, people don't worry much about the problem until there's a Times Beach or until the local landfill is pronounced a Superfund site or until an incinerator is proposed for the community.

That's why all of us need to do a better job of bringing the hazardous waste issue to light.

Specifically, we should base our actions on four imperatives.

The first imperative is to be credible in conduct.

In the days before Love Canal, industry's game plan for dealing with the public could be summarized in two words: Don't lie.

Sounds good at first glance.

But what it really meant was a closed technical society whose people saw no loss in saying nothing, and no gain in saying anything.

But when our private mistakes became public tragedies, we were forced to come clean—scrubbed raw by public outrage.

Now I'm not glad that certain tragedies occurred.

But I like to think some good came out of them, because they made us realize that our credibility marches in lockstep with our accountability to the public.

Public Approval

Nowadays, when it comes to building new plants—like an incinerator—we're seeking the public's approval before the first spade of earth is turned.

For example, a Phillips subsidiary—Incinatrol—is planning to build two hazardous waste incinerators in Texas.

These incinerators will take most any type of waste—except nuclear waste—and vaporize it at temperatures of up to 24 hundred degrees.

That's hot enough to break apart the molecular structure of most chemicals.

What's left are carbon dioxide and salt water—and these are non-toxic.

These incinerators will even shred and burn the steel drums that the waste comes in and make them environmentally safe for landfill. . . .

Our second imperative is to be clear in communication.

People want simple answers to complex questions.

And if we don't give them simple answers they'll go to someone who will—even if that someone is less qualified and less likely to know the whole story. . . .

Our third imperative is to be realistic in our expectations.

As important as incineration is in helping solve America's trash problem we'll sleep a lot easier at night if we don't expect the American people to fall at our feet in humble thanks.

Benjamin Franklin once said: "To serve the public faithfully, and at the same time please it entirely, is impossible."

Probably the best we can hope for is some measure of public trust.

By now, most of you have heard of the NIMBY factor—

NIMBY being an acronym for "Not in my back yard."

Our society today wants all the advantages of our modern world without any of the risks.

We want enough energy to run our microwave ovens and satellite dishes without any power plants, strip mines or oil wells in our back yards.

And we want our trash picked up every Tuesday and Friday without landfills or incinerators in our community.

The NIMBY factor makes the siting and permitting processes

for incinerators very tough.

So it's important to remember that being credible in conduct and clear in communication will not automatically lay the NIMBY factor to rest.

Our expectations need to be realistic.

The fourth imperative is to be responsible in risk.

Having been burned by Three Mile Island, the greenhouse effect, the scare over Chilean grapes, and a host of other troubling events, our society in many respects has exchanged free enterprise for frightened enterprise.

Henry Fairlie wrote an article called "Fear of Living," which appeared in an issue of *The New Republic.*

Fairlie calls our modern-day fear of risk, "Strikingly an American phenomenon."

He says, "In America, the threshold of tolerable risk has now been set so low that the nation is refusing to pay the inevitable costs of human endeavor."

Carry this fear of risk to its illogical end

—And all airplanes should be grounded—because sometimes one crashes.

—All ladders should be banned—because sometimes a person falls off one.

—And all oil development should be stopped—because sometimes a tanker runs aground.

The truth is, there are risks in everything we do.

And the reason we take risks, is that the rewards outweigh them.

Risks and Rewards

There are risks—and rewards—in incineration.

And if incineration is going to be a more widely accepted part of our solution to the waste problem, those of us who build and operate incinerators must first do all we can to minimize the risks and then educate the public about the remaining balance of risks and rewards.

We all tend to fear what we don't understand.

And we resist what we fear.

So educating the public—that is, placing the risks and rewards of incineration in their proper context—will help calm the fears of a community.

We also need to involve our communities in the decision-making process, so the risks and rewards are shared.

And we must understand, as Thoreau once said, that it takes two to speak the truth—one to speak and another to listen.

I'll close with this:

This summer [1989], we'll celebrate the 20th anniversary of the [first] landing on the moon.

As we celebrate, we're sure to be reminded that three men

163

lost their lives in the first Apollo spacecraft.

And while their loss was tragic, we must also remember that their deaths left us undeterred.

The Eagle landed a year and a half ahead of schedule.

Henry Fairlie described that conquering spirit as:

"The American gusto that blew like a fresh wind around the globe. . .showing what could be accomplished in so short a time by a nation that did not shrink from risk."

Fear of Risk

Twenty years from now will our fear of risk have buried us beneath a mountain of trash?

I don't think so.

Not if science, industry, the government and the public begin now to establish an integrated waste management system.

This system would feature source reduction to limit the generation of waste, recycling programs to reprocess wastes into useful items, treatment and incineration to reduce the volume of waste and to generate energy, and new landfill technologies to dispose of other wastes in an environmentally safe manner.

"Incineration is a controlled and officially sanctioned 'toxic waste leak' through stack emissions and ash disposal."

Toxic Waste Should Not Be Incinerated

Greenpeace

The following viewpoint is by Greenpeace, one of America's foremost environmental organizations. In the viewpoint, the authors write that toxic waste incinerators spew carcinogenic chemicals, metals, and dioxins into the atmosphere, thereby jeopardizing human health. Even with a burning efficiency above ninety-nine percent, the authors assert that incinerators would annually emit thousands of pounds of dangerous toxins into the air. The authors also claim that government management of hazardous waste incinerators is inadequate and potentially unsafe.

As you read, consider the following questions:

1. Why do the authors argue that it is impossible to accurately measure the performance of waste incinerators?
2. According to the authors, what are some of the toxic by-products of incineration?
3. How do the authors use the term "fugitive chemicals"?

From "Hazardous Waste Incinerators," a 1987 factsheet published by Greenpeace. Reprinted with permission.

"Land-based hazardous waste incinerators are stationary point sources which emit pollutants into the air, land, and water media. Emissions may occur as part of the incineration process, as part of the scrubber operations, or as fugitive emissions. Uptake of emissions by terrestrial life may occur through air, water, soil, or via the food web."

—EPA Science Advisory Board, April 1985

Environmental Protection Agency reported that U.S. industries produced nearly *600 billion pounds* of hazardous waste in 1983. Each year, more hazardous waste is produced. What can be done to protect the general public and their air, water, and soil from this enormous quantity of toxic chemicals?

Today hard experience is teaching what common sense has known all along: hazardous materials must be kept out of the air, water and soil. Every state has groundwater and surface water supplies contaminated by hazardous waste, communities destroyed by toxic waste dumps, and men, women and children who are suffering from exposure to discarded industrial chemicals.

Public demand has resulted in better protection for water and soil. Beginning in the early 1970s, Congress passed a series of laws curtailing direct discharge to water and shallow land burial of hazardous waste. However, regulating air emissions of hazardous chemicals has barely begun.

Landfills in the Sky

EPA and industry plan a massive expansion of incineration capacity during the next few years. According to the Office of Technology Assessment, some 20% of hazardous waste is supposedly suitable for incineration but only 1% of hazardous waste is currently being incinerated. To burn all wastes classified as burnable, existing incinerators must go to maximum capacities and maximum operating times . . . and many more communities will be targeted as sites for new hazardous waste incinerators. The people in these communities want answers.

Scientists—those who work for EPA and industry—agree that hazardous waste incinerators emit toxic chemicals into the air. They also agree that there are both short-term and long-term health effects from accumulations of toxic fallout from incinerators. But damages to public health and the environment cannot be accurately predicted because of lack of information.

Incinerators have been operating for years, but little is known about their effects because they tend to be located in developed areas where the effects of their toxic air emissions are not easily distinguished from the effects of other toxic air emissions.

166

Scientists, who are conducting incineration research for the EPA, are concerned that "the formation and release of (products of incomplete combustion) PIC during incineration may . . . pose a significant risk to the public," as stated in the EPA's report "Inhalation Pathway Risk Assessment of Hazardous Waste Incineration Facilities."

Reprinted by permission: Tribune Media Services.

In this same report, scientists warned that "the human health risk from incineration of carcinogenic heavy metals (such as chromium, cadmium, and beryllium) may be significant."

In their review of the EPA's program of hazardous waste incineration, the EPA Science Advisory Board issued this warning, "Based upon the data submitted for its review and observations made during site visits of operating facilities, the Committee is concerned . . . about the reliability of operating large-scale land based incinerators. . . ."

Monitoring the Burn

No reliable method exists to measure or monitor the performance of hazardous waste incinerators. As one EPA report says, "The complexity of the incineration process, the differences in incinerator designs, and the difficulties in monitoring changing operating conditions make the accurate prediction of absolute incineration performance an essentially impossible task."

EPA requires destruction and removal efficiencies (DREs) of 99.99% ("four 9's") of some hazardous waste and 99.9999% ("six 9's") for critical items, such as PCBs [polychlorinated biphenyls]. Unfortunately, DREs are not measured during actual, routine operations when real waste is being burned. DREs are determined during a one-time-only "trial burn" of selected chemicals under carefully controlled conditions.

The stack gas samples that are collected and analyzed in trial burns are usually no more than 1/650,000th of one day's output of stack gas. Unless major modifications are undertaken, an incinerator is permitted to operate for 10 years on the basis of this one trial burn. Reassessments of DREs during the remainder of the incinerator's operating life are not required.

According to an EPA report, this trial burn method provides "only a 'snapshot' of the incinerator's efficiency during the trial burn." This same report warns, "No information is obtained about how the incinerator's performance might fluctuate with future changes in operating conditions or waste feed characteristics."

The EPA Science Advisory Board expressed concern on this issue as follows:

> Research on the performance has occurred only under optimal burn conditions and sampling has, on occasion, been discontinued during upset conditions which take place with unknown frequency. Even relatively short-term operation of incinerators in upset conditions can greatly increase the total incinerator emitted loadings to the environment.

Even if the trial burn DREs could be achieved routinely, communities near incinerators are exposed to significant quantities of unburned wastes that escape in the stack gas. In an EPA-contracted study of ten commercial hazardous waste incinerators in 1986, the average incinerator had a feedrate of 6,100 pounds/hour, operated 6,037 hours/year, and burned 36,865,000 pounds of liquid hazardous waste in that one year.

At a 99.99% DRE for all of this waste at all times—no upsets, no loss of efficiency in startups and shutdowns, and no variations in waste feedstreams—at least 3,686 pounds of unburned waste was blown out of the stack of that average incinerator in one year.

Incomplete Combustion

When a hazardous waste—a chlorinated organic solvent, for example—is burned, most of it breaks down into carbon dioxide, water and chlorine. Of these, only the chlorine is toxic. But the hot molecules also rearrange and recombine into many new, relatively complex chemicals, so-called "products of incomplete combustion" (PICs). *One EPA study cautions that these PICs "are more difficult to destroy and may be more toxic than the parent compound."*

Among the more notoriously toxic PICs that were identified in the EPA's study of eight hazardous waste incinerators were benzene, chloroform, tetrachloroethylene, and naphthalene, as well as formaldehyde, phosgene, dioxins and furans. . . . And these were only a fraction of the chemicals that are actually present in stack gases. Another EPA study questions "whether the 90-99 percent of the hydrocarbons which have not been identified could result in a significant risk to human health."

When EPA evaluated the performance of eight incinerators, they found metals at varying concentrations in all stack gases. The metals come from the waste itself and from waste containers, such as metal drums that are routinely burned at some incinerators. Another EPA study cautions, "Stack releases of heavy metals (such as arsenic, chromium, and lead) are independent of DRE since heavy metals are not destroyed by incineration processes."

Midwest Research Institute found that as much as 53% of the heavy metals burned in an incinerator are released in the stack gases. Metals not emitted in stack gases are deposited in the incinerator ash.

Among the eight incinerators evaluated, one incinerator was emitting lead at the rate of 23 pounds per day into the air—almost 6,000 pounds per year at average operating times. The emission rate of cadmium was 67 pounds per year, while the rate for nickel was 452 pounds per year.

Fugitive Chemicals

Unburned waste, newly-formed toxic PICs and heavy metals are not the only toxic air pollutants released at incinerators. Fugitive emissions, chemicals that escape during transportation, storage and processing, may be an even greater problem. The EPA Science Advisory Board cautions that ". . . fugitive emissions and accidental spills may release as much or more toxic material to the environment than the direct emissions from incomplete waste incineration."

At one large commercial incinerator burning pesticide-related wastes, gross fugitive emissions were estimated at 10,000 pounds per year. Ninety-three percent of the chloroform and 62% of the toluene found in the air at this incinerator were fugitive emissions. In other words, thirteen times more chloroform escaped from storage tanks, leaky valves, etc. than was blown out of the incinerator stack.

Besides burning waste, hazardous waste incinerators also generate waste: fly ash that goes up the stack, bottom ash that is left in the incinerator—and residues from air pollution control devices.

When a common hazardous waste, such as organic liquid, is burned, most of the waste is vaporized, but as much as 9% remains as an ash. When solid hazardous waste is burned, as much as 29% remains as ash, according to an EPA report. This incinerator ash carries toxic heavy metals and PICs. In one ash study, 37 toxic PICs were found at levels ranging from 0.1 to 500 parts per million (ppm). Metals in the ash included lead, 5,000 ppm; arsenic, 27 ppm; cadmium, 61 ppm; and nickel, 7,300 ppm.

Toxic By-Products

Incineration is the process in which combustion is used to destroy toxic materials. In addition to producing carbon, oxygen, and water, incineration produces air pollution and residual ash containing dioxin and other toxic substances.

Jon Naar, *Design for a Livable Planet*, 1990.

Using these measurements, the ten incinerators evaluated by the EPA in their 1986 study could have produced at least 33 million pounds of ash, containing 165,000 pounds of lead and 241,000 pounds of nickel. The most common method of disposal for such ash is burial in landfills.

Some incinerators have air pollution control devices, such as scrubbers or filters, to capture a portion of the gaseous pollutants emitted. Stack gas scrubbers do not reduce the quantity of toxic emissions from an incinerator, they simply shift them from one medium, air, to another, water or soil. Scrubber water is routinely treated and discharged into ponds or the facility's wastewater discharge while solid filters are usually buried in landfills.

Inadequate Oversight

Very little is known about the complex mixtures of toxic chemicals that are burned in incinerators. Accurate chemical analyses are so difficult that, according to another EPA report, "Except in settings where an incinerator is dedicated to a particular chemical process waste stream, a detailed quantitative makeup of the waste being burned is unknown."

According to criticisms leveled by their own Science Advisory Board, EPA's oversight of hazardous waste incineration has been inadequate at best.

In their review of EPA's hazardous waste incineration program released in April 1985, the Science Advisory Board was blunt: ". . . the Agency continues to experience difficulties both in assessing and managing hazardous waste incineration programs."

The Board identified areas where critical information needs

were ignored: ". . . the Agency did not assess a number of scientific issues relating to the incineration of liquid hazardous wastes. . .," ". . . inadequate resources were devoted to a holistic and scientific review of these technologies regarding their environmental impacts and acceptability. . ." and . . ."to date, the sampling of stack gas emissions has not occurred in a manner which would allow appropriate scientific evaluation."

In addition, the EPA has not established, much less implemented, any firm guidelines for incinerator construction and operation. For instance, in an EPA-funded survey of eight incinerators, "(o)perating temperatures ranged from 650 to 1450 C and calculated residence time varied from 0.07 to 6.5 seconds."

EPA restricts only six categories of the many hundreds of air contaminants emitted by incinerators. Based on a limit for each contaminant, the restrictions are insensitive to the cumulative effect of the total emissions, the buildup of bioaccumulative toxic fallout and the effect of other pollution sources in the area.

Hazardous waste incineration is riddled with unknowns, but one thing is certain—the health and the environment of communities in which incinerators are sited are at risk. Incinerators release unknown quantities of unknown chemicals, presenting health threats of unknown magnitude and unknown duration to the people and ecosystems of neighboring communities.

Incineration's appeal lies in its ability to make hazardous waste seem to vanish into the air. With increasing restrictions on other forms of disposal, incineration is being promoted as a simple and cheap "permanent" solution to the vast quantities of hazardous wastes produced. In reality, incineration is a controlled and officially sanctioned "toxic waste leak" through stack emissions and ash disposal.

The Quick Fix

Incineration involves very real risks and very real uncertainties for the host communities. Incinerating hazardous wastes does not stop their spread through the environment, but it does make liability for toxic contamination more difficult to prove.

Hazardous waste incineration facilities are known to emit toxic chemicals and metals into the air. Incinerators only aggravate the hazardous waste problem by providing the illusion of a "quick fix" for those who are so eager for an easy answer that they ignore the risks associated with this immature technology.

Given the serious concerns voiced by the scientific community and the experiences of communities where incinerators have been sited, the current enthusiasm for incineration can only be regarded as an incredible lack of reason, an hysteria of industry and government.

"If. . .Congress were to give private industry an incentive to concentrate on developing technology, we would stand a greater chance of restoring. . .landfills to their original state."

Private Industry Could Clean Up Toxic Waste

Amal Kumar Naj

The creation of Superfund laws in 1980 was supposed to give the Environmental Protection Agency the power and money to clean up America's toxic waste sites. However, most scientists and environmentalists have realized the problem is much larger than legislators envisioned when drafting Superfund. To remedy the situation, writers like Amal Kumar Naj advocate allowing private industry to solve the problem. In the following viewpoint, Naj, an environmental issues reporter for *The Wall Street Journal's* New York bureau, argues that only by fostering free-market competition in toxic waste cleanup can the EPA hope to succeed. He contends that federal toxic waste legislation is inefficient, expensive, and ineffective.

As you read, consider the following questions:

1. Why does Naj believe companies have little control over the cleanup technologies used at toxic waste sites?
2. In the author's opinion, what are the benefits of creating a free-market approach to toxic waste cleanup?
3. According to Naj, why are stringent environmental standards unfair to business?

In 1980 Congress authorized the Environmental Protection Agency to locate toxic waste sites and force the parties responsible to clean them up. Eight years later, the results are dismal: Of the 27,000 or so sites that have been identified so far—2,500 of them requiring urgent attention—only about three dozen have been cleaned up and 275 are in early cleanup stages.

The 1980 Superfund Act, by most accounts, hasn't healed the wounds from America's industrial past. The toxic waste cleanup program needs a new focus and sharper guidelines.

The years of effort to secure cleanups have exposed some fundamental flaws in the program. Chief among them is that the act itself encourages a bewildering amount of litigation, much of it delaying tactics by the companies. Superfund's success ultimately depends upon the development and commercialization of technology for effective, permanent cleanups, but this isn't getting very much attention.

The law is structured in such a way that the EPA enforces it by initiating cleanups on its own, using a multibillion-dollar trust fund established by Congress, if the parties responsible won't volunteer or can't be tracked down. The agency then sues to recover the money.

No Control

The EPA controls the selection of the technology for treatment of the contaminants and the cleanup standards to be attained. Moreover, companies are liable even years after the work if the treatment is found to be inadequate or if the regulators tighten the cleanup standards after the work already has been done.

The problem with this approach is that companies have very little say on, and hence very little control of, a situation that requires them to spend tens or hundreds of millions of dollars. The average cost of cleaning up a site has been running at about $25 million, and some companies, such as Westinghouse, Allied-Signal and Monsanto, face liabilities in 40 to 100 sites. A conservative estimate is that it will cost about $100 billion to clean up the nation's hazardous waste sites. The Office of Technology Assessment, the investigative arm of Congress, says $500 billion—up from its 1985 estimate of $300 billion—will be needed over the next 50 years.

Companies readily acknowledge that it is worth spending millions of dollars on lawyers to put off spending hundreds of millions of dollars on cleanups. "The only way [left] for the companies to negotiate is through litigation," says Jerome Strauss, director of the hazardous waste division at Versar Inc., an environmental engineering firm in Springfield, Va. "Otherwise the companies feel they are being stabbed in the back."

Consider: Shell Oil along with its insurers spent $40 million in legal fees before agreeing to spend several hundred million dollars to clean up a vast site near Denver, and five other companies spent a total of $16 million in legal fees before agreeing to clean up a St. Louis site at a cost of $14 million. Some companies are suing each other over their shares of the liability—since many sites contain wastes from several companies. Then there are the suits that companies have filed against their insurers to get them to pick up the tab, and the suits with which insurers have retaliated; altogether 300 such suits are working their way through the courts.

Nature Calls

Meanwhile, the EPA's selection and administration of technology have come under harsh criticism. The Office of Technology Assessment has said the EPA's cleanup efforts are too lenient. After examining 100 sites, it said in a June 1990 report that the EPA often chose technologies that didn't result in permanent cleanups, or it selected "permanent" technologies that hadn't been proved to be such. "Many good, permanently effective waste treatment technologies are on the market but, too often, are not fully examined, or are not selected for use," the report also said.

174

"Even after eight years, cleanup technology is a new and fast-changing field and the work force [at the EPA] is relatively young and inexperienced, [and] people in contractor firms also lack experience," the report added.

It's hard to say how much of the caustic tone of the report was motivated by finger-pointing by Congress, which is saying to its constituents, in effect: Look, we gave the EPA all this money, and it's the EPA that's bungling. Winston Porter, head of the EPA's hazardous waste treatment division, bristles at the mention of the report.

"That report is superficial and incomplete," he says. But he concedes that "there's a lot of room for improvement" in the Superfund program.

The environmental agency is in a tough position: In a 1986 amendment of the Superfund Act, Congress required the EPA to give preference to permanently effective cleanup technologies that at the same time are cost-effective. Some of the "permanent" technologies that would clean up all of the contaminants are so expensive—given the state of their development—that most of the fund will be consumed by just a few sites. The Office of Technology Assessment, on the other hand, asserts that the EPA, in an attempt to spend its money on a large number of sites, often miscalculates cost or inflates the numbers to reject a better technology.

Foster Competition

The dispute aside, what's clear is that Congress hasn't created incentives or an environment that will foster a competitive rush for new, effective technologies.

As the EPA has found, even the most sophisticated and well-designed treatment is fraught with uncertainties. The landfills—packed with metals, acids, organic compounds, solvents and numerous other deadly substances for decades—are each so different in character that they defy common technological solutions. Incineration doesn't work for many sites, because it would let off poisonous gases; sometimes chemical treatment doesn't remove the deadly substances; and oftentimes each identified toxic element has to be targeted and extracted in a process so complex as to make treatment impractical.

In any one year, the EPA has been able to test and approve only 10 to 20 treatment technologies. If Congress were to allow the companies themselves to select the cleanup technologies—leaving the EPA to monitor cleanup standards—this would more than likely lead to competitive bids from environmental engineering firms and the companies that put the stuff in landfills in the first place. And more than likely, the result would be cost-efficient, permanently effective technologies. Without such a change, Congress will find itself in the untenable position of considering subsidies to foster development and commercialization of the technologies.

Of course, no amount of technological development will do much good if the companies aren't sure what cleanup standards they must attain. The 1984 amendment set ground-water quality goals established under the Safe Drinking Water Act for the Superfund sites. But they cover only 22 chemicals. Federal and state regulators continue to struggle with the issue of acceptable risk for the vast majority of other chemicals and metals.

Sometimes they set standards based on available research studies. But "many times the numbers are pulled out of thin air," says A. Patrick Nucciarone, an environmental attorney with Hannoch Weisman in New Jersey and former chief of the environmental protection section of the U.S. Attorney's Office in that state.

Conflicting Standards

The result is a hodgepodge of enforcement decisions, especially with states playing an increasing role in cleanup efforts. Olin Corp., for instance, spent $3.5 million to clean up mercury contamination at its Saltville, Va., plant site in an agreement with state authorities. But the EPA said the standard wasn't satisfactory. The company now figures it will have to spend an additional $10 million to $15 million.

Some environmentally conscious states, on the other hand, are using cleanup criteria more stringent than those of the federal government. For instance, New Jersey's permissible radioactive emission standard is three times stricter than the federal standard. To avoid conflicts, it may make sense for a company to comply with the higher of the two cleanup standards. "But that means a jump in the order of two to five times in the cleanup cost," says Mr. Nucciarone. "Sometimes it can't be justified, because the lower standard doesn't threaten the ground water."

Congress must decide the acceptable level of risks from toxic wastes—in other words, how clean is clean. While in theory it would be preferable to reduce the risks to zero, the current high price of such a standard wouldn't allow much of a cleanup of America's graveyard. If, however, Congress were to give private industry an incentive to concentrate on developing technology, we would stand a greater chance of restoring most of the poisonous landfills to their original state.

"It would be useful to stick to the tactics of mass struggle in trying to protect and improve regulations and leave nothing to the market forces."

Private Industry Could Not Clean Up Toxic Waste

Jay Berry

Many environmental activists, including some associated with Greenpeace and Earth First!, blame private industry for toxic waste in America. Jay Berry, an environmental writer for *People's Weekly World*, a newspaper of the Socialist Workers Party, supports that position. In the following viewpoint, Berry states that private industry must shoulder the cost of toxic waste cleanup, but must not be given the authority to supervise the process. Berry believes that private corporations cannot be trusted to work in the public's best interest. He contends that the market approach condones pollution.

As you read, consider the following questions:

1. In Berry's opinion, why is it ludicrous to measure the danger of toxins by their weight?
2. According to the author, how does a free-market strategy obscure the true issues?
3. What does Berry say are the ultimate effects of toxic pollutants?

Jay Berry, "Environmental Progress—Less than Meets the Eye," *People's Daily World,* July 7, 1990.

In a sobering look at our record on eliminating toxic pollutants, ecologist-activist Dr. Barry Commoner has shown that major gains have been made in the case of only a few such substances. Regarding such air pollutants as nitrogen oxides and sulfur oxides, only modest gains were registered, and these came before 1982—i.e., before the Reagan-Bush Environmental Protection Agency and Occupational Safety and Health Administration. In water quality, on balance no gains have been made at all. Major gains were registered with regard to a few substances, such as DDT [dichloro-diphenyl-trichloro-ethane], lead and asbestos.

Commoner's book, *Making Peace with the Planet*, contains much worthwhile information. He had to compile an overview of the environmental picture himself, although this is supposed to be done by the President's Council on Environmental Quality. President Reagan zapped this group. Looking at his record, it is no wonder.

A Corrupt Process

After surveying the substances for which there have been major improvements, Commoner concludes that the way to go forward is to change entire production processes to stop generating toxic pollutants. Lead levels, for example, went down because lead was removed from gasoline and paint. DDT levels declined because the chemical was replaced by other pesticides. It is Commoner's view that the regulatory process is too slow, and too permeated by corruption and sleazy corporate lawyers to be effective.

All the battles in which the people have made major gains involved much public awareness and mass struggle. There were many campaigns and television shows dealing with DDT, lead and asbestos. Lead was the focus of activity for many community groups, and asbestos for many trade unions. OSHA's first act was to promulgate an emergency standard for asbestos.

Over [1988-89], the media have begun to describe toxic hazards by listing the number of tons or pounds of pollutants emitted by a given company. This has led Big Business to suggest that the best way to combat toxic pollution is to rely on the market. Companies would be allowed to discharge a certain amount of pollutants "free," while having to pay a tax on the amount of pollutants emitted above this ceiling. They could also trade or sell their "pollution credits" to other companies. The beginnings of such a strategy are embodied in a bill before the Minnesota legislature. Under this bill, companies would be required to pay a pollution tax of 2 cents per pound for the emission of toxins.

These trends make no sense at all from the point of view of the people exposed to the noxious substances.

First, it is nothing short of ludicrous to measure the danger of a chemical by its weight. Would you measure the danger posed by some animals by their weight? A few ounces of mosquitoes carrying the malaria parasite could wipe out thousands of people, while an 8-ton elephant might be completely harmless. The same is true for chemicals. For example, the dioxin TCDD is about a million times more toxic than most other dangerous solvents. Dioxin, an impurity in herbicides, is given off by garbage incinerators and electrical fires involving PCBs [polychlorinated biphenyls]. It is the most potent known cancer-causing agent and was the worst ingredient in the chemical soup affecting the residents of Love Canal. Dioxin has caused many cancers in Vietnamese civilians and U.S. troops exposed to defoliants and herbicides. One pound of that chemical is enough to kill 10 million people. Under the proposed Minnesota law, a company would have to pay a tax of 2 cents for giving off this much dioxin. For $8 it could emit enough dioxin to kill every person on earth.

© Simpson/Rothco. Reprinted with permission.

There are other things terribly wrong with the market-forces approach. For example, it implies that there is nothing inherently wrong about discharging pollutants, and that it is just as acceptable to trade the right to pollute as it is to trade bubble gum cards. Also—and this pertains mainly to substances on which progress has been made—the "free market" strategy makes it difficult for people to understand the entire problem and to fight for reasonable goals. People can understand that a certain amount of asbestos causes lung damage, and a certain amount of vinyl chloride causes cancer. On the other hand, people would find it difficult to translate tons of emitted pollutants, or pollution tax rates, into needed levels of health protection.

Moreover, it would be impossible to focus on the practical goal of reducing exposure to lead to levels that will not cause reproductive damage and nervous disorders in children.

Tooth and Nail

Finally, the proposed tax system could be used to forestall any regulation for the most toxic substances, such as dioxin, which are dangerous in very small quantities. Adopting that system would amount to unilateral disarmament by the people who breathe and drink water.

To keep the record straight, it should be noted that corporations. . .have continued to fight tooth and nail against environmental policies that adversely affect the bottom line.

They have also spent money lavishly to keep us from understanding the seriousness of the hazards. For example, in the case of asbestos, whose capacity to cause cancer and severe lung disease has been amply documented and which still causes about 20,000 deaths per year, the industry continues to fund "research" purporting to show that North American asbestos is safe. One such study was published in scientific journals and received wide media exposure.

Another striking example is the case of dioxin. . . . The [EPA] put out documents purporting to show that people could be exposed without harm to levels a thousand times higher than those at Love Canal. It continues to release documents claiming that dioxin is not a cancer-causing agent, and that it cannot cause cancer in humans. Other Reagan administration officials were mobilized to attack studies showing that dioxin caused human cancers and to stall and disrupt studies that would demonstrate this fact.

Toxic pollutants continue to take their toll on the American people. Hundreds of citizens' groups have documented high rates of cancer and birth defects in the neighborhoods of waste dumps and chemical plants. . . .

A lot of work needs to be done to halt pollution-induced disease. For starters, it would be useful to stick to the tactics of mass struggle in trying to protect and improve regulations and leave nothing to the market forces.

"The ideal option is waste reduction—not to generate toxics in the first place. "

Ending Production of Toxic Waste Is the Only Solution

David Sarokin

While many grassroots environmental organizations battle for safer toxic waste disposal sites, others suggest a different solution: source reduction. Advocates of source reduction claim that the only solution to toxic waste is to never produce it. In the following viewpoint, David Sarokin writes that source reduction is safer, cleaner, and more economical than treating toxic wastes after they have been created. He argues that industry needs incentives, government-sponsored or otherwise, to stop toxic wastes at their source. Sarokin is an environmental consultant in New York and was a staff member at INFORM, a nonprofit environmental research organization.

As you read, consider the following questions:

1. Why does Sarokin call hazardous waste disposal and destruction the "least desirable" options?
2. In the author's opinion, is the obstacle to source reduction economic? Why or why not?
3. What does Sarokin consider the greatest obstacle to toxic waste reduction efforts?

David Sarokin, "Going to the Source," *Greenpeace,* vol. 12, no. 1, 1988. Reprinted with permission.

In 1986, the state's siting commission informed the citizens of New Jersey of its recommendations: 11 towns had been selected as possible sites for the construction of hazardous waste treatment or disposal facilities. The response of the people was a unanimous "NO!" At public hearings and citizen rallies the cry was the same: "Take your landfills and incinerators and put them someplace else. We don't want them here!"

Also familiar, and at first glance reasonable, was the response of the commission. In essence, it went like this: "We have hundreds of thousands of tons of hazardous wastes to dispose of—wastes that come from the creation of material we all use, materials that improve our quality of life, materials no one wants to do without. Industry has to keep manufacturing; the wastes have to go somewhere. Let's make sure they are managed safely in state-of-the-art facilities."

It is an argument repeated daily in communities around the world. The outcome of the dispute depended on the individual circumstances, but the polar stand-off between the "siters"—those that wanted to see some form of "safe" disposal—and the "NIMBYs"—those that cried "not-in-my-backyard"—was invariable.

Waste Reduction

Until now. Today, there is a third variation on the old stand-off, one that derives from a new way of thinking about how to solve the toxic waste crisis. Today, the response from communities around the world is more enlightened, more pointed and far more promising. Citizens are asking: Are landfills and incinerators really needed? Why do hazardous wastes have to be generated in the first place? Can't industry, with all its expertise and creativity, find a way to eliminate hazardous wastes? Let's do everything in our power to minimize hazardous wastes before we start talking about disposal facilities.

This idea is called waste reduction. It was born in the common sense realization that the generation, not the disposal, of toxic wastes is the problem. It has seized the imagination of environmentalists, industrialists, and governments around the world. It is the "upstream solution"—a way to deal with the problem at the source rather than "downstream"—at the end of the pipeline. And it has profound implications for environmentalists, industry and the world.

In the U.S., 20 states have programs in place to encourage industrial waste reduction, and the federal government is considering expanding its fledgling national program. The United Nations Economic Commission for Europe held its first conference on Non-Waste Technology in 1976 and has continued its activities since then. The governments of Austria, Denmark, France and the Netherlands, to name a few, provide funds to promote industrial waste reduction efforts.

The idea of waste reduction, at least in scientific and policy circles, is not new. More than a decade ago, the U.S. Environmental Protection Agency established a preferred hierarchy of waste management practices.

The Basic First Step

Industry needs to use fewer poisons and in small quantities. Pollution prevention; toxics-use reduction. Those principles are the sine qua non, the basic first step to ground water protection, air quality enhancement, drinking water safety, revitalization of the Great Lakes and other damaged watersheds, solution of the waste disposal crisis (if it's not toxic, there's no problem burying it in a landfill), and a host of other benefits the nation has been seeking for decades.

Peter Montague, *The Workbook*, July-September 1989.

The ideal option is waste reduction—not to generate toxics in the first place, wherever and whenever possible. The second alternative is recycling—for wastes that cannot be reduced, industry should find ways to reuse them. The third choice is destruction—the wastes that remain despite the best efforts to reduce or recycle should be destroyed where possible through effective treatment operations. Disposal—in pits, lagoons, deep wells and at sea—is the least desirable method of dealing with wastes.

"Downstream" Mentality

Since establishing this hierarchy, the U.S. EPA is just beginning to pay attention to waste reduction. Canada also is starting to explore the reduction option. Although a number of European countries have voiced support for waste reduction, the impact of their programs is difficult to gauge. And only a handful of waste generating companies have set up waste reduction programs. Governments, industry and, to some extent, environmentalists have focused almost all their attention, time and resources on the disposal and destruction of hazardous wastes—the lowest rungs on the waste management ladder.

How one chemical company came to employ source reduction in its plant illustrates the problems with the "downstream" mentality. A chemical plant that manufactures resins—the industrial "glue" used to hold together plywood, particle board and other products—used large quantities of toxic chemicals such as phenol and formaldehyde as its major raw materials. These and other chemicals found their way into the plant's wastewater which, after on-site treatment, was discharged to the local sewage treatment plant.

That might have been the end of the story right there, had not the sewage treatment plant, because of end-of-pipeline regulations, imposed stringent restrictions on the amount of toxic chemicals it would accept in the wastewater. The company's treatment facility, an evaporation pond, was filling up with sludge faster than expected, and the cost of sludge disposal was skyrocketing. Management thought of building a bigger pond, but that was too expensive as well. Besides, they were getting increasingly worried about the legal liability the company would face if groundwater beneath the pond was contaminated.

Through a variety of unique circumstances, the company was forced to consider reducing its production of toxics. For the first time in almost 30 years of resins production, the plant management took a hard look at where the wastes were coming from and what could be done to curb production.

The results were startling. Through a combination of waste reduction measures that were neither expensive nor technologically difficult, the plant reduced its generation of hazardous wastes by 93 percent and saved itself over $50,000 in sludge disposal costs. Some steps were as straightforward as flushing a chemical loading hose with water before disconnecting it to prevent toxic chemicals from dripping on the floor.

Attitude Adjustment

This plant's accomplishments are encouraging, but the point of the story is this: nothing prevented the company from using the same waste reduction techniques 10, 20 or 30 years ago. The obstacles are not technological nor economic. It was simply a matter of attitude, encouraged by a flawed regulatory structure and the availability of cheap, out-of-sight disposal solutions, that determined how much attention and creativity the company focused on handling hazardous wastes.

It is only when the plants find themselves with their backs against the wall—the full on-site disposal pond, a state or government regulation, the threat of lawsuits and the growing price of the disposal option—that the upstream solution is explored.

Originally, "waste management" meant little more than finding the most convenient river or empty spot of land to dump materials. But as the use and discharge of chemicals skyrocketed (U.S. production of organic chemicals in particular grew at a rate ten times that of overall industrial production), it became clear that we are poisoning ourselves.

Now, many environmentalists are convinced that, for many toxic chemicals, no currently available disposal options are safe enough. Incinerators, sewage treatment plants and other forms of treatment produce emissions that are themselves sources of pollution. "What emerges is a paradox," says Michael Royston, author of *Pollution Prevention Pays*. "It takes resources to remove pollution; pollution generates residue. It takes more resources to dispose of this residue, and disposal of residue also produces pollution."

A Pivotal Difference

There is a pivotal difference between waste reduction and both of the other two generic options—treatment and land disposal. The latter remain faithful to the end-of-pipe concept on which our entire environmental protection system was founded. Waste reduction, which everyone agrees in principle to be the best option, is fundamentally different because it prevents pollution, rather than just controlling it. Waste reduction is not simply another attempt at regulatory reform within the pollution-control framework.

Joel S. Hirschhorn, *Science for the People*, September/October 1988.

Solving the waste production problem involves two basic steps: first, toxic components can be replaced with non-toxic ones. For example, since PCBs [polychlorinated biphenyls] were banned as a health hazard several years ago, private industry has shifted to a variety of non-toxic alternatives. Secondly, by changing manufacturing processes, the volume of wastes produced can be significantly reduced.

The debate among source reduction advocates now is whether to use the carrot or the stick, or both. Should we institute a negative regulatory structure or establish government financing for information exchange and technical assistance? Whichever course is taken, we must insist that incentives be created to either encourage active waste reduction through financial penalties and other inducements, or require it, through new permit programs or other government mandates.

The Private Sector

Opposing these measures is the long tradition of business-as-usual in the private sector. Many companies are ignoring readily available non-toxic substitutes. The very way industrial plants are staffed reflects the downstream bias: production staff, those who generate the wastes, are kept entirely independent of waste management staff, those who must find a place to put it. Successful waste reduction measures at one company are not always spread throughout the industry, partly due to a lack of dialogue on waste reduction, and partly due to industry's tendency to label everything they do a "trade secret."

Governmental regulations are unevenly enforced, riddled with loopholes (many toxics are not regulated at all) and overwhelmingly biased toward affecting what comes out of the pipeline, not the processes by which the wastes are produced. And most companies are simply not yet devoting the resources needed to identify and implement waste reduction steps.

The greatest obstacle to serious waste reduction efforts, however, is the availability of waste disposal capacity. As long as companies have landfills, deep wells, and sewage treatment plants for their wastes, there is little incentive to attempt a waste reduction strategy. This is especially true when these disposal options are cheap. It is no surprise that, in the U.S., most of the hazardous waste generated goes into the least expensive disposal route, deep well injection.

Not enough work has been done in this area to know if we can completely eliminate the need for incinerators and the like, but one thing is clear. Waste reduction can take us a long way towards minimizing the generation of hazardous wastes if only we make the effort to fulfill its potential.

Understanding Words in Context

Readers occasionally come across words they do not recognize. And frequently, because they do not know a word or words, they will not fully understand the passage being read. Obviously, the reader can look up an unfamiliar word in a dictionary. However, by carefully examining the word in the context in which it is used, the word's meaning can often be determined. A careful reader may find clues to the meaning of the word in surrounding words, ideas, and attitudes.

Below are excerpts from the viewpoints in this chapter. In each excerpt, one word is printed in italicized capital letters. Try to determine the meaning of each word by reading the excerpt. Under each excerpt you will find four definitions for the italicized word. Choose the one that is closest to your understanding of the word.

Finally, use a dictionary to see how well you have understood the words in context. It will be helpful to discuss with others the clues which helped you decide on each word's meaning.

1. Chemicals found on the site include high levels of toxins and *CARCINOGENS* like toluene, benzene, and lead. Cancer levels in the area have not yet been measured.

   CARCINOGEN means:

   a) harmful to autos   c) cancer-causing
   b) a corrosive agent   d) illegal chemical

2. A study was conducted by Rutgers University at the *BEHEST* of people living near the landfill site who wanted to know the extent of the problem.

   BEHEST means:

   a) expense   c) objection
   b) command   d) outcry

3. On-site cleanups require a thorough understanding of the physical, chemical, and *HYDROGEOLOGICAL* properties of the dump site to avoid contaminating neighboring drinking wells.

HYDROGEOLOGICAL means:

a) underground water
b) surface water
c) foundation
d) subterranean

4. By not knowing the behind-the-scenes work, some observers think that the most *TANGIBLE* result of the Superfund law is to create more studies and delays.

TANGIBLE means:

a) annoying
b) concrete
c) superficial
d) immediate

5. The sewage treatment plant imposed *STRINGENT* restrictions on the amount of toxic chemicals it would accept in wastewater, thereby limiting the amount of toxins industries could release.

STRINGENT means:

a) strict
b) legislated
c) environmental
d) court-ordered

6. The *INGESTION* of toxic emissions by animal and plant life may occur through air, water, soil, or via the food web, causing dire health problems.

INGESTION means:

a) touching
b) acceptance
c) rejection
d) taking into the body

7. Research on the performance of incinerators has occurred only under *OPTIMAL* conditions with specially selected waste.

OPTIMAL means:

a) visual
b) experimental
c) excellent
d) scientific

8. The Office of Technology Assessment said that private contractors receive money from polluters in transactions that are hidden from public *SCRUTINY* and accountability.

SCRUTINY means:

a) observation
b) standards
c) forums
d) protest

Periodical Bibliography

The following articles have been selected to supplement the diverse views presented in this chapter.

Harry Anderson	"The Global Poison Trade," *Newsweek*, November 7, 1988.
James Bovard	"Some Waste Cleanup Rules Are a Waste of Resources," *The Wall Street Journal*, February 15, 1989.
Betsy Carpenter	"Superfund, Superflop," *U.S. News & World Report*, February 6, 1989.
Susan Chollar	"The Poison Eaters," *Discover*, April 1990.
Joel S. Hirschhorn	"Cutting Production of Hazardous Waste," *Technology Review*, April 1988.
Marguerite Holloway	"How Mercury Slid by the E.P.A.," *The Nation*, February 19, 1990.
John Holusha	"Putting the Torch to Toxic Wastes," *The New York Times,* June 21, 1989.
Ted Peters	"Not in My Backyard! The Waste Disposal Crisis," *The Christian Century*, February 15, 1989.
Stephanie Pollack and Seth Shulman	"Toxic Responsibility," *The Atlantic Monthly*, March 1989.
Linda Rocawich	"Toxins on Tap?" *The Progressive*, May 1989.
Michael Satchell	"Uncle Sam's Toxic Folly," *U.S. News & World Report*, March 27, 1989.
Ronald Smothers	"Plans on Waste Disposal Seem to Dim the Outlook," *The New York Times*, October 27, 1989.
Rochelle Stanfield	"New Technologies Aim to Make Toxic Wastes Permanently Harmless," *The New York Times*, July 19, 1988.
David Stipp	"Environmental Crime Can Land Executives in Prison These Days," *The Wall Street Journal*, September 10, 1990.
Bruce Stutz	"Environment: Cleaning Up," *The Atlantic Monthly*, October 1990.
Bill Turque and John McCormick	"The Military's Toxic Legacy," *Newsweek*, August 6, 1990.
Philip J. Yenovkian	"Protecting Americans from Hazardous Materials," *USA Today*, March 1990.

How Serious Is Air and Water Pollution?

THE ENVIRONMENTAL
CRISIS

Chapter Preface

In 1969, the Cuyahoga River in Cleveland, Ohio, caught fire because its waters were so heavily polluted with toxic petrochemicals. However, Cleveland was not the only city in the 1960s that had such dangerously polluted sites. Smokestacks billowed toxic chemicals freely into the air and fish died by the thousands in polluted rivers and streams in industrial cities across the country. Today, these gross ecological problems are largely under control. Environmental optimists say this proves that the earth's air and water quality have improved. Others, however, claim that these improvements are cosmetic and hide the problems that still exist. Thus, the extent of air and water pollution and its threat to human health remain serious points of contention among scientists, environmentalists, corporate leaders, and community activists.

The authors in the following chapter present evidence to defend their opinions of the seriousness of air and water pollution.

"The weight of evidence indicates that. . .our water supply is safe. "

America's Water Supply Is Safe

Melvin A. Benarde

In the past decade, sales of bottled water have skyrocketed, due in large part to the public's concern about the purity of America's fresh water. Many scientists and hydrologists argue that this concern is unwarranted. In the following viewpoint, Melvin A. Benarde, the associate director of the Environmental Studies Institute at Drexel University in Philadelphia, writes that the nation's drinking water supply is safe. He describes the hydrological cycle, America's groundwater supply, and how completely pure water is unattainable and unnecessary for good health. Benarde maintains that the government-established water quality standards protect citizens from cancer-causing contaminants.

As you read, consider the following questions:

1. According to Benarde, why is groundwater better than surface water?
2. In the author's opinion, how much pure water exists in the world?
3. How does Benarde define "safety" concerning water quality?

Water and its pollution command attention and wide discussion. Considering, however, that most discussions generate more heat than light, they are often more cathartic than productive.

Among the critical issues competing for public attention is the need to maintain water resources of high quality and generous quantity. A growing population and simultaneously expanding industrial and agricultural bases, as well as concomitantly increasing energy needs, with their waste by-products, require immense quantities of water.

The increasing importance of groundwater is reflected in the staggering amounts withdrawn each day. Withdrawals have increased from about 20 billion gallons per day (bgd) in 1945 to approximately 95 bgd in 1985. Although this represents an increase (almost 12% per year), the preponderant upturn in usage more than likely began in the early 1960s. This means that demands for water have been rising far faster than is generally conceded or perceived.

The types of use to which groundwater is put, along with estimates of the quantities withdrawn, are as follows:

Irrigation	63	bgd
Industry	13	
Drinking	12.5	
Rural, home and stock watering	3.5	
	92.0	bgd

Projections suggest that by the year 2020, 135 bgd will be withdrawn. Will it be there? Perhaps the question should be posed with a qualification. Will it be there in usable form? Or will it be so contaminated as to be unfit for consumption?

Before discussing groundwater pollution, such essential questions as What is it? and Where does it come from? require consideration.

The Hydrologic Cycle

The earth's water cycle is a complex closed system of heroic proportions that maintains a balance between water in the atmosphere and water in and on the earth. Most of the earth's water is stored in the saline waters of the world's oceans. Fresh water for the most part is frozen in glaciers, with smaller amounts contained in lakes or underground. Every molecule of this water will move through the hydrologic cycle.

Each year some 95,000 cubic miles of water evaporate. Approximately 75,000 cubic miles fall back as precipitation—rain, snow, sleet, and hail—into the oceans, lakes, and rivers, and onto the land. Responding to the complex of mighty forces from the rotation of the earth, the radiant heat of the sun, and the gravitational effects of the earth and the other eight planets of the solar system, we have then an endless cycle of evaporation and precipitation.

At any instant, about 0.005% of the total supply moves through the cycle. In the United States, a drop of water spends an average of 12 days passing through the air, then may remain in a glacier for 40 years, in a lake for 100 years, or in the ground from 200 to 10,000 years. Eventually, every drop moves through the cycle. The hydrologic cycle uses more energy in 24 hours than humans have generated throughout their total existence. The awesomeness of this energy use should not be quickly dismissed or forgotten. Nor must it be forgotten that the *total supply of water never grows or diminishes*. That is crucial to comprehension of the entire issue.

Safe from Cancer

The chances of getting cancer from drinking water are extremely low. Over a 70-year life span, the chance of being in a fatal traffic accident is 3 million times greater than the chance of contracting cancer from drinking water. Drinking water standards for substances believed to be carcinogenic are generally placed at a level that would cause a 1-in-a-million cancer risk over a 70-year life span.

Kristine M. Napier, *Assessing the Quality of America's Water*, 1988.

The water we use and drink today was doubtless contained in barrels carried on the Santa Maria, Pinta, and Nina as Columbus sailed west in 1492. This endlessly recycled water was the same consumed by Caesar and Cleopatra as they sailed serenely down the Nile. And the hunter-gatherer-artists of the upper Paleolithic period more than 18,000 years ago, who lived in and painted the caves at Altamira in Spain and Lascaux in France, drank the same water. In fact, we are all drinking "used" water.

Groundwater

Potable (drinkable) water exists in the ground at some depth and at some quantity nearly everywhere on earth. Gravity attracts the water from the skies, pulls it beneath the surface, distributes it among permeable layers, and influences the direction in which it flows.

The amount of drinkable water stored within the first half mile of the surface is at least 20 times greater than the amount held in all our rivers and streams. The major source of this vast supply is rain.

Water from rain-soaked surfaces slowly percolates through the earth's layers at a rate of from several inches to several feet per day. A common misconception has it that groundwater consists of large underground rivers and lakes similar to those aboveground. Instead, the seeping or percolating water may reach rock, sand, or gravel formations where it collects as if in a saturated sponge. This collection, at various depths, is referred to as groundwater, and the collection area is called an aquifer. Aquifers may be small and extend a few miles, or, as in the case of the Ogallala aquifer, they can spread over many states.

The great advantage of groundwater as a drinking water source has always been its comparative purity. Unlike surface water, groundwater ordinarily needed little or no treatment to safeguard its quality. There are other advantages: the large storage potential of aquifers, replenished by rainfall, mitigates the need for expensive reservoirs and long-distance transmission lines.

Unfortunately, industrial and agricultural expansion has created monumental problems of waste disposal. Each year some 70 billion gallons of waste are disposed of from both accidental and purposeful "spills" and waste chemicals are being leached into the soil and then into major aquifers.

Nearly 50% of the population of the United States depends on groundwater as their primary source of drinking water. The quality of this water, a national resource, can be adversely affected by the chemicals and microbes scattered throughout our environment, which it contacts as it migrates across and through the surface of the land. Consequently, the level of pollution is related to the degree of contamination of the soil, as well as to the waste effluents pouring into streams, lakes, and rivers. Accordingly, groundwater contamination has become one of the nation's most pressing environmental concerns. . . .

What Is Safe?

The question of ultimate concern and most often asked is: Is our drinking water safe? Few individuals would be satisfied with anything less than a clear, affirmative response. "No" or "maybe" would be terribly uncomfortable. Interestingly enough, many are convinced that it is not safe. Before rendering my own opinion, or better still, allowing you to formulate your own, a look at the available evidence seems reasonable. Also reasonable at this juncture is the question, What do we mean by "safe"?

This seemingly simplistic question is hardly that. But neither is it so convoluted or abstruse as to be beyond consideration. Much of the confusion and misconception about the nature of "safe" and "safety" in decision making at all levels would be dispelled if their meaning were understood and agreed upon.

Before "safe" or "safety" can be defined, the specter of risk must be raised, and along with it the question of whether we are willing to take chances. Of course we are. We do it every day. Often many times a day. Inherent in choice is concern for risk.

195

Are we willing to take risks? Again, of course we are, but assuredly not all. What about acceptable risks?

If we can go that far, we can define "safety" as a judgment. That's the key—a personal and individual judgment about the acceptability of risk; and in turn we can define "risk" as a measure of the probability of harm to our health. Safety then is a value judgment of how much risk we as individuals, or collectively as a community or society, will accept, and risk is a quantitative assessment of the degree of harm to health that may be anticipated.

Consequently, a chemical, a process, a drive to the beach, or a plane trip from Chicago to Miami is safe if its risks are judged to be acceptable, or unsafe if they are judged to be unacceptable. For many people leaving the ground is completely out of the question. Obviously, this definition differs markedly from that in most dictionaries where "safe" is defined as "free from risk"—a definition both misleading and unrealistic. Nothing we do can be totally without risk, neither taking a bath, crossing the street, eating a meal, having a baby, playing a round of golf, nor jogging through the park. There are only degrees of risk and, thereby, degrees of safety. . . .

"Safe" then is anything people decide is safe. On what basis have some people decided our drinking water is unsafe?

Pollution

Having thus suggested a view of safe and safety, the concept of pollution as it relates to water deserves fuller consideration.

Pollution is not an all or nothing concept. Pure water does not exist outside analytical laboratories. Rivers, streams, and lakes are natural habitats for a wide variety of plants and animals. When they die, the organic and inorganic chemicals of which they are constituted pollute the water. Runoff from land as a result of rain or flood and leaf fall during the year add additional contaminants. Consequently, natural bodies of water cannot be thought of as "pure" in either a biological or chemical sense.

Microbiologists and sanitary engineers consider water pollution as a problem of oxygen deficit; the lower the dissolved oxygen, the greater the pollution. The public often takes a broader view. Anything added to water is a pollutant. Thus, discarded bottles, tires, shoes, and egg crates, along with the rest of the trash that careless members of our society choose to toss away, are considered pollutants.

These things are unsightly and aesthetically unappealing, but they have little or no effect on the dissolved oxygen in the water. To a smaller but highly vocal segment of the population, pollution refers to anything other than chemically pure water, which, of course, has never existed on this planet. . . .

Obviously an effort to provide a safe water supply is being

made. Regulations and standards are one way of approaching the goal. Standards, however, generally derive from a series of calculations, most of which are based on mathematical models with very weak biological bases. What biological data enter the model are usually animal data, and that can be orders of magnitude above the range of environmental or "real" exposure. Thus, caution in interpretation is required. Nevertheless, many of the calculations, or "extrapolations" as they are often called, are all the decisionmakers have to work with. Consequently, the decision as to which level to peg a standard is often a judgment call.

Water Quality

[Water quality] standards set limits on the amounts of specified chemical and biological materials permitted in water supplies. This means that every community supply serving 15 or more connections or 25 people must ensure that its water meets these minimum standards. Even noncommunity supplies such as trailer parks, camping sites, and roadside motels with their own sources are included in the regulations. Most public drinking supplies, particularly the larger ones, already meet these standards.

To help states comply, Congress directed the EPA [Environmental Protection Agency] to provide the states with both financial and technical assistance. As of June 24, 1977, every water supply would require periodic testing. From then on, "Notice of Violation" has become a regular occurrence. Just what does this mean in terms of the safety of a supply?

The limits or standards set for each chemical, as well as bacterial level, were based on the amount of each substance planners calculated most individuals would consume over a lifetime without adverse health effects. The limit was based on consumption of 2 liters of water (or water-based beverages such as tea, coffee, and soft drinks) every day for a lifetime. Of course, this allows for a large margin of safety. The fact that a violation is noted for a water supply is not necessarily cause for alarm. Rather, it is a device to call attention to deficiencies in the system. This was Congress' way of giving anyone who wants it "the right to know" about their particular supply. Unfortunately, neither Congress nor the EPA authorized an education campaign to provide an understanding of the meaning of the "standards" and "violations." Nevertheless, two sets of standards have been established: the National Interim Primary Drinking Water Regulations (NIPDWRs) along with the National Secondary Drinking Water Regulations (NSDWRs).

The NIPDWRs set what the EPA believes are achievable levels of quality to protect health. They are referred to as "interim" because research is ongoing and as new developments occur, changes may be made. Standards have been set for ten chemicals, six pesticides, bacteria, radioactivity, and turbidity.

The NSDWRs control contaminants in water that for the most part affect the aesthetic qualities relating to public acceptability. These regulations are not federally enforceable but are intended as guidelines for each state and by extension for individual localities.

As we approach the waning years of the 20th century the weight of evidence indicates that biologically, chemically, and epidemiologically our water supply is safe. Psychologically, that may not be the case. Too many people prefer to believe otherwise.

Water Supply Is Safe

[Researcher J.H.] Lehr concedes that in certain areas of the country (industrial areas in New York, New Jersey, and New England) much more than 1% of the groundwater has been polluted, but there is still a considerable amount available that is not contaminated. Lehr estimates that, nationwide, groundwater pollution is having an impact on less than 5% of the population. He predicts that within the next 10 years the percentages of groundwater polluted and population affected will both increase less than 10% and then decline during the following decade. By the year 2000, Lehr believes the nation will have reduced new emissions into groundwater by more than 90% of present levels.

Ruth Patrick, *Groundwater Contamination in the United States*, 1987.

With our ability to test for smaller and smaller concentrations of chemicals (we are not able to identify contaminants in the parts per trillion range) the recurring questions are: What do these levels mean? and What is their implication for human health? (Current analytic capability permits detection of dioxin levels of parts per quadrillion [ppq]—that is 1 followed by 15 zeros. Other than telling us that the substance is present in these close to molecular quantities, it does little more for us. If we can find no adverse health effects at the ppm or ppb level, surely amounts in the ppq range can not be expected to be harmful.)

Perhaps the questions can be answered by asking another. If untoward health effects are not observable at the parts per million (ppm) level, will they become manifest at the parts per billion or the parts per trillion level—six orders of magnitude less? Let us restate that. Can chemicals undetectable at one level become harmful when newly developed sophisticated analytical techniques are able to detect them at far lower levels? That is what has happened over the past 20 years. Chemists are closing in on detecting the presence of molecules, but does that make the environment or the water supply less safe? Hardly.

At the levels found in groundwater and surface waters, they do not induce pathologic, malignant, or mutagenic changes in laboratory animals or microbial and tissue culture test systems. They do, however, create headlines and doubt about the safety of the water supply.

Good Health

On the other hand, to load test animals with concentrations five, six, or seven orders of magnitude above those found in some of the country's water supplies creates a dilemma of another sort. How does one translate those studies into human terms—human protection? These analytic innovations notwithstanding, as we approach the second millennium, and move into the 21st century, the health of the American people is at its highest level. Never before in the history of our country has the general well-being been better, and the future indicates still further improvement for more people. Unfortunately, too many of us prefer to believe otherwise.

There is yet another problem: the lack of understanding between a threat to health and the citation of a water supply for violation of noncompliance with standards of the Safe Drinking Water Act. A great breakthrough will have occurred when the American people understand that difference and also accept the fact of their generally high level of health.

"The number of chemicals threatening the safety of our drinking water [is] almost countless."

America's Water Supply Is Unsafe

Gary Null

Gary Null holds a doctorate in human nutrition and public health science and is the author of over twenty books on fitness, diet, and the environment. Null also hosts a health-oriented television program and "The Gary Null Show" on radio. In the following viewpoint, Null argues that America's water supply is contaminated by hundreds of carcinogenic chemicals. He writes that leaking gas storage tanks, chemical plants, fertilizers, lead pipes, and fluoridation programs have polluted the nation's drinking water. Null contends that over half of America's aquifers are tainted by the runoff from hazardous waste sites and many more contain trace residues of pesticide.

As you read, consider the following questions:

1. According to Null, how much gas does it take to contaminate 75,000 gallons of water?
2. In the author's opinion, what health problems can fluoride cause?
3. Why does Null write that dioxin is so dangerous?

From *Clearer, Cleaner, Safer, Greener* by Gary Null. Copyright © 1990 by Gary Null and Omni Publications, Inc. Reprinted by permission of Villard Books, a division of Random House, Inc.

Up until recently, an abundant supply of safe drinking water has been taken for granted by most people. Today, hazardous-waste sites are leaking and contaminating the underground aquifers that supply more than 53 percent of the nation's drinking water, including 97 percent in rural areas.

The following are a few other alarming facts about the safety of our drinking water:

• A 1982 EPA [Environmental Protection Agency] survey of large public water systems supplied by underground aquifers found 45 percent of them to be contaminated with organic chemicals;

• In New Jersey, every major aquifer is contaminated by chemical pollutants;

• In California, pesticides contaminate the drinking water of more than 1 million people;

• On Long Island, more than 4,000 wells are contaminated with Temik, a potent pesticide used in the region for potato farming;

• Underground aquifers surrounding almost all of the nation's nuclear-weapon facilities have been contaminated with radioactive waste and other toxic chemicals. Some of the most severely affected areas include those surrounding Fernald, Ohio; the Mound Facility near Miamiburg, Ohio; Livermore, California; and Hanford Reservation near Richland, Washington. In Texas, the Pantex Facility has not established sufficient safeguards to protect the Ogallala Aquifer, the main source of drinking water for Amarillo, from its waste. The Savannah River Plant near Aitken, South Carolina, has contaminated that area's most important aquifer. . . .

Gas and Degreasers

The following are some of the contaminants, how they commonly find their way into our water supplies, and how they can affect our health:

Benzene: A clear, colorless liquid derived from petroleum. It is used in the manufacture of pesticides, detergents, pharmaceuticals, paints, plastics, and motor fuels, and is widely used by industries as a solvent. Benzene is a potent carcinogen. It enters our water supply primarily as industrial waste, and agricultural runoff, and through leaky fuel tanks.

Some 40 percent of the nation's groundwater may be contaminated by gasoline, the complex chemical structure of which contains not only benzene, but also many other dangerous substances like ethylene dibromide (EDB). One gallon of gasoline can contaminate 75,000 gallons of water with these toxic chemicals. The EPA estimates that nearly a quarter of the 2.5 million gasoline storage tanks across the nation may be leaking. Most of these tanks have already outlived their normal life expectancy, but the oil companies have been slow to replace them. In some contamination situations, the companies have compensated people whose water supply was contaminated by the leaks, but they are settling these matters out of court and hence have not made any admission of guilt. Around Denver, for instance, Chevron bought up 41 homes and relocated residents at a cost of $10 million when groundwater was found to be contaminated by gasoline leaks. Mobil and Exxon spent $1 million to build a new water system in Canobe Park, Rhode Island, when existing water supplies became tainted by gasoline.

"We don't bother buying pesticides anymore. We just spray the crops with our groundwater."

© Simpson/Rothco. Reprinted with permission.

Trichloroethylene: Also known as TCE, this chemical has accumulated in the environment from the disposal of dry-cleaning materials, the manufacture of pesticides, paints, waxes, varnishes, paint stripper, and metal degreasers. Minute amounts of this chemical are suspected of causing cancer. For residents of Des Moines, Iowa, levels of this deadly chemical in their drinking water climbed to more than 18 times the federal standard of

50 parts per billion in 1983. The cause: A local company had used the chemical in the sixties as a solvent to remove grease from brakes and wheels. When it came to disposing of the stuff, the company sprayed it on its parking lot to control dust and dumped the rest down the drain. . . .

Lead and Fluoride

Lead is one of the most prevalent and most toxic forms of water pollution. It is extremely toxic to children and pregnant women, and can result in delayed physical and mental development in babies and mental impairment in children. Excessive lead can also lead to nervous-system damage, hearing loss, anemia, and kidney damage. Even in small amounts the metal can inhibit red blood-cell formation and cause low-weight births. Lead usually enters our water by leaching out of lead pipes and lead solder pipe joints.

The Centers for Disease Control (CDC) estimates that 10.4 million children are exposed to excessive amounts of lead in their drinking water. According to EPA senior scientist Joel Schwartz, "The more we learn about lead, the more we find adverse effects at lower and lower levels. Drinking water is now a major source of lead for a sizable portion of the population.". . .

Fluoride: For nearly 40 years, respected organizations like the American Dental Association and the U.S. Public Health Service have promoted the claim that fluoridation prevents dental cavities. Responding to these claims, cities around the country have added this chemical to their drinking-water supplies, usually at levels of about one part per million.

There are no published studies showing that fluoride reduces tooth decay. What we do know is that excessive fluoride causes skeletal damage, and a disorder called fluorosis in which teeth develop white spots and become brittle. There is also mounting evidence that fluoride causes cancer. According to Dean Burk, a senior researcher at the National Cancer Institute, in the United States alone more people have died in the last 30 years from cancer connected with fluoridation than all the military deaths in the entire history of the United States. . . .

Dangerous By-Products

Nitrate, a chemical by-product of nitrogen fertilizers commonly used on farms, is believed to contaminate about 20 percent of the nation's wells. In Kansas, 29 percent of farm wells sampled in 1986 contained high levels of nitrates, while drinking water in 50 percent of the communities showed levels of the chemical in excess of federal standards. Nitrates are associated with "blue baby syndrome," a potentially fatal blood disease in infants.

Polychlorinated biphenyls or PCBs: These chemicals belong to a family of substances called halogenated aromatic hydrocarbons.

This family also contains such chemicals as DDT and TCDD (or dioxin), which are among some of the most toxic chemicals known to man. Like the chlorofluorocarbons (or CFCs) that are so damaging to the ozone layer of our atmosphere, the properties of these chlorine derivatives making them so attractive to industry are the same properties causing environmental havoc. They are extremely stable, so they remain in the environment for a long time, are heat-resistant, durable, nonflammable, and nonconducting. PCBs have been widely used in transformers and other electrical equipment, pesticides, heat-exchanger fluids, paints, plastics, adhesives, and sealers. High levels of these chemicals have entered waterways throughout the country either by industrial dumping or sewage systems. Some of the most contaminated areas include the Great Lakes; Escambia Bay, Florida; Waukegan Harbor, Illinois; the Chesapeake Bay; San Francisco Bay; Puget Sound; and the Hudson River. . . .

Contaminated Water

Organic contaminants in ground water are an increasing problem. Synthetic organic chemicals enter the soil as a result of: chemicals in agriculture; leakage from landfills, waste storage ponds and underground storage tanks; and spills. The fact that manufactured organics are found in ground waters in concentrations of potential concern indicates that the assimilative capacity of the soil has been exceeded for such compounds.

Examples: Some 17 million families in the U.S., about 30% of the population, use septic tanks or other types of subsurface seepage to dispose of their wastes. So 3.5 billion gallons of waste is being introduced into the soil each day. Inevitably, some of it seeps into ground water.

The Washington Spectator, September 15, 1989.

Dioxin is one of the most toxic chemicals known to man. . . . This substance is so lethal that Canada has set its safe limit at 20 parts per *trillion,* while New York State sets an even more cautious standard of 10 parts per trillion. Despite the concern over even traces of this substance, the EPA still has not included it on its list of regulated chemicals. In concentrations as low as one part per billion, dioxin can be fatal; at lower levels (measured in parts per trillion or quadrillion) it can cause cancer, serious skin rashes, and a host of systemic disorders.

Citizens around the Great Lakes have been waging an ongoing battle with industry, particularly the giant Dow Chemical, concerning the emission of toxic substances that can combine to form dioxin. At Dow's Midland, Michigan, production facility, the company uses as much as sixty-three million gallons of water each day for its manufacturing processes. Dioxin is formed as a by-product of a number of chemicals, many of which are manufactured by Dow at this site and released in its waste water into small receiving streams. The company has even admitted that dioxin is present in the dust and soil surrounding its Midland site. Because of its extreme toxicity, even state-of-the-art equipment may fail to detect traces of the chemical. So, while licensing authorities regulating waste emissions have imposed stricter guidelines on Dow, without an outright ban on all dioxin-producing emissions, keeping levels of the chemical within safe limits appears improbable.

Chlorine was introduced in 1913 to disinfect water by killing bacteria and viruses. In a never-ending battle to fight pollution, water authorities across the country have been adding increasing amounts of chlorine to "purify" our drinking water. In Cincinnati, for example, by 1970, the Cincinnati Water Works had increased its use of chlorine 200 percent during a 15-year period. This may seem like a responsible reaction. If the water is dirtier, add more of a longtime dependable cleanser. Unfortunately, it does not work that way. Though a glass of water may look and smell clean as a result of chlorine treatment, it is becoming increasingly apparent that water is not made safe by remedial purification. Instead, the only way to have clean water is to keep it from getting polluted in the first place.

Widespread Cancer

But that is only part of the chlorine problem. When it is used in high levels, chlorine can cause genetic damage and several forms of cancer. This is partly because of the toxic character of the chlorine itself, but also stems from extremely dangerous by-products that are formed when chlorine-treated surface waters interact with organic matter. These by-products, called tri-halomethanes (THMs), are much more toxic than the chlorine itself and are recognized carcinogens.

According to the U.S. Council on Environmental Quality, "The wide practice of chlorinating public drinking water appeared to increase the risk of gastrointestinal cancer over an individual's lifetime by fifty to one hundred percent."

The number of chemicals threatening the safety of our drinking water [is] almost countless. I have attempted to familiarize you with a few of them and to give you some idea of how they can find their way into your water supply. These examples are merely illustrative. Drinking-water contamination can take place almost anywhere in the country.

"The air has been so bad that it again needs a warning label: caution, breathing may be hazardous to your health."

Smog Poses a Serious Health Threat

Sharon Begley

The hot, smoggy summer of 1988 induced numerous air quality warnings and caused many environmental scientists to claim that air pollution had triggered an irreversible global warming trend. The following viewpoint by Sharon Begley was written at the height of the 1988 smog alerts. Begley, a science reporter for *Newsweek* who frequently covers environmental issues, writes that the high ozone levels present in smog pose a serious health threat. She contends that even limited exposure to polluted air causes damage in human lungs, especially to people with respiratory problems, those who work outside, athletes who exercise heavily, and children. Begley also argues that the nation's crops and forests are damaged by urban air pollution.

As you read, consider the following questions:

1. According to Begley, what physical effect does ozone have on the lungs?
2. How are plants affected by smog according to the author?
3. In Begley's opinion, what must be done to reduce the smog level?

Welcome, sulfur dioxide, Hello, carbon monoxide, The air, the air is everywhere.

—From the 1967 musical "Hair"

It was a song of the '60s about a problem of the '60s, air so dirty you could see it, taste it, practically feel it. But as emission-control devices became standard issue on cars and factories, the air began to look cleaner, and for many Americans the problem of air pollution became as anachronistic as moral outrage over nude actors. This summer [1988] the miasma of corrosive ozone and other pollutants that has blighted many of the nation's cities has changed all that. The air has been so bad that it again needs a warning label: caution, breathing may be hazardous to your health. "If you can't see pollution, you tend to assume the government is doing its job," says David Hawkins of the Natural Resources Defense Council, an environmental group. "This summer is a reminder that it's not."

A Lethal Mix

The heat wave and stagnant air have landed a devastating one-two punch. Sunlight and heat literally cook up pollutants, forming ozone when hydrocarbons (from such sources as gasoline vapors) and nitrogen oxides (mostly from vehicles) react. The hotter the day, the more ozone; the longer air stays put, the longer smog and ozone hover. In the summer of 1988, 76 cities registered ozone readings at least 25 percent above the Environmental Protection Agency's limit of 120 parts per billion (ppb). Atlanta has topped the standard 21 times and New York, 27 times. In July 1988, Chicago suffered its first "yellow alert" in a decade: Illinois EPA asked 34 industries to shut down some operations for the day to keep the air breathable. New England's ozone levels are almost triple those of 1986. All told, "the ozone is the worst in the 10 years we've been keeping data," says EPA Administrator Lee Thomas.

Yet many other air pollutants have been slashed dramatically since passage of the Clean Air Act in 1970. Emissions of sulfur dioxide, mostly from oil- and coal-burning power plants, are down 37 percent. Particulates, from myriad combustion and industrial sources, have decreased. Phasing lead out of gasoline has reduced lead levels by 90 percent. But the bad air around us, says Stephanie Pollack of the Conservation Law Foundation of New England, "indicates that we have not made as much progress as we had assumed. There should be fewer pollutants to cook by now." In fact, for all the progress, 75 million urbanites live where ozone regularly exceeds federal limits and 41.4 million live where carbon monoxide (CO) is too high.

The easy fixes have been made. Eliminating all hydrocarbons and CO from car exhaust may be technologically impossible. Catalytic converters and other devices have cut emissions by 96 percent and "it's not feasible to go to zero emissions," says Gordon Rinschler of Chrysler. Other sources—gas stations, dry cleaners, bakeries—are much harder to control than the quintessential filthy plume from a steel mill. Says EPA's Bruce Jordan, head of the air-standards unit, "This is probably our toughest problem: emissions from so many small and diverse sources."

" DARLING! THAT WAS HIS FIRST COUGH. "

Reprinted from "Politics for Life," published by the Green Party, London, England.

Ozone exacerbates breathing problems for the country's 10 million asthmatics, but it harms healthy respiratory systems, too. The gas damages cells in the lungs' airways, making the passages inflamed and swollen. New studies suggest that even legal levels of ozone hurt. In one experiment for the EPA, healthy men exercised six and a half hours on a stationary bicycle or treadmill for 50 minutes at a stretch, breathing 120 ppb ozone. After several sessions, their lung function had declined 12 percent and it hurt to breathe deeply.

Ozone Scars

The damage does not go away when clean air blows in. In a study of campers in New Jersey, scientists at Rutgers University found that the time it took children's lungs to recover equaled the time they breathed pollution. Other studies have found that ozone seems to scar the lungs and increase the incidence of infection, perhaps permanently. "There is some suspicion that chronic exposure may lead to long-term damage in lung tissue," says Thomas Stock of the University of Texas School of Public Health. Animal studies suggest ozone impairs the immune system. Based on such findings, EPA's Thomas predicts the agency will change the ozone standard—meaning that "safe" air isn't.

Although the latest concern about dirty air was prompted by smog, unseen chemicals may be worse for human health. "You can have the clearest day with the bluest skies and still have concentrations of [toxics] that can be very harmful," says J. David Thornton of Minnesota's pollution-control agency. The unseen pollutants include cancer-causing benzene and heavy metals such as cadmium. Some 5 billion pounds of synthetic organics, such as pesticides and other toxic chemicals, escape into the air every year. "We're dealing with a toxic chemical soup," says environmental expert Samuel Epstein of the University of Illinois Medical Center. Most of its ingredients, linked to ills from leukemia to heart disease, are not covered by the Clean Air Act.

Green things breathe too, and each year ozone causes an estimated $1 billion to $5 billion in losses to U.S. soybean, corn, peanut and cotton crops. The gas stunts growth by reducing photosynthesis and forcing a plant to redirect its energy to making repairs. Ozone also makes plants more susceptible to pests, says Gary Lovett of the New York Botanical Garden.

Eastern Forests

Nowhere are the signs of air pollution starker than in the Eastern forests. Dying trees pervade the Appalachian crests. On North Carolina's Mount Mitchell, the highest peak in the East, Fraser firs stand bare in the hazy sunshine. More than 40 percent of the red spruces, many older than the United States, are dead. On New York's Whiteface Mountain, the spruce population has been slashed in half. Droughts and pests are partly responsible, but two other main suspects in the arboricides are ozone and acid rain, which together do more harm than either alone. According to Robert Bruck of North Carolina State University, ozone readings atop Mitchell regularly surpass the danger point (55 ppb) for trees. Such levels may destroy the chlorophyll necessary for photosynthesis. Ozone also degrades the waxy surfaces of the conifer's needles, letting nutrient-leaching acids into the inner tissues. The mountaintop forests, says Bruck, "may act as the canary in the miners' shaft," warning that woods at lower elevations may soon die, too.

If the cost of pollution is clear, the solutions aren't. The ubiquitous smog in southern California shows how hard it is to clean the air, and Los Angeles has good company. Houston says it has cut emissions of ozone-forming hydrocarbons about 50 percent since 1970, but it is still second only to L.A. in the number of days it violates the ozone standard. For many areas, part of the trouble is that pollution shows no respect for political borders. Denver has banned hydrocarbon-emitting wood stoves and mandates low-polluting gasoline during the winter, but is still regularly engulfed in smog. The mile-high city sits where four airflows converge, so as long as its neighbors pollute, Denver suffers.

The Health Costs

The most alarming effect of mass motorization may not be the depletion of fossil fuels but the large-scale damage to human health and the natural environment. Researchers at the University of California estimate that the use of gasoline and diesel fuel in the United States alone may cause up to 30,000 deaths every year. And the American Lung Association estimates that air pollution from motor vehicles, power plants, and industrial fuel combustion costs the United States $40 billion annually in health care and lost productivity.

Michael Renner, *Current*, June 1989.

Tough policies and lots of money, though, can turn the pollution tide. Beginning in the 1960s, Pittsburgh switched from coal to oil on industrial boilers and from oil to gas for home heating. It required steel mills, power plants and chemical factories to spend millions for scrubbers and other controls. Hard times in the steel industry helped cut emissions, but so did fining companies that violate pollution laws $10,000 for a first offense, $2,500 a day thereafter—U.S. Steel once got socked with a bill for $750,000. The county has also gone to court to keep potential polluters from expanding. . . .

Politics goes only so far; ultimately the cost of clean air may be changing our lifestyles. "It's easy to go out and sue big faceless corporations," says EPA New England administrator Michael Deland. "Now the problem is us—you, me, our cars, our wood stoves." As researchers pin down the damage pollution causes humans and other living things, Americans will have to decide whether it's worth taking the steps necessary for everyone to breathe free.

"A review of the information about ozone pollution shows the problem to be. . .less severe than we have been led to believe."

Smog's Threat to Health Is Uncertain

Peter L. Spencer

Peter L. Spencer is the managing editor of *Consumer's Research*, a monthly magazine that investigates issues of importance to American consumers. In the following viewpoint, Spencer questions the accuracy of smog-monitoring methods and claims that ozone's threat to human health is exaggerated. Spencer believes the ozone levels of 1988 were unusually high due to a hot summer, not to substantial increases in air pollutants. He maintains that even the air in Los Angeles, home of the nation's worst smog, is clean 97 percent of the time. Spencer argues that slight health improvements do not justify the overwhelming cost of significantly reducing ozone levels.

As you read, consider the following questions:

1. What influence does weather have on ozone levels according to the author?
2. Does Spencer believe that ozone's health effects are long-term? Why or why not?
3. According to the author, how much would it cost to reduce ozone levels drastically?

Peter L. Spencer, "Clearing the Air on Urban Smog," *Consumers' Research,* March 1990. Reprinted with permission.

From all the attention given it by the media and the federal government, smog in our cities would appear to be a serious and pervasive problem—and one that is getting worse.

"The problem is immense. We must address it now," said Environmental Protection Agency (EPA) Administrator William K. Reilly. Congress, at this writing, is hard at work on amendments to the Clean Air Act that aim to reduce urban ozone—the main component of smog—to improve this situation. Requiring tighter controls on industry, auto emissions, and an increase in the use of alternative "clean burning" fuels, among others, these amendments are expected to cost between $7 billion and $20 billion a year to implement—the brunt of which will be borne by consumers.

Is the problem so urgent as official pronouncements would have us believe? Are the proposed solutions worth the cost?

A review of the information about ozone pollution shows the problem to be (a) less severe than we have been led to believe, (b) improving, not getting worse, and (c) of a radically different nature from that suggested by the usual publicity on the subject.

Urban ozone is not emitted directly into the air, but is produced by a complex chemical/physical reaction involving sunlight, nitrogen oxides (NO_x), and volatile organic compounds (VOCs). When measuring pollution, therefore, it is possible to track trends both in ozone levels and these chemical "precursors." And doing this reveals an improving situation, not a deteriorating one.

According to the EPA's analysis of air quality trends (released in April 1989) the levels of NO_x, VOCs, and ozone have all declined in the years from 1978 through 1987. The emission levels of VOCs and NO_x declined 17% and 8% respectively, and there was a 17% drop in ozone levels.

In addition, the EPA report found the number of days in which the federal air-quality standard for ozone was exceeded declined, on average, 38% over the decade. . . .

Bad Weather

Nevertheless, official tallies show the number of mostly urban areas that don't meet federal air-quality standards for ozone on the rise. There are 101 areas, harboring some 150 million people, on the current EPA listing (which runs through 1988), 37 more than the 1987 listing. Further, 31 of these areas, which include many of America's largest cities, are classified as serious to severe, in terms of ozone pollution.

Why the increase in cities cited for violating pollution standards at a time when the pollutants have been in decline?

A chief explanation for this, according to data from the CEQ [Council on Environmental Quality], is the role played by the extremely hot temperatures in areas of the country in 1988. The nature of ozone formation makes it highly susceptible to the weather—that is, sunlight, temperature, and wind conditions. In any given year, abnormal weather can affect ozone levels drastically. Abnormal periods of hot weather, for instance, will show a large increase in ozone levels, as warmer temperatures increase ozone formation. The EPA "nonattainment" tallies, however, do not adjust for such abnormal conditions.

Dramatic Improvements

Between 1975 and 1986, every indicator of air quality improved dramatically: Sulphur dioxide was down 40 percent, carbon monoxide down 40 percent, suspended particulates down 22 percent, lead down 85 percent and ozone down 20 percent.

So why are we so sure things are getting worse? Because in September 1988, after the hottest U.S. summer since 1940, the Environmental Protection Agency rushed out with preliminary data showing surface ozone—smog—soaring out of control. . . .

Yet the only reason ozone readings suddenly soared was not auto emissions, which fell, but temperatures, which rose.

That was immediately proven in 1989, when temperatures fell, and so did ozone exceedences, by about 65 percent to what could be the lowest recorded level.

Warren T. Brookes, *Conservative Chronicle,* February 1, 1990.

Aberrant weather, in fact, is largely responsible for the increase of 37 cities in the EPA's listing of nonattainment cities. Because 1988 was the third hottest summer since 1931, cities experienced large numbers of days in which the ozone standard was exceeded.

According to Dr. Kay Jones, author of the CEQ report on ozone status and trends, cities showing such abnormal "exceedences" in 1988 showed dramatically lower counts in 1989, a year more closely representative of normal temperatures. For example, Baltimore, which had 34 ozone exceedence days in 1988, had only two in 1989; Chicago, with 27 in 1988, fell to three; Cincinnati fell from 27 to two; and Washington, D.C., from 30 down to three.

Only two areas—Houston, Texas, and Los Angeles, California, show chronic ozone problems, says Dr. Jones. Los Angeles is in a class by itself, due to its year-round warm weather and unique topography. "The aggregate population exposure in the Los Angeles Basin and [surrounding counties] and Harris County, Texas, [where Houston is located] overwhelms the rest of the nation. These areas account for 88% of all the U.S. population exposed to ozone levels above. . .the standard," he says. (Like Los Angeles, Houston has year-round mild-to-hot temperatures and a large, auto-intensive population spread out over a big geographical area.)

Misleading Information

In addition, the method used by the EPA to determine whether a city meets federal standards for ozone pollution can make the situation seem worse than it actually is.

Areas suspected of ozone problems are required by the EPA to set up monitors to check ozone concentrations on an hourly basis during smog season (typically from May through September, but year-round in Los Angeles). Maintained by state and local authorities, these monitors are usually placed at locations likely to have poor air quality.

If the standard—which is set at 0.12 parts per million (ppm)—is violated for at least an hour on four separate days over a three-year period, the area is classified as "nonattainment."

In other words, all it takes is one monitor to show four high hourly readings (spread anywhere over 36 months) to put an entire area on the "polluted" list. For example, Birmingham, Alabama, which is classified as "moderately" polluted in the EPA listing, showed no exceedences in 1987, only four in 1988, and none in 1989. Because of the three-year average, it will stay on the polluted list even if it shows no exceedences again in 1990.

Further, ozone concentrations are not uniform over an area, according to scientists, but vary considerably according to location and time, depending on weather conditions, mixes of pollutants, etc. One area of a city can show above-standard conditions, even though most of the region is relatively in the clear.

As David Gushee, Senior Environmental Specialist at the Congressional Research Service points out, in most nonattainment cities "all of the monitors show levels below 0.12 ppm most of the time, even in smog season. During high ozone episodes, many of the monitors continue to show levels below 0.12 ppm even while standard-breaking levels are being recorded on one or a few monitors elsewhere in the metropolitan area."

A Falsely Grim Picture

From these readings, the EPA calculates the number of days a city violates ozone standards. But this can also paint an unnecessarily grim picture. Because ozone exceedence days are measured according to hourly readings, a single hour over the standard counts as a full day, even though the bulk of the day might show levels below the standard.

Los Angeles, for instance, is shown typically to exceed ozone standards on more than 140 days per year. But an analysis of

EPA data by the American Petroleum Institute found that in Los Angeles—which by far has the largest ozone problem—readings were above the standard less than 3% of the total number of hours monitored (from 1981 to 1985). That is, residents of L.A. were breathing air that met ozone standards about 97% of the time. All other cities showed even larger percentages of "clean" air.

Inflated Concern

According to health experts, the health effects of ozone pollution and acid rain are, for the most part, short term and minor. Little is known as to their long-term health effects.

Even toxic air pollutants affect a tiny percentage of the population (primarily those living near industrial plants), and cause few cancers compared to the total number of cancer cases reported (3,000 out of a total of 900,000 cancers annually). And even the 3,000 number is, according to some scientists, inflated.

John W. Merline, *Consumer's Research*, March 1990.

What's more, the EPA's characterization of cities as having "moderate," "serious," and "severe" ozone problems can be misleading. Such classifications are not based on average ozone readings throughout an area, but on the fourth highest reading over the three-year surveillance period. According to the CEQ: "The frequency of high ozone observations above the 0.12 ppm standard diminishes rapidly with increasing concentration."

Health Effects

In light of these observations, what are the risks associated with exposure to ozone pollution?

According to a review of EPA and medical studies, the Office of Technology Assessment (OTA) concludes that above-standard ozone levels can cause some short-term respiratory distress, characterized as coughing, painful breathing, and shortness of breath in some people who exercise outdoors. (Indoor ozone readings don't reach high enough levels to be threatening.) The heavier the exercise and the longer the exposure, the more likely the chance of an adverse health effect. In most cases, symptoms clear up in less than six hours.

Long-term exposure to high ozone levels—in people who work outside, for example—might pose a risk of lung damage, but evidence to this effect is inconclusive, according to the OTA.

While about half of Americans live in areas that exceed the ozone standard at least once a year, only a minority of these people are at risk of adverse effects. As the OTA explains: "Ozone in

215

a city's air. . .does not necessarily equal ozone in people's lungs. Concentrations vary with time of day and exact location. People vary in the amount of time they spend indoors.". . .

The economic benefits of eliminating ozone's health effects might total between $500 million and $4 billion, according to the OTA, assuming all areas can be brought into attainment. These are rough estimates based on what people say they'd be willing to pay to be free of ozone's short-term symptoms.

The Costs

However, the costs involved in the proposals now being considered to reduce ozone pollution would run anywhere from $7 billion to $20 billion a year. And even the most expensive proposals, using currently available technologies, will not bring the most severely affected areas into attainment, according to the OTA. (Many areas are expected to meet the standard in the next several years—according to current trends—without additional pollution controls.)

And some of the pollution control methods proposed—such as switching to alternative fuels and installing vapor recovery devices on cars—may bring adverse health effects of their own.

Furthermore, there is much scientific uncertainty about the effectiveness of current technologies in reducing ozone. According to Dr. Philip Abelson, deputy editor of the journal *Science*, while the EPA has relied on reducing man-made sources of pollutants (with minimal effect in some areas) natural sources might be contributing significantly more to high ozone concentrations in some areas than previously thought.

As the previous discussion would suggest, the information on ozone is far from complete. As Dr. Abelson says: "If EPA is to regulate intelligently, it must be better informed about the differing circumstances and mechanisms that exist in the various rural and urban areas."

"Alcohol and ether fuels can . . . improve octane in our cars with little adverse effect on human health or the environment."

Alternative Fuels Can Reduce Air Pollution

Samuel S. Epstein

Samuel S. Epstein is a doctor and professor of occupational and environmental medicine at the University of Illinois College of Medicine in Chicago. In the following viewpoint, Epstein writes that American motorists must switch to alternative fuels or suffer the ill effects of poisoning through gasoline vapors, oil spills, and urban smog. He supports a change from gasoline to cleaner fuels such as ethanol and methanol to improve public health and urban air quality. Epstein contends that new laws and economic incentives are needed to encourage the use of alternative fuels over "dirty," oil-based products.

As you read, consider the following questions:

1. List the numerous costs associated with gasoline use that Epstein cites.
2. In the author's opinion, what effect does benzene have on humans?
3. According to Epstein, who pays the hidden costs of America's dependence on oil?

Samuel S. Epstein, "Health Requires That We Replace Gasoline," *Los Angeles Times*, March 17, 1989. Reprinted with permission.

The time for tough, fundamental decisions on motor fuels is long overdue.

The relatively low retail price charged the U.S. taxpayer for gasoline totally fails to reflect its hidden costs. Apart from the strategic and security costs of dependence on foreign imports, the environmental and public-health costs are prohibitive. These include:

—The contribution of gasoline combustion to global warming.

—Spills from offshore and tundra drilling and marine accidents.

—Contamination of surface and ground waters by drilling muds, hazardous refinery wastes and effluents and leaking storage tanks.

—Leukemia and brain and other cancers in refinery workers.

—Atmospheric emissions from refineries responsible for cancers in neighboring communities.

—Emissions from the gasoline distribution system and vehicle refueling, evaporative and exhaust emissions producing carcinogen-laced urban smog responsible for cancer as well as heightened respiratory and cardiovascular disease.

Benzene

Gasoline is more dangerous than ever. With the phase-out of lead additives, the aromatic content of gasoline has doubled, particularly in super premium (93 octane) gasoline. The principal aromatic hydrocarbons—benzene, toluene and xylene—make up more than 40% of gasoline. Benzene is also produced by combustion of aromatic hydrocarbons even in benzene-free gasoline. Automobile-related emissions are responsible for 85% of the increasing national benzene emissions, about 130,000 tons per year.

Consumers are now routinely exposed to 1 part per million (p.p.m.) benzene during full-service gasoline refueling, and 3 p.p.m. at self-serve pumps. This exceeds the 1 p.p.m. exposure standard above which the Occupational Safety and Health Administration requires that workers be warned and protected. Based on inhalation tests in rodents, the Environmental Protection Agency estimated in 1984 that the probability of developing cancer following lifetime exposure to 1 p.p.m. benzene or gasoline is about 1% and 0.1%, respectively. The Senate Environment and Public Works Committee concluded that exposure to such levels is responsible for about 220 extra cancers per year in the Los Angeles Basin alone.

Apart from the excess risk of leukemia and cancer, Dow Chemical Co. in 1980 reported genetic damage in workers exposed to only 1 p.p.m. benzene. It is the overwhelming concensus of the independent scientific community that there is no way of setting safe exposure levels or tolerances to any chemical agent such as benzene that can induce genetic damage or cancer. It is clear that gasoline, in all phases of production, use and disposal, is a major source of environmental and occupational carcinogens and preventable cancers.

Helioflores © 1989 Cartoonists & Writers Syndicate. Reprinted with permission.

In 1984 the American Petroleum Institute identified a new class of carcinogens in gasoline even more potent than benzene. Long-term inhalation of unleaded gasoline by rodents induced liver and kidney cancers that were associated with isoalkanes in gasoline. The significance of these findings, which API initially suppressed and subsequently trivialized, is underscored by the 142% increase in kidney cancer in American males from 1950-1985.

Ozone

Aromatic hydrocarbons, especially xylene, also contribute to the formation of the urban ozone soup, a major cause of respiratory disease, particularly in the young and elderly. Ozone is formed when volatile organic compounds react in the presence of heat and sunlight.

Are these problems the price we must pay for efficient transportation and progress? Despite industry propaganda, few modern automobiles need 93 octane gasolines, costing 10 to 20 cents per gallon more than regular (87 octane) unleaded. The bottom line: The petroleum industry sells gasolines we don't need that are slowly killing us and destroying the environment.

Economical and safer alternatives to gasoline are readily available. EPA-approved alcohol and ether fuels can replace aromatics and improve octane in our cars with little adverse effect on human health or the environment. Eventually, these fuels could completely replace gasoline. Fuel ethanol, used in Brazil for years, has been sold in this country as "gasohol," 10% agriculturally derived ethanol and 90% gasoline. Despite the petroleum industry's claims that ethanol and methanol are too expensive, compared to the retail and hidden price we pay for gasoline, these fuels are a true bargain.

The problem lies in the petroleum industry's resistance to fuels not produced from a barrel of crude oil. Much of today's petroleum industry is free-ranging and multinational, indifferent to the security interests of their customer nations, especially when supplies are cheaper elsewhere. Yet, according to the National Security Defense Council Foundation, the petroleum industry expected U.S. taxpayers to ante up an extra $36.25 to defend every barrel of oil that came out of the Persian Gulf, a cost never included in the price of gasoline at the pump. On an annual basis, this totaled $14.7 billion or roughly the annual budget of U.S. Department of Energy.

Tough Legislation Needed

These true externalized costs of gasoline must be reflected in tough legislation and incentives for the expanded use of safer, clean-burning fuels, coupled with draconian penalties on "dirty" fuels. Such measures would improve public health, enhance air quality, reduce dependence on foreign oil, boost U.S. agriculture and reduce the federal budget deficit.

In the last analysis, the multinational petroleum industry is a reckless corporate citizen that holds the world at ransom. Time and again, when a choice between profit and human health or the environment or national security must be made, the industry will choose profit every time. The expeditious phase-out of runaway petroleum technologies and ultra-hazardous, obsolete, gasoline fuels must become an immediate national priority.

"*Ozone formation in Denver would increase by more than 13% if ethanol fuel were used year-round.*"

Alternative Fuels Cannot Reduce Air Pollution

Anthony Woodlief

For years scientific and environmental magazines have heralded the imminent arrival of alternative fuels to run America's vehicles. Aside from a very limited use of natural gas and ethanol, however, alternative fuels have made little impact. Writers like Anthony Woodlief of the Competitive Enterprise Institute in Washington, D.C., think the reluctance to abandon gasoline is justified. In the following viewpoint, Woodlief writes that methanol, ethanol, and natural gas offer poor performance and no discernible improvement in toxic emissions. Woodlief argues that while alternative fuels may reduce the level of certain pollutants related to petroleum use, they create new health concerns.

As you read, consider the following questions:

1. According to Woodlief, what health problems can methanol cause?
2. Why does the author oppose the use of ethanol?
3. In Woodlief's opinion, what are the drawbacks to using natural gas instead of gasoline?

Anthony Woodlief, "The High Cost of Clean Cars," *Consumers' Research,* March 1990. This material originally appeared in "The Clean Fuels Myth," a Competitive Enterprise Institute publication by Anthony Woodlief. It is reprinted here with the author's permission.

In June 1989, President Bush released his clean air plan for improving air quality in the United States, particularly in urban areas. One aspect of this plan, the clean fuels program, is described by the White House as "perhaps the most innovative and far-reaching component" of the proposal. The clean fuels program would phase in alternative fuels, most notably ethanol, methanol, and possibly natural gas, in at least nine major U.S. cities, including Houston, New York, Chicago, and Los Angeles. The program would also require car companies to produce alternative fuel vehicles, with the goal of one million new clean-fueled vehicles on the market every year by 1997.

The clean fuels program primarily addresses the urban concentrations of carbon monoxide (CO) and ozone that result from gasoline vehicle emissions. CO is a primary emission of gasoline vehicles, while ozone is formed from the photochemical reactions of other emissions, namely nitrogen oxides (NO_x) and volatile organic compounds (VOCs). CO is toxic in high concentrations, and can cause respiratory problems. Ozone can cause respiratory problems as well.

Fuels that produce less of the pollutants common to gasoline without generating other forms of pollution would merit the label "clean fuels." Unfortunately, the clean fuels advocated in the Bush plan do not meet these criteria.

Methanol

Methanol is produced mostly from coal and natural gas. Engines running on methanol produce aldehydes, among them formaldehyde, a probable carcinogen. Although methanol may produce a 34% to 83% reduction in reactive hydrocarbons (a class of VOCs) and thereby reduce smog formation, formaldehyde is photoreactive and contributes to the formation of smog, which can offset any reduction in these hydrocarbons.

Nitrogen oxide is not significantly reduced with methanol use, and neither is CO, judging from tests of conventional vehicles modified for methanol.

Aside from the pollutants it generates, methanol raises other serious health concerns. It is toxic and absorbed into the skin more easily than gasoline. Its vapors weigh as much as air, increasing the possibility of methanol poisoning in the case of accidental leakage, because the vapors would remain close to the ground.

Methanol is as much as 25 times as toxic as gasoline, which means large increases in poisoning fatalities, along with increases in methanol-induced blindness, if methanol is used widely.

Since methanol blends are more volatile than gasoline, they can cause explosions in the engine, or in the fuel tank if it is damaged in an accident. Methanol's colorless, almost invisible flame makes the fires from such explosions a double threat.

Aside from the effects of methanol on humans, it is damaging to conventional gasoline vehicles' fuel delivery systems as well. It is corrosive, eventually destroying both conventional automobile engine metals and rubber hoses. The result is a more expensive vehicle, since equipment resistant to methanol's corrosiveness must be used. Estimates of methanol conversion costs range from $600 to $1,900 per automobile.

The Danger of Methanol

Extrapolation of existing data indicates that 195 additional methanol deaths will occur each year if methanol fuels become widespread without the simultaneous introduction of effective methods to prevent accidental pediatric ingestion and siphoning. In addition, there will be a $50 to $100 million annual increase in acute health care costs for poisonings from fuels, excluding the costs of extended hospitalizations for complications of methanol poisoning, chronic care and rehabilitation for severe permanent blindness or neurologic impairment, and loss of life.

Toby Lovitz and William O. Robertson, *Consumer's Research*, March 1990.

Methanol is more expensive to produce than gasoline. A probable pump price for methanol is estimated at 72 cents to $1.15 a gallon. Since methanol has a lower energy content, getting 50-60% of the mileage of gasoline, this pump price is equivalent to $1.30 to $2.07 for a gallon of gasoline.

Ethanol

Ethanol is an alcohol fuel usually made from corn, although other biomass such as sugar cane or beets can also be used. Ethanol is blended with gasoline, usually in a 10% ethanol/90% gasoline mixture, which increases the amount of oxygen in the fuel and reduces lead and CO emissions, while reducing mileage by only about 2%. This blend is estimated to be capable of reducing CO emissions by about 22% if used nationwide.

There is an emissions trade-off, however, because ethanol can increase total VOC emissions by more than 25%. A Colorado study estimated that ozone formation in Denver would increase by more than 13% if ethanol fuel were used year-round.

Furthermore, a study in Brazil, where ethanol blends are used widely in concentrations of up to 100%, shows that aldehyde emissions from ethanol vehicles are four times higher than from gasoline vehicles. In addition to ozone, these aldehydes create peroxyacetyl nitrate, which damages plants.

The estimated cost of a gallon of ethanol, taking into account production, shipping costs, and capital expenditures, is $1.10 to $1.80 more than a gallon of gasoline. Since each gallon of the fuel bought at the pump will probably contain at most a 10% mixture of ethanol, the blend will cost an estimated 11.1 to 17.3 cents per gallon more than straight gasoline.

Because ethanol is produced primarily from corn, widescale ethanol production is expected to raise food prices in the United States an estimated $6 billion to $8.6 billion.

Natural Gas

Compressed natural gas (CNG) is distinguished from liquid natural gas such as propane by the fact that it is gaseous. The EPA [Environmental Protection Agency] has found that CO emissions from CNG vehicles were 50% to 80% lower than from gasoline vehicles, with total VOCs reduced a similar amount. Nitrogen oxide emissions, however, ranged widely from no change to increases of up to 80%.

On an energy-equivalent basis, natural gas vehicles get 20-30% of the mileage of gasoline vehicles. In addition, steel storage tanks weighing seven-and-a-half times as much as a conventional gasoline tank are necessary to hold the natural gas equivalent of five gallons of gasoline.

Dr. James Cannon, of the environmental group INFORM, writes: "Most natural gas vehicles have room for only two or three [fuel tanks]. This limits their driving range to less than 300 miles between refills while adding up to 500 pounds to the car and consuming more than half of the usable trunk space in cars using steel tanks."

Furthermore, the additional weight from these tanks cuts down on the mileage of natural gas vehicles even more, adversely affecting handling, braking, and acceleration as well.

The pump price of natural gas is estimated at 63 to 88 cents for the equivalent of a gallon of gasoline. This estimate still makes the cars only marginally cost effective, and uneconomical if other costs of its mandated use are considered. For example, the refueling stations necessary to meet just 14% of the U.S. transportation needs are estimated to cost $12 billion.

In addition, one study places the cost to convert a vehicle to run on natural gas at $1,500 to $2,300.

Evaluating Sources of Information

When historians study and interpret past events, they use two kinds of sources: primary and secondary. Primary sources are eyewitness accounts. For example, the diary of an environmental activist detailing her experiences fighting polluters would be a primary source. A book about the environmental movement written by a journalist who quotes the activist's diary in his book would be a secondary source. Primary and secondary sources may be decades or even hundreds of years old, and often historians find that the sources offer conflicting and contradictory information. To fully evaluate documents and assess their accuracy, historians analyze the credibility of the documents' authors and, in the case of secondary sources, analyze the credibility of the information the authors used.

Historians are not the only people who encounter conflicting information, however. Anyone who reads a daily newspaper, watches television, or just talks to different people will encounter many different views. Writers and speakers use sources of information to support their own statements. Thus, critical thinkers, just like historians, must question the writer's or speaker's sources of information as well as the writer or speaker.

While there are many criteria that can be applied to assess the accuracy of a primary or secondary source, for this activity you will be asked to apply three. For each source listed on the following page, ask yourself the following questions: First, did the person actually see or participate in the event he or she is reporting? This will help you determine the credibility of the information—an eyewitness to an event is an extremely valuable source. Second, does the person have a vested interest in the report? Assessing the person's social status, professional affiliations, nationality, and religious and political beliefs will be helpful in considering this question. By evaluating this you will be able to determine how objective the person's report may be. Third, how qualified is the author to make the statements he or she is making? Consider the person's profession and how he or she might know about the event. Someone who has spent years being involved with or studying the issue may be able to offer more information than someone who simply is offering an uneducated opinion; for example, a politician or layperson.

Keeping the above criteria in mind, imagine you are writing a paper on the effectiveness of laws governing air and water pollution. You decide to cite an equal number of primary and secondary sources. Listed below are several sources that may be useful for your research. *Place a P next to those descriptions you believe are primary sources. Place an S next to those descriptions you believe are secondary sources.* Next, based on the above criteria, *rank the primary sources, assigning the number 1 to that which appears the most valuable, 2 to the source likely to be the second-most valuable, and so on, until all the primary sources are ranked. Then rank the secondary sources, again using the above criteria.*

		Rank in
P or S		Importance
_____	1. A report entitled, "Coal-fired Power Plants and Smokestack Emissions," written by the Nuclear Regulatory Commission.	_____
_____	2. A television interview with the captain of a barge that dumps waste in the ocean.	_____
_____	3. An article by a science reporter for *Newsweek* on progress made in cleaning up toxic-waste sites.	_____
_____	4. A book entitled *Air Pollution Is Killing Our Children.*	_____
_____	5. The testimony of the director of the Environmental Protection Agency before a Senate subcommittee reviewing the Clean Air Act.	_____
_____	6. The final report of a ten-year study by a noted environmental scientist claiming that America's air and water is becoming cleaner.	_____
_____	7. Viewpoint five in this chapter.	_____
_____	8. A "60 Minutes" story on the health effects of smog in Los Angeles.	_____
_____	9. A critique of current environmental legislation by analysts at the conservative Heritage Foundation.	_____
_____	10. An independent lab report on groundwater quality publicized by Greenpeace.	_____
_____	11. A *New York Times* article that quotes an Exxon executive saying that new, reformulated gasoline will reduce air pollution.	_____

Periodical Bibliography

The following articles have been selected to supplement the diverse views presented in this chapter.

Jerry Adler	"Troubled Waters," *Newsweek*, April 16, 1990.
Sharon Begley	"Keep Holding Your Breath," *Newsweek*, June 4, 1990.
Alex Blinder	"Two Cheers for Bush's Plan to Clean Up the Clean Air Act," *Business Week*, July 10, 1989.
Business Week	"Managing Earth's Resources," June 18, 1990.
Vicky Cahan	"The Clean-Air Fight Gets Dirtier," *Business Week*, March 5, 1990.
George J. Church	"Smell That Fresh Air!" *Time*, June 26, 1989.
Gary Cohen and Kenneth R. Sheets	"Costs and Benefits: Fresh Questions About Clean Air," *U.S. News & World Report*, July 30, 1990.
Otto Friedrich	"Scrubbing the Skies," *Time*, April 16, 1990.
William Greider	"Whitewash: Is Congress Conning Us on Clean Air?" *Rolling Stone*, June 14, 1990.
Donald E. Harleman	"Cutting the Waste in Wastewater Cleanups," *Technology Review*, April 1990.
John Harris	"How to Sell Smoke," *Forbes*, June 11, 1990.
Peter Jaret	"Air Quality: Unacceptable," *Health*, March 1989.
Francesca Lyman	"Clean Cars," *Technology Review*, May/June 1990.
Paul W. McCracken	"Gasoline Prices Are Much Too Low," *The Wall Street Journal*, October 10, 1990.
John G. McDonald	"Gasoline and Clean Air," *Vital Speeches of the Day*, August 15, 1990.
Ed Rubenstein	"Clearing the Air," *National Review*, March 5, 1990.
Linda Saunders	"Uneasy Riders," *Health*, February 1990.
Joy Williams	"Save the Whales, Screw the Shrimp," *Esquire*, February 1989.
Timothy E. Wirth	"Clean Fuels, Clean Air," *The New York Times*, March 8, 1990.

6 CHAPTER

How Can the Environment Be Protected?

THE ENVIRONMENTAL
CRISIS

Chapter Preface

Since the first Earth Day more than twenty years ago, the federal government has enacted several laws to protect the environment. Some have been remarkably successful, while others seem to be failing. For example, regulations mandating cleaner-burning cars and improved gas mileage have greatly reduced auto emissions. However, other initiatives, like the Superfund toxic waste cleanup program, have been multibillion dollar disappointments. Superfund, despite its price tag, has effectively dealt with only a handful of sites while thousands continue to leak toxic pollutants into the environment.

Some suggest that government action, like the Superfund legislation, can never properly protect the environment. Instead, they recommend a market-based system that places the burden of responsibility on private industry. Promoters of this solution believe industry will respond quickly and be more efficient and economical than the government would be in protecting the environment.

In the following chapter, authors from various disciplines offer their solutions to the environmental crisis. Their areas of expertise range from public policy to environmental science to philosophy. Though they disagree over methods, the writers agree that strong measures must be taken to protect and preserve earth's environment.

"A national environmental strategy and set of policy goals and objectives remain imperative."

Government Intervention Can Protect the Environment

Robert Gottlieb and Helen Ingram

Robert Gottlieb teaches in the Urban Planning Program at the University of California at Los Angeles. He writes for *The Wall Street Journal,* and is the author of several books, including *A Life of Its Own: The Politics and Power of Water.* Helen Ingram is a professor of political science at the University of Arizona at Tucson and the author of several books on the environment and natural resources, including *Environmental Politics and Policy.* In the following viewpoint, Gottlieb and Ingram contend that increased local government control over environmental concerns is necessary to protect the environment. They argue that ordinary citizens active in local governments can regulate and preserve the environment.

As you read, consider the following questions:

1. According to the authors, government environmental policymakers face many conflicting problems. What are they?
2. What form of political action do Gottlieb and Ingram advocate to save the environment?
3. How do the authors think government and grassroots organizations can work together to preserve the environment?

Reprinted from *Winning America,* Marcus Raskim and Chester Hartman, editors, with permission from the publisher, South End Press, 116 Saint Botolph Street, Boston, MA 02115.

Environmental policy today is at a crossroads. Attempts. . .to undo the legislation and regulatory policies established during the 1970s have backfired. Environmental groups have grown in numbers and reach, and Congressional initiatives have increased. In some cases, this has led to more legislation, greater funding for environmental programs, and increased regulations.

Yet environmental problems have, for the most part, remained intractable. Legislative and regulatory approaches have often been inadequate in addressing a growing set of concerns that touch the very fabric of our urban and industrial society. Target dates, such as those established by the Clean Air Act, have come and gone, without anticipated goals having been reached. While the current regulatory approaches look to tradeoffs, cost-benefit analysis, and risk assessment procedures, among others, to try to reduce or at least contain the degradation at hand, it is not even clear whether such goals will ever be met for particular contaminants, such as ozone, in those cities, such as Los Angeles or Denver, where dirty air appears to have become a permanent fixture of the urban design.

The basis for environmental policy continues to evolve around how best to accommodate the dual objectives of environmental protection and economic growth. Government policymakers are continually beset by the apparently conflicting pressures regarding environmental degradation, reindustrialization (whether high tech or old tech), job creation, and community fears regarding environmental and/or economic decline. Policy questions frequently are posed as a choice between contrasting objectives: jobs versus community versus environment. Those environmental groups who accept such a framework are faced with either selecting the route of tradeoffs and compromise, and accepting some level of degradation as an inevitable byproduct of industrialization, or choosing the environment over jobs and economic growth; that is, either enter the corridors of power and likely alienate part of the environmental constituency or be considered marginal in terms of the present political discourse. It is an unhappy predicament somehow incommensurate with the overwhelming public sentiment in favor of large-scale and more definitive action to address hazardous wastes, air and water contamination, pesticide use, solid waste disposal, and countless other environmental problems of our contemporary urban/industrial society.

Protective Laws

The established environmental movement of the 1970s and 1980s prided itself on developing a legislative and regulatory agenda over the years. This consisted of specific initiatives in a range of policy areas, much of which translated into laws and administrative programs designed to protect the natural environment. Efforts, such as the 1985 *Environmental Agenda for the Future* put together by the ten largest established environmental groups, represented an elaboration of this already developed program. Their approach, furthermore, has been dictated by the politics of the lobbyist, where agreements are crafted by various interest groups in a give-and-take process in which the giving often exceeds the taking when the power of money is involved.

The Government's Proper Role

Controlling pollution is a proper role for government. Government regulation is needed when firms do not bear the full costs of their actions. A firm that pumps sulfur dioxide or other toxic compounds into the air or water does not bear the consequences. The costs and risks may be borne by individuals thousands of miles away who have no way to force the polluting firm to stop its practices or to compensate its victims for the damage they suffer.

So we share the conviction that pollution should be reduced and that government has to guide that process.

Martin Feldstein and Kathleen Feldstein, *Los Angeles Times,* July 23, 1989.

There is, however, a more grassroots-oriented environmentalism on both a more local and unyielding basis. These movements will frequently insist that a particular project such as an incinerator or a power plant be stopped. They exhibit less willingness to compromise, although their focus is usually limited to the specific matter at hand. Thus, they develop little by way of national program or agenda. Still, many of these movements have begun to make tentative efforts toward developing networks and coalitions. In the process, they have established the outlines of a statewide or national approach, albeit one confined to particular issues.

A national environmental strategy and set of policy goals and objectives remain imperative in face of a declining environment and untempered forms of industrialization. Between the political constraints of the national lobbyist and the limits of a localized campaign, there needs to emerge a form of action—and theory—that links grassroots mobilization with attacking the structure of the problem on the state, national, and even international levels. Such an approach—a new environmental politics—would indeed entail the obvious ("think globally, act locally"), as well as the less obvious ("think globally, act globally") and the most immediate ("think locally, act locally").

232

Programs and improvements come about largely through the influence of social movements and community action. Legislative initiatives, regulatory actions, and court interventions have been framed in part by the public's concern and activity; such is likely to be the case in the future as well. Environmental "improvements" in this light reflect the state of environmental politics. . . .

Government Acts

During the 1970s, [the] environmental organizations were successful in establishing what came to be called the "environmental agenda," aided largely by the enormous swelling of public environmental sentiment. This included the major legislative initiatives of the decade such as the Clean Air Act, Safe Drinking Water Act, the Endangered Species Protection Act, the Resource Recovery and Conservation Act, and the Comprehensive Environmental Response, Conservation, and Liabilities Act (better known as Superfund). These bills and several others signed into law during the 1970s sought to address the problems of pollution and contamination as well as the protection of scenic and natural resources.

Environmental organizations also developed a series of complex and interactive relationships with a host of new administrative bureaucracies such as the Environmental Protection Agency and the Council on Environmental Quality, complementing the relations established by the previous generation of conservationists and preservationists with such agencies as the National Park Service, the Soil Conservation Service, and the U.S. Forest Service. Environmental groups were also successful in transforming a range of legal rulings and legislative initiatives, such as the California Friends of Mammoth ruling in 1972 and the 1969 National Environmental Policy Act, into a whole new field of environmental law where, for example, the production and review of environmental impact statements became an industry unto itself.

The election of Ronald Reagan seemed to threaten that agenda. The new administration, under the banner of deregulation, attempted to either reduce or restructure bureaucracies, limit spending levels for "clean up" legislation, and separate certain key constituencies such as hunters and fishermen and the tourism trade as a whole from the scenic protectionists among the environmental groups. While Jimmy Carter had overestimated the clout and reach of the environmental groups, particularly in the West, Ronald Reagan underestimated the elevation of environmental values among the public at large. The hard-edged rhetoric used by the President and certain of his key officials, such as James Watt and Anne Gorsuch, during much of

Reagan's first term, had the immediate effect of reinvigorating environmental organizations, many of which had been ready to proclaim the end of the Environmental Decade. Most of the administration's attempts to halt expenditures, roll back legislation, or delay implementation of regulations had only limited success. In certain instances, such as passage of the Safe Drinking Water Act Amendments in 1986, Congress, responding to the strong public concerns that had evolved around the issue of groundwater contamination, restructured this legislative initiative to forestall Reagan administration regulatory backbiting, specifically referring to the efforts of the Office of Management and Budget to undermine EPA standard-setting.

Environmental Standstill

For the most part, however, environmentally sensitive legislators were too busy fighting the Reagan administration's attempts to march backward to push forward with new laws or approaches. Reauthorizations of existing laws became pitched battles, with changes mostly a matter of detail. Much of the significant policymaking of the Reagan years took place within the bureaucracy, far from public, and often from Congressional, scrutiny. It is not surprising that the development interests tended to fare best in restricted forums where legal and technical expertise, which can be purchased, are at a premium.

Political Possibilities

The United States. . .must modernize technologies and practices in every economic sector, from more fuel-efficient cars and energy-efficient appliances to manufacturing that relies on recycled material, to a second green revolution requiring fewer fertilizers and pesticides. The emerging consensus for environmental protection is opening the door to solutions once considered politically impossible.

Albert Gore, *The New Republic*, November 6, 1989.

Rather than insisting upon opening agency forums and broadening conflict, some environmental groups actually cooperated in restricting public access. A great deal was made of new opportunities for negotiation and environmental mediation. Emphasis was put upon finding common ground for agreement, not upon distinguishing environmental and development viewpoints. Leaders of environmental groups were congratulated for their growing maturity, reasonableness, and sound management of what had become large-scale organizations. Instead of publicly regretting the lack of substantial accomplishment in cleaning up the environment, environmental leaders satisfied themselves that the network of regulatory laws put in place in the 1970s was not dismantled.

The apparent failure at full-blown deregulation and dismantling of legislation, however, did not prevent the emergence of a number of new or revised approaches, some of which were embraced by both Reaganites and environmental groups. These placed the environmental issue on the level of competing technologies and reallocation of resources and minimized the role of both the government and public action. Reaganites emphasized the move toward privatization and private markets in place of government intervention, a position which attracted those environmentalists who had come to focus on government subsidies as a major source of environmental abuse. In the area of solid waste management, for example, growing environmental concerns over landfills, which in turn contributed to the price escalation of the fees per pound of waste, helped stimulate the reappearance of the incineration industry. Privatization-oriented measures, such as tax breaks and the reduction of federal grants, aided that shift, which the environmental movement was slow to address. During the late 1970s, in fact, several environmental groups even welcomed the development of this "waste-to-energy" technology, only to modify their positions later as community and neighborhood groups, worried about air contaminants, hazardous ash residue, and local neighborhood impacts, took the lead in opposing this newly touted technical solution.

The Private Sector

The focus began to shift to the private sector as the problems of regulation, expensive and inefficient subsidies, and the costs of cleanup multiplied. Water markets, for one, were identified by some in the water industry—that unique collection of public agencies and private interests—as the best way to salvage longstanding water policies designed to stimulate irrigated agricultural production and urban development. A number of environmental groups identified with this approach, calling it a "win-win" alternative to the construction of new and potentially environmentally destructive facilities. Yet markets also allowed pricing inequities to continue, even providing an additional benefit for those landowners wishing to either bail out of the system or maneuver to obtain an additional profit from arrangements that had amounted to billions of dollars in federal transfer payments to western agriculture. The buyers, meanwhile—the rapidly expanding urban complexes in places like San Diego, Denver, and Phoenix—saw markets as the way to sustain development plans in the face of newly emerging "slow growth" movements. These movements were different from the environmental constituencies, more distinctly neighborhood- and community-oriented, focused on the urban and industrial environment, though not unsympathetic to fears about abuse of the natural environment.

Power of the People

Positive and constructive action with respect to environmental issues has, for the most part, come from individual citizens and public-interest groups. Laws have been passed, recycling programs instituted, and products banned from the market primarily at the behest of citizen action. This is one illustration of the power held by the people.

We also hold the power of the vote. Through our votes, we elect representatives, and through our votes we can remove them and change the political structure. We need to realize that environmental issues require strong leadership, people dedicated to serving the public interests in the long-term rather than the short-term objectives of powerful industry lobbies.

Gary Null, *Clearer, Cleaner, Safer, Greener,* 1990.

These new social movements have compounded the complexity of the environmental agenda. They have raised concerns about toxics and hazardous wastes. They worry about residential groundwater contamination and carcinogenic water disinfection byproducts more than protecting in-stream flows. They have placed questions of housing, transportation, air quality, and even economic development on the agenda, which the traditional environmental agenda either had failed to address or addressed inadequately. These questions, however, are fundamental environmental issues. They reflect patterns of industrialization and urbanization, the primary sources of environmental degradation.

Environmental issues are social issues; the natural environment and the human environment are intricately linked in this industrial age. Some groups have begun to connect apparently disparate concerns such as environmentalism and feminism into a new discourse that places the abuses of industrialization in the context of daily life. Furthermore, unlike the traditional agendas of the nationally-oriented environmental organizations, the focus of many of these community, neighborhood, and various "single issue" groups is local. Their issues are as much about community and democratic control as about "natural" environmental degradation, where the focus tends to be on national and bureaucratic solutions.

236

These divergent forms of environmental politics help to develop larger perspectives on the environment and future political approaches. Traditional environmentalism, aside from its long-standing interest in scenic protection, has developed as a crisis-oriented, reactive form of politics, seeking to address questions of "clean-up" and more effective regulation of the extraordinary brew of new products and production processes that have heightened the potential of large-scale environmental deterioration. Though this environmentalism also seeks to promote concepts of conservation and "source reduction," these are often articulated in the form of programs to make urban and industrial interests more efficient in their operations, rationalizing rather than restructuring the production process.

The Grassroots Movement

In contrast, the more populist, grassroots environmentalism promotes the concept that the needs of the community, and, in its more radical form, the workplace, take precedence. Traditional environmentalism has focused primarily on protecting nature and rationalizing the system while reducing its more obvious environmental abuses. Grassroots environmentalism, dealing with everyday problems from toxics to growth, has questioned how the system functions, at least on a local and single-issue level. . . .

What is most striking about these grassroots movements is their democratic thrust, similar in some ways to the emergence of the student, civil rights, and women's movements a generation earlier. Instead of embracing expertise, they have become examples of how to develop "self-taught experts." Instead of seeking to lobby or litigate more effectively, they have become advocates of popular action and citizen lawsuits, influencing legislative debate by their mobilizing efforts rather than lobbying skills. They have become organizations of members, in neighborhoods and communities, rather than groupings with organized mailing lists and membership dues which are situated in offices that take the place of communities. Most important, they have begun to demand an accounting of how actions by industries and developers, the government as well as the private sector, affect people in their day-to-day lives and impact both the environments around us and the larger natural—and social—environment.

There is a rich historical tradition related to what can be called a democratic and populist environmentalism. These were the movements that emerged in the late 19th century to address the extraordinary abuses of early industrialization and urbanization, when issues of foul air, dirty water (which killed thousands of people in countless epidemics of infectious diseases), the horrendous noises and din of the new industrial and urban order, the suffocating and overcrowded cities, and the problems of rotting and infected foods dominated the urban and industrial landscape. Rivers, streams, mountains, and wilderness were, to be sure, casualties of this new order, part of the same package of development. The movements that emerged—public sanitarians, municipal housekeepers, social feminists, both "sewer socialists" and radical syndicalists, and a range of other reformist and revolutionary movements of the moment—represented an environmental tradition much as John Muir and Gifford Pinchot did with their romantic and utilitarian impulses.

Today, the issues of the industrial and urban order are more complex and yet more extensive in their impact on peoples' lives and environments. The new grassroots movements of the 1980s are part of a range of efforts that seek to address the consequences of this order, whether in terms of nuclear politics, economic dislocation, or the problems of the environment writ large or small. In this sense, environmentalism can be seen not as an "interest group" seeking better regulation or protection of scenic resources, but as an essential component of a new democratic politics. It is a politics where "risk" is no longer just a question of what contaminant we are prepared or not prepared to live with, but a question of dealing with the hazards of an undemocratic society where the decisions that affect our lives are made elsewhere.

"America's wilderness areas and sensitive animal life are threatened not by big business, but by government bureaucrats."

Government Intervention Cannot Protect the Environment

The Heritage Foundation

Free-market supporters and corporate leaders generally believe that government regulation of any industry is ineffective and inefficient. To them, this is especially true of federal environmental cleanup programs such as Superfund. The only way to stop pollution, they claim, is to allow industry to police itself. In the following viewpoint, the authors contend that government agencies actually impede progress in ending pollution. The Heritage Foundation is a conservative think tank based in Washington, D.C.

As you read, consider the following questions:

1. According to The Heritage Foundation, how can environmental goals be reached effectively and efficiently?
2. Why do the authors oppose making the federal government responsible for environmental problems?
3. What obstacles to environmental reform do the authors say remain?

Excerpted from "Environment," in *Issues '88,* edited by Mark Liedl. Copyright © 1988 The Heritage Foundation. Reprinted with permission.

America's wilderness areas and sensitive animal life are threatened not by big business, but by government bureaucrats and pernicious economic incentives created by government. The reason is that "public ownership" of national parks, forests, and wilderness areas in reality means ownership by nobody. Instead, control is vested in the hands of federal agencies that respond to bureaucratic incentives. Often these are destructive of environmental goals. Anti-pollution policy suffers from a similar disregard of incentives, resulting in policies costly to business and ineffectual in reaching policy goals.

A Shift in Policy

Federal policy should shift to create positive incentives to reach environmental goals effectively and efficiently. To do this the fiction of public ownership should be replaced with the reality of responsible ownership by nongovernmental entities. Example: environmental organizations could manage wilderness areas. The private sector, meanwhile, could be required to pay the full cost of gaining access to forest and range lands. The responsibility for hazardous waste programs could be moved to the states and local communities as much as possible, to encourage innovative approaches and to discourage communities from merely passing the buck, and the bill, to Uncle Sam. Finally, privatization and other market-based strategies could introduce strong incentives for efficient pollution policy.

Create a Wilderness Board to administer wilderness areas. For decades the management of wilderness areas in the U.S. has provoked bitter political disputes. Wilderness advocacy organizations take every opportunity to get Congress to classify sensitive tracts as wilderness areas. This blocks virtually any commercial use of these tracts. Those who oppose such efforts invariably are denounced as antienvironment. Yet it is possible to balance use and conservation in many sensitive lands. Environmentalists would understand this if they were given the responsibility for running wilderness lands. If they effectively "owned" the land, through a long lease arrangement with the federal government, they would have the incentive to raise revenues from less sensitive lands to purchase more sensitive areas. As with a private museum, the environmental groups could buy and sell tracts for their "collection," and augment their revenues with commercial activities that did not conflict with their primary purpose. In fact, several organizations, such as The Nature Conservancy, already own land privately and obtain revenue by permitting carefully controlled mineral exploration.

A Wilderness Board should be established, consisting of environmental organizations. This Board would manage public lands, making day-to-day decisions over operation of the lands and decisions regarding sales and purchases of lands. The Board would be required to report to Congress, which would have oversight responsibility.

End Forest Service destruction of forests. The U.S. Forest Service is the nation's largest road builder. The Forest Service road network is more than eight times as long as the federal interstate system and has scarred America's woodlands. Having spent billions of taxpayers' dollars to build these roads, to give access to commercial timber companies, it then sells wood below cost. And in its efforts to give away timber, the Forest Service encourages both the "clear cutting" of forests, which leads to huge gaping holes on thousands of otherwise scenic hillsides, and also the deforestation of sensitive high-elevation timberlands.

"THE GOOD NEWS IS, THERE'S A SHIP COMING – THE BAD NEWS IS, IT'S THE E.P.A...."

The more roads that the Forest Service builds and the more clear-cut areas that must be replanted, the bigger the Forest Service's budget and workforce. Since the Forest Service does not in any sense own forests, the long term damage to the value of forests from its actions, and the artificial economics of timber sales do not concern it.

More productive management of the nation's forests would result from transferring ownership to conservation organizations, or selling essentially commercial forests—with assurances for public access—to commercial timber companies. In both cases, the new owners would have a direct interest in preserving the value of the forests to protect their investment, and in ending uneconomic destruction of trees.

Increase state and local control of hazardous waste policy. The cleanup of hazardous waste dumps is rapidly becoming the nation's most expensive public works program. Billions of dollars are committed to dealing with the results of toxic emissions. Few Americans would dispute the need to deal with the hazardous waste problem, but it should be done by states and local governments, not the federal government and its Superfund program. Federal responsibility simply allows local officials to escape the obligation to take quick and decisive action before a problem reaches crisis proportions. Meanwhile, paying for cleanup through taxes on all firms, as now is the policy, imposes a double cost on responsible firms which already control their toxic pollution, while allowing the worst polluters to evade the cost of their actions.

Two Steps Necessary

Two steps are needed to make hazardous waste policy effective, fair, and economical. First, it must be made clear that it is the responsibility of state and local governments close to the scene to take the initiative in controlling toxic dumping and dealing with its consequences. Second, future hazardous dumps could be limited by instituting a tax on dangerous waste products rather than on all firms in industries producing toxic waste. This would encourage firms to find the least costly way of reducing or safely disposing of waste, and it would place the heaviest tax burden on the worst offenders.

Use market mechanisms, such as a production rights market, to achieve pollution goals. Virtually all Americans want pollution reduced. And virtually all Americans want to keep their jobs. Yet laws forcing businesses to reduce pollution increase business costs and thus reduce employment. Government policy, moreover, discourages firms from finding the least costly method of reducing pollution. Typically, regulations require a firm to meet a particular emission standard or to install a particular anti-pollution device, irrespective of immediate or long-term cost.

A better anti-pollution policy would mandate industry-wide reductions in pollution, but allow firms more flexibility to meet these standards. The whole industry could reach the standard by encouraging firms that could reduce pollution substantially, but inexpensively, to cut pollution the most. Meanwhile, some other firms, for whom meeting the standard would mean heavy costs and job losses, would be able to exceed the standard. In this way, pollution could be reduced at the lowest possible industry-wide cost. And individual firms would be permitted to find the least costly way of reducing pollution, rather than installing particular equipment.

Command, Control, and Fail

Too often, environmental programs protect bureaucratic jobs more successfully than they protect the environment. But even if bureaucrats truly had the greatest of desires to protect the environment, the public-works method would still be thwarted. Since, by its very nature, a command-and-control approach is centrally planned and directed, it is ill equipped to handle decentralized problems. By its very nature, pollution (and other environmental problems) occurs under widely differing local conditions.

There can never be enough bureaucrats, with sufficient expertise, to design and implement the details of an ambitious environmental policy. Neither is there sufficient money to make such programs succeed.

Kent Jeffreys, *The World & I,* June 1989.

The way to achieve industry-wide standards while minimizing harm to some firms would be by a "production rights market." The total permissible pollution would be set for an industry, or a group of firms in a particular area, and licenses would be sold for the right to contribute to that total. The revenues collected would be used by government to deal with such effects of pollution as health problems or corrosion of buildings. Polluting firms would have to purchase the licenses but could trade them between each other. The result would be that firms easily able to reduce pollution would do so to avoid licensing costs, while other firms would prefer to pay license fees, rather than facing heavy costs and layoffs. The overall standard would be achieved.

Review Environmental Protection Agency grant incentives to encourage private sector financing and operation of wastewater plants.
The privatization of municipal wastewater treatment plants, which clean and treat sewage, is a recent success story. Cities such as Chandler, Arizona, and Auburn, Alabama, which have contracted with private firms to construct and operate wastewater treatment plants, have reduced costs by about 20 to 30 percent. Because these competitive private firms are more innovative and less costly, the integrity of the water supply is better protected. As such, wastewater treatment privatization has won accolades from environmental groups and local taxpayers.

The federal grant program, however, discourages privatization. Cities must forfeit their federal funds for wastewater plant construction if they seek private financing. This can make privatization unattractive to cities even when the cost of a privately built wastewater plant is less than the specifications required by an EPA grant. To reverse these perverse incentives the federal government should allow cities to receive 20 percent of a project's cost if it is privately owned and financed. The cost to the federal government would be far less than the 55 percent federal funding that cities can receive for publicly owned plants. But because of the significant savings that can be achieved through private design and financing, even with the smaller grant many cities would find it more economic to use the private sector.

Innovative Solutions

Environmental protection policy and procedures need to be improved. This can be achieved through innovative policies which replace bureaucratic plodding with aggressive free market incentives. While government has a role to play in environmental protection, so does the marketplace. And while pollution control is an important goal, there is a cost in achieving it. This cost is in jobs. Consequently, policymakers should focus on the least costly way of achieving reasonable standards. Such an approach would improve environmental protection, resulting in more cleanup for current expenditures or the same cleanup for less cost.

Environmental reform in the 1990s offers the welcome opportunity of building a partnership between conservatives and traditional liberals. Recently, environmental groups such as the Audubon Society have recognized the value of partnership with the private sector to achieve conservation goals. And increasingly, such environmentalists are admitting that government is not always the right answer.

Barriers to Improvement

One obstacle to innovative environmental solutions is the mindset that the private sector is, by definition, the enemy of a clean environment. This, of course, has served as the rationale for a massive buildup of public sector regulatory industries. Although this mindset has moderated somewhat among certain conservation groups, it remains a significant obstacle to reform. Another obstacle is the federal bureaucracy. A more free market approach to conservation and environmental protection will mean less government spending, and thus fewer bureaucrats.

Congress is another barrier. Federal control over the environment means power for members of Congress. Whether it comes in the form of grass roots support from environmental groups or campaign contributions from industries seeking favors, these benefits are something that politicians do not want to relinquish. And finally, special interests would oppose changes in the status quo. These are of two types: First is the environmentalist on the leftist fringe of the movement who opposes anything that would lessen government control. Second are the lobbyists and industries which benefit from regulatory policies. Many firms, for example, have learned that environmental policies provide an excellent opportunity to tilt the competitive playing field to favor their interests. Rust Belt industries lobbied hard for "grandfather clauses" in the Clean Air Act which create a bias against new plants in the South and Southeast. Similarly, the restriction on the use of low sulfur coal results from the effective use of environmental laws to benefit the "dirty coal" sector and its union allies. Conservatives should use such examples to explain the environmental risks of relying so heavily on federal environmental regulations. . . .

Government Failures

The problems of current environmental programs must be understood. The current effort to reform federal water policies, to reduce forestry subsidies, and to rethink the sewage grant program was preceded by research projects and articles documenting how these programs were wasting money and endangering the environment. Similar studies are needed for other environmental programs. The public must learn how the Superfund has become a vast public works boondoggle, and how the Clean Air Act encourages the use and continued operation of older, more polluting plants. Also more studies are needed detailing the ways in which environmental regulators discourage the development and introduction of less polluting technologies.

"Direct action in the ecology movement is one way to. . .create a situation in which corporations, developers and government agents are willing to negotiate."

Radical Activism Can Help Protect the Environment

Bill Devall

Bill Devall is a teacher in the Department of Sociology at Humboldt State University in Arcata, California. He is also one of the leaders of the "deep ecology" movement, whose members oppose the development of roads, bridges, and cities that destroy nature. Deep ecologists believe that nature is as important, or more important, than humans. They support any actions that prevent human civilization from encroaching on nature. In the following viewpoint, Devall writes that environmental activists are justified in damaging logging equipment, pulling up survey stakes, and sinking fishing vessels to protect the environment. Devall equates these activists with the followers of Mohandas Gandhi and Martin Luther King Jr. who used civil disobedience to achieve social justice.

As you read, consider the following questions:

1. Why does Devall consider environmental activists different from political terrorists?
2. How does the author define direct action, monkeywrenching, and ecotage?
3. What parallels does Devall draw between monkeywrenchers and those that risked their lives to save Jews during the Holocaust?

Excerpted, with permission, from *Simple in Means, Rich in Ends: Practicing Deep Ecology* by Bill Devall, 1988; Gibbs Smith, Publisher, Layton, Utah.

A small group of men and women kneel in front of an advancing bulldozer on a road being built by the U.S. Forest Service on Bald Mountain in the Kalmiopsis wilderness of southwestern Oregon. They have made repeated appeals to U.S. Forest Service officials to abandon their plans to build this road into a pristine forest area. They are now engaged in a nonviolent protest against the destruction of an incredibly wild and biologically diverse area.

In San Francisco, lawyers for Native American and environmental groups go to the federal courthouse to file for an injunction against the Forest Service. They are seeking to prevent the government from building a road through the sacred high country of the Siskiyou Mountains in northwestern California.

Political Activism

At Fishing Bridge in Yellowstone National Park, protesters dressed in bear costumes pass out leaflets to visitors. The protesters are denouncing the destruction of grizzly bear habitat by the National Park Service and calling on the agency to engage in a different kind of policy—managing visitors to the park rather than managing bears by killing ones that cause "problems."

Since 1984, many people who eat beef objected to using beef from Latin America, raised on pasture lands which had previously been rain forests. This beef was imported to the U.S.A. and used by some fast food restaurants. Boycotts and protests at some of these restaurants by concerned environmental activists led at least one company to decide against further purchases of the beef.

These are just a few of the types of action which are labeled *political activism* in the environmental movement. The deep, long-range ecology movement is only partly a political movement. Political activism, however, is one way of demonstrating solidarity with our bioregion, with some other species of plants or animals, and solidarity with each other in the movement. We set limits on corporations and governments by our activism and at the same time affirm the integrity of places close to our hearts.

Grassroots activism is a basic thrust of the Green movements, bioregional movements, restoration movements, and environmental movements such as Earth First! Grassroots environmental movements are based on the principles of nonviolence and direct action.

Nonviolent Direct Action

"They have the power," I'm told. "What can I do that will matter? They can do anything they want."

"They"—the military, economic elites, corporations—do have a certain type of power that should be acknowledged. But we are not trapped in their type of power. The problem is this: by accepting theirs as the only legitimate source of power, we deny our own. When we say we can't do anything important we usually mean we can't see how we can achieve our goals. We get stuck on the goal and not the process.

Civil Disobedience

I have no desire to tell anyone what to do. But do something. Pay your rent for living on this beautiful, blue-green living earth. Don't have children. Live more simply. Recycle. Write members of Congress. Support environmental groups that file lawsuits and lobby—and then demand that they take a stronger stand. Commit civil disobedience to thwart the destruction of the planet, or support those who do. Sneak around at night and pull up survey stakes. You know what you can do. Do it.

Dave Foreman, *Mother Jones*, April/May 1990.

Empowering ourselves means recognizing and acting from our own source of power. Right action includes words, acts and feelings true to our intuitions and principles.

For some people this means living our daily lives in a simple but rich and full way—saying grace at meals, growing a garden, riding a bicycle to work. Others may participate in nonviolent direct action; Greenpeace, the international environmental group, has engaged in many nonviolent campaigns. In Australia, in the late 1970s, activists protesting proposed dams on the Franklin River of Tasmania staged effective nonviolent protests over many months. Anyone contemplating this type of direct action can learn many lessons from reading the history of the Tasmanian wilderness campaign. . . .

Direct action in the ecology movement is one way to generate tension, to expose myths and assumptions of the dominant mindset, to create a situation in which corporations, developers and government agents are willing to negotiate. The activist is saying, "We seek negotiations. We are not interested in vandalism or terrorism. We are not seeking vengeance nor threatening the safety of citizens." Disabling a bulldozer which is posed to invade habitat of an endangered species is an act of resistance, not vandalism. Standing between seals and seal hunters is an act of resistance—creating tension—not an attack on sealers. . . .

Sea Shepherds

In November 1986 under the cover of early winter darkness, two volunteers working with the Sea Shepherd Conservation Society entered two boats used by the Icelandic whaling industry in Reykjavik Harbor. The volunteers sent the vessels to the bottom of the harbor by opening the seacocks and flooding the engine rooms. They also considered sinking a third ship but found a night watchman aboard (the Sea Shepherd Society has pledged it will not injure any person in its protest actions). During the same action, they sabotaged the whale processing plant in Reykjavik Harbor and destroyed the computer room of the Icelandic whaling industry.

Rod Coronado, the young man who planned and executed the raid on Reykjavik, is a defender of whales who agreed to follow the Sea Shepherd Society guidelines for action in the field: no explosives; no weapons; no action that has even a remote possibility of causing injury to a living being; if apprehended, do not resist arrest in a violent manner; be prepared to accept full responsibility and suffer the possible consequences of your actions.

Paul Watson, spokesperson for the Sea Shepherd Society, declared that the action "was done to strike a blow against the whaling industry." Iceland had continued to defy decisions from the International Whaling Commission concerning the number and type of whales that could be harpooned annually.

The action against the Icelandic whaling fleet was not the first by the Sea Shepherd Society against illegal whaling. In 1979 the *Sea Shepherd* rammed a "pirate" whaling vessel, the *Sierra,* off the coast of Portugal. Both vessels were towed to the Portuguese port of Leixoes and the *Sea Shepherd* was later confiscated. Paul Watson and the two other crew members who remained on board during the ramming escaped from the country. Volunteers later went back to Portugal to attach a magnetic mine to the hull of the *Sierra.* It sank quickly.

Unconventional Defense

The Sea Shepherd Society is not alone in taking unconventional action in defense of animals. Under the banner of animal liberation, small groups have invaded laboratories of colleges and universities to liberate primates and other animals used in experiments. In 1985 in Hawaii two dolphins were liberated from captivity.

Protests against certain logging practices have occurred in Australia, Oregon, Texas, California, and other areas. Protesters, chaining themselves to bulldozers or climbing trees, have refused to disperse when ordered by police and have been arrested. In the Solomon Islands in the South Pacific, villagers attacked and burned the logging camp and equipment owned by a multinational corporation which had been granted a timber lease to the island by the central government.

Actions such as these have been aggressively reported by the news media. Some groups, such as Greenpeace, have actively sought publicity for their nonviolent encounters with the Russian whaling fleet and with officials of the French government. In 1985, instead of stopping their nuclear weapons testing in the South Pacific, the French government tried to stop Greenpeace protests. In that instance the Greenpeace vessel *Rainbow Warrior* was being outfitted in an Auckland, New Zealand, harbor in preparation for a voyage into the French nuclear test zone in the South Pacific. On orders from officials at the top level of the French government, agents of the French intelligence agency entered New Zealand on false passports and attached a bomb to the Greenpeace vessel. The explosion sent the *Rainbow Warrior* to the bottom of Auckland Harbor and killed a crew member, Fernando Pereira, who was preparing to sail with Greenpeace into the French nuclear test zone. The *Rainbow Warrior* was refloated but could not be restored to seaworthy status. It was towed into the South Pacific and sunk.

Monkeywrenching

Monkeywrenching. Ecotage. Ecodefense. Billboard bandits. Unauthorized heavy equipment maintenance. Desurveying. Road reclamation. Tree spiking.

Monkeywrenching is a step beyond civil disobedience. It is nonviolent, aimed only at inanimate machines, and at the pocketbooks of the industrial despoilers. It is the final step in the defense of the wild, the deliberate action taken by the Earth defender when all other measures have failed, the process whereby the wilderness defender becomes the wilderness acting in self-defense.

Earth First! Introductory Tabloid, December 21, 1987.

For over a hundred years the conservation-environmental movement was remarkably resistant to use of protest demonstrations or direct action as tactics in campaigns. From the days of John Muir, environmentalists relied on letter writing campaigns, appeals to elected officials, and publicity campaigns to arouse the sympathy of the public for an endangered area. In comparison to other movements of equal vigor, such as the labor movement, the environmental movement has been remarkably free from violence and street demonstrations.

Thoreau in his famous essay "On Civil Disobedience," written after he spent the night in jail for refusing to pay a tax levied to support the War in Mexico in 1845, provided strong defense for the moral claims of civil disobedience when one is acting from deeply held convictions. Gandhi and Martin Luther King, Jr. greatly developed strategies and philosophies for civil disobedience campaigns. In the later part of the twentieth century, grassroots environmental movements have begun to use civil disobedience. To better understand these campaigns, it is necessary to define some phrases which some politicians and news media have been using disparagingly.

Direct action is action taken in defense of a forest, river, or specific species of plants or animals, in which the protester has no monetary or private property interest, but has a concern as part of his or her ecological self and makes a statement with his or her body. To paraphrase Gandhi: I serve no one but myself, but my *self* is broad and deep. A protest march in front of a U.S. Forest Service [office] or blocking public access to roads leading to a logging site is direct action when the protesters are attempting to call attention to the integrity of a primeval forest. Sailing a vessel into an area of ocean decreed by a government as a "prohibited zone" to protest government policies is direct action. So is sitting in a small boat between whales and whalers' harpoons.

Monkeywrenching is the purposeful dismantling or disabling of artifacts used in environmentally destructive practices at a specific site—dismantling fishing gear or logging equipment, for example.

Ecotage is disabling a technological or bureaucratic operation in defense of one's place. It is self-defense. According to the dictionary, ecotage is a combination of ecology and sabotage. Ecology comes from combining the Greek *oikos,* a household, and *logy,* to study; *saboter* means to damage machinery with wooden shoes. Ecotage, as used there, means actions which can be executed without injury to life.

Sam Lovejoy, who engaged in antinuclear ecotage in New England, wrote that ecotage is directed, targeted, and ethical action in defense of living systems. It is not action which could be considered vandalism or random attacks on technology. . . .

Powerful Actions

Monkeywrenching and ecotage are powerful (and personally empowering) actions which require the participant to "step outside of the system," in the words of Dave Foreman, and take responsibility for defending a piece of territory to protect its integrity. "Maybe it [monkeywrenching] is not going to stop everything. Maybe it's not going to change the world, but it's going to buy that place, those creatures, some time. And maybe that's the best that can be done."

Monkeywrenching calls us to a place in our own minds that we have perhaps not visited before, a place of alertness, attention, perception to the whole situation. Foreman's book, *Ecodefense,* is concerned primarily with what he calls "strategic monkeywrenching," which he says is thoughtful, deliberate and safe for participants and other people who might be in the area.

251

Strategic monkeywrenching is used only when attempting to protect areas which are not legally protected as wilderness but have great beauty, biological diversity, integrity of place and wilderness, and are threatened by some specific action such as road construction, natural resource exploration or energy developments.

Defending Our Home

If the wilderness is our true home, and if it is threatened with invasion, pillage, and destruction—as it certainly is—then we have the right to defend that home, as we would our private quarters, by whatever means are necessary. (An Englishman's home is his castle; the American's home is his favorite forest, river, fishing stream, her favorite mountain or desert canyon, his favorite swamp or woods or lake.) We have the right to resist and we have the obligation; not to defend that which we love would be dishonorable. The majority of the American people have demonstrated on every possible occasion that they support the ideal of wilderness preservation.

Edward Abbey, *One Life at a Time, Please,* 1988.

According to Foreman, strategic monkeywrenching is based on the following principles:

1. It is nonviolent. "It is not directed towards harming human beings or other forms of life."

2. It is not organized by a formal group. "It is truly individual action."

3. It may be a project of a small affinity group.

4. It is targeted. The focus of activity is specific; for example, stopping or delaying destruction in a specific area as part of a larger strategy to obtain official protection.

5. It is timely. It has a proper place in the total campaign. Monkeywrenchers make a clear and accurate assessment of the political situation.

6. It is dispersed. There is no central clearinghouse of information on monkeywrenching. No records are kept of operations.

7. It is diverse. Many kinds of people are involved. It is nonelitist. It is *not* paramilitary action.

8. It is fun. "There is a rush of excitement." It can also be very dangerous.

9. It is *not* revolutionary. "It does not aim to overthrow any social, political or economic system. It is merely nonviolent self-defense of the wild."

10. It is simple. "Use the simplest tool and method."

11. It is deliberate and ethical, *not* vandalistic or unpremedi-

252

tated. "They keep a pure heart and mind about it. They remember that they are engaged in the most moral of all actions: protecting life, defending the Earth."

Public Awareness and Personal Risk

Animal rights or animal liberation advocates used strategic monkeywrenching and ecotage to rescue hundreds of laboratory animals from cruel and painful experiments. Widespread publicity concerning their actions has aroused a storm of discussion concerning ethical responsibilities of scientists and students toward these animals. Furthermore, the discussion has extended to other facilities such as zoos, fur companies, slaughterhouse operations, and cosmetic corporations using animals to test chemicals. The ripple effect has led to widespread public awareness of behavior that was considered "usual" or "ordinary." Ecotage and monkeywrenching tactics used by animal rights advocates helped unveil some of the assumptions of the dominant society and led to constructive dialogue.

Specific techniques of monkeywrenching and ecotage are discussed at length in Foreman's book and in the "Ned Ludd" column of the *Earth First!* journal. Techniques should be selected after considering moral and technical factors and the competency of the persons taking part.

I see an analogy between rescuers of Jews and homosexuals in Nazi-occupied Europe and strategic monkeywrenching in the late twentieth century. As part of Dr. Samuel Oliner's academic study of helping behavior during the Holocaust, he interviewed a sample of people who had been rescued, some of the rescuers, as well as people living in the same area as rescuers who did not risk themselves to help victims. Oliner found a number of similarities among rescuers, including an openness of character, willingness to take risks, spontaneity in the desperate situation, personalizing the situation through empathy with victims, and creativity. He collected many stories of ordinary people who, in extraordinary situations, found ways to help another person not of their own race or religion. These same traits can be applied to practitioners of deep ecology, who are, in a sense, rescuers of the environment.

"Violence sabotages legitimate environmental groups."

Radical Activism Cannot Help Protect the Environment

Doug Bandow

Environmental organizations like Greenpeace and Earth First! have used civil disobedience as a means of achieving change in environmental policy. Many observers believe that the tactics used by these groups are hurting their cause. In the following viewpoint, Doug Bandow, a senior fellow at the Cato Institute, a libertarian think tank in Washington, D.C., writes that the radical fringe of the environmental movement endangers human lives in misguided attempts to protest current environmental policy. Bandow argues that mainstream environmentalists must condemn the fringe element and work toward alternative, non-violent solutions to the environmental crisis.

As you read, consider the following questions:

1. How does Bandow define "deep ecology"?
2. What message does the author believe should be sent by mainstream environmentalists to the ecoteurs?
3. What alternatives to ecotage does Bandow promote to protect the environment?

Excerpted, with permission, from "Ecoterrorism: The Dangerous Fringe of the Environmental Movement," by Doug Bandow, The Heritage Foundation *Backgrounder*, April 12, 1990.

Due to the twentieth anniversary of Earth Day, environmental activists and private citizens alike are reflecting on the state of the earth's ecology and what policies best can make the world cleaner. One environmental matter, however, is receiving little attention. Individuals and scattered bands of environmental or ecological radicals, usually called ecoterrorists, have been sabotaging industrial facilities, logging operations, construction projects, and other economic targets around the country. They have inflicted millions of dollars in damage and have maimed innocent people.

These ecoterrorists are a tiny, fringe group. They in no way represent America's broad environmental movement. Yet, mainstream environmentalists and the press remain strangely silent about the atrocities committed by the ecoterrorists. By failing to police their own movement, and by failing to denounce loudly and openly the ecoterrorists, mainstream environmentalists risk bringing their entire movement into disrepute. It thus is time for mainstream environmental groups and their supporters in Congress to disassociate themselves from those who use violence in the name of the environment and to see that they are brought to justice.

Eco-sabotage

In the early 1970s a lone environmental activist, identified only as "The Fox," engaged in a sustained campaign of eco-sabotage, also termed ecotage, against Chicago-area firms. For three years he committed acts ranging from vandalizing the offices of corporations to more serious and dangerous crimes such as plugging industrial drains and smokestacks. Around the same time, a group in Minnesota called the "Bolt Weevils" and one in Arizona called the "Ecoraiders" carried out similar activities.

The concept of ecoterrorism gained some attention in the book *Ecotage!*, a "do-it-yourself" guide published in 1972 with the support of Environmental Action. Based on the results of a contest soliciting eco-sabotage ideas, this book extolled the activities of "The Fox," who, it argued, "deserves special credit because he has put his ideas into action, whereas for many, ecotage will remain a fantasy." The book also praised "the Billboard Bandits in Michigan, the Eco-Commandoes in Florida," who carried out their own disruptive activities, and contended that "if Thomas Jefferson, Patrick Henry and George Washington were alive today they'd be ecoteurs by night."

While authors Sam Love and David Obst explained that "we are not advocating that those who buy this book go out and try each one of the tactics included," they added that "it is important for readers to become aware that such ideas do exist and that there are already groups actively involved in implementing some of them."

A few years later, environmental activist Edward Abbey romanticized ecotage in his novel, *The Monkey Wrench Gang*. In this story, four people roam the West wreaking havoc, destroying power poles, railroad lines, billboards, and any other signs of civilization that mar the landscape. The book concludes with the blowing up of a bridge over the Colorado River. The book's message: those genuinely concerned about the environment are entitled to use virtually any tactic, perhaps excluding murder, to stop development. Abbey, who died in 1989, became the spiritual adviser and symbol for activists who turned to outlaw resistance. "If opposition is not enough, we must resist. And if resistance is not enough, then subvert," he said.

Violent Terrorists

Earth First! is an environmental terrorist organization which not only advocates sabotage, violence and terrorism, it provides its followers handbooks and newsletters on how to perfect their craft. Don't be fooled by the Earth First! euphemism for the sabotage it advocates: "monkey wrenching." These are not juvenile pranksters, and their antics are hardly "monkey business."

Earth First!'s ultimate objective is to frighten all users off of the public lands, keeping them from their lawful pursuits. Timbermen, cattlemen, wool-growers, oil and gas prospectors, miners, off-road vehicle enthusiasts, ski resort owners and others have been targets of Earth First!-style violence.

William Perry Pendley, *The Los Angeles Daily Journal*, August 17, 1990.

In 1981, Dave Foreman, a former lobbyist for the Wilderness Society, founded "Earth First!" This group, Foreman admits, was formed "to inspire others to carry out activities straight from the pages of *The Monkey Wrench Gang* even though Earth First!, we agreed, would itself be ostensibly law-abiding." Strictly speaking, Foreman calls "Earth First!" a movement rather than an organization; there are no membership lists nor officers, for instance. But the group, with about 10,000 people receiving its newsletter, provides a focal point for those interested in destructive and violent forms of protest. "Earth First! as an organization does not support or condone illegal or violent activities" runs a disclaimer in the newsletter. However, it adds: "what an individual does autonomously is his or her own business."

Yet Foreman joined environmental activist Bill Haywood to write *Ecodefense: A Field Guide to Monkeywrenching*, a book that has sold more than 10,000 copies. While purporting to be for "entertainment purposes only," its 311 pages offer detailed advice on how, illegally and violently, to sabotage attempts to develop land and other resources. It describes how to drive spikes into trees to shatter chainsaws and saw millblades when these cut the trees and logs. This "tree spiking" can injure lumberjacks and mill workers severely. Road spikes are recommended to flatten tires. Methods for destroying roads, disabling construction equipment, and cutting down power lines "are discussed. In one chapter, the authors explain that power lines "are highly-vulnerable to monkeywrenching from individuals or small groups."

During an Earth First! demonstration at the Arches National Park in mid-1981, power lines in nearby Moab, Utah were cut. Foreman said that Earth First! was not directly responsible for such acts, but he added that "Other people in Earth First! have *done* things, not as Earth First! though. . . Earth First!, a group, is not going to do any monkey-wrenching. But if people who get the Earth First! newsletter do that, that's fine."

In a later interview he went even further, arguing that monkeywrenching "is morally *required* as self-defense on the part of the Earth."

Underlying the activities of many members of Earth First! and probably most ecoterrorists is the ideology of "Deep Ecology," which places the protection of nature above the promotion of humankind. The principles of Deep Ecology were first enunciated in 1972 by Norwegian philosopher Arne Naess. California sociologist Bill Devall and philosopher George Sessions of Sierra College in California are among the more prominent American Deep Ecologists. Naess advocates "a long range, humane reduction [in the world's population] through mild but tenacious political and economic measures. This will make possible, as a result of increased habitat, population growth for thousands of species which are now constrained by human pressures." According to environmentalist Alston Chase, a newspaper columnist and chairman of the Yellowstone National Park Library and Museum Association, who does not support Naess's views, "poets, philosophers, economists, and physicists joined the ecologists in a search for a new beginning." Through what Chase describes as a "swirl of chaotic, primeval theorizing, patterns began to form, and themes resonated," particularly the notions that nature is sacred and everything within the universe is interconnected. . . .

Injury to the Innocent

While most of the actions of ecoteurs to date mainly have destroyed property, injury of innocent people is now becoming part of the ecoterrorist record. Spiking trees with metal or ceramic spikes, the latter of which are not detected by metal detectors, is common in the western U.S. Incidents have also occurred in Canada and Australia. In May 1987, a young California sawmill operator was severely injured when a spike shattered a band saw. A local Earth First! official blamed the sawmill for jeopardizing its workers' lives. Earth First! leader Foreman said workers fearing injury could quit and that to him, "the old-growth forest in North Idaho is a hell of a lot more important than Joe Six-pack." Loggers in California and Oregon since have been injured.

No Room for Activists

We will continue to monitor Earth First!, and as long as the group continues to advocate violence we will oppose their efforts to meet on public lands. There is no room in America for terrorists who use violence and fear to achieve their political objectives. People like the followers of Earth First! who engage in those activities cannot cloak themselves in the First Amendment.

William Perry Pendley, *The Los Angeles Daily Journal*, August 17, 1990.

Northwest Forestry Association spokesman Mike Sullivan of Portland, Oregon, says that spiking incidents have been reported throughout the Northwest. After the injury of the California mill worker, the Forest Service said it planned to step up efforts to prevent spiking, but argued that the practice was "not a great epidemic." Though spiking has increased during the mid-1980s, explains Forest Service spokesman Jay Humphries, "there is still less than 100 incidents a year. Most of the illegal activity and threats to Forest Service land are related to marijuana growing, not environmental ecotage."

Many loggers remained unconvinced. In 1988, one Washington lumber mill lost $20,000 worth of blades from cutting spiked trees.

In another incident involving personal injury, demonstrators, some armed with knives and clubs, attacked Forest Service personnel involved in herbicide spraying in the Siskiyou National Forest.

Combatting Ecoterrorism

Increased enforcement has been the traditional response to ecoterrorism. Companies are more vigilant in protecting their equipment; the Forest Service tries to watch more closely for saboteurs of trees, roads, and equipment. In 1988, Congress passed a bill offered by Senator James McClure, the Idaho Republican, making tree spiking a federal offense. In 1989, Representative Charles (Chip) Pashayan, the California Republican, introduced legislation to stiffen penalties and create a reward program for informers against tree spikers.

In 1989, too, the Washington Contract Loggers Association created a Field Intelligence Report to track the activities of ecoteurs and has established a reward program for information leading to the apprehension of such criminals. Similarly, the Mountain States Legal Foundation, based in Denver, Colorado, established an ecotage hotline. In the first two months of hotline operation, Foundation President William Perry Pendley received reports of ecotage from California, Colorado, Idaho, Nevada, Oregon, and Washington. Mountain States also established a clearinghouse to file civil damage actions against saboteurs and to assist the government in prosecuting violators.

Adequate penalties are a necessary part of any effort to combat ecoterrorism. Yet western forestland and deserts are too sparsely populated to be patrolled and defended effectively against the determined ecoterrorists. The best defense against ecotage is for mainstream environmentalist community and political leaders and for businessmen to speak out frequently on the issue.

A Necessary Message

The message should be twofold: 1) violence is not justified as a response to perceived wrongs to the environment, and 2) the protection of human life remains society's paramount responsibility.

Particularly important is the role of the major environmental groups. Though none of them endorse ecotage, few have shown much enthusiasm for publicly criticizing the practice. Some even aid violent ecoteurs. David Brower, past executive director of the Sierra Club and current chairman of Friends of the Earth, gives Earth First! office space and has defended the organization's activities. "I think the environmental movement has room for lots of different views broadcasting on many channels," said Brower. "I'm certainly not going to be against civil disobedience."

Brower has said that "Earth First! makes Friends of the Earth look reasonable. What we need now is an outfit to make Earth First! look reasonable." When challenged to disavow ecoterrorists in 1983, the Sierra Club's then-executive director and now chairman Michael McCloskey responded that "we no more have an obligation to run around denouncing extremists using the environmental movement than Republicans and Democrats have an obligation to go around spending most of their time condemning the views of left or right wing extremists."

McCloskey ignores the fact the Republicans and Democrats have done just that. They overwhelmingly reject the use of violence to achieve their goals. They never have supported the use of tactics that may maim and even kill. And when such cases occur, these political movements have acted to disassociate themselves with the culprits. In the 1950s, the American labor movement purged itself of most communist members and influence. In 1989, George Bush and Republican Party Chairman Lee Atwater denounced the election of former Ku Klux Klan leader David Duke as a Republican to the Louisiana State Legislature and expelled him from the national party.

The political organizations closest to the terrorist group's ideological views should separate themselves from its activities and to help mold a broad social consensus against its activities. The Sierra Club and other organizations, because they are committed to many of the goals of Earth First!, have a special duty to discourage violence committed in the name of the environment. . . .

Better Alternatives

Environmental destruction underwritten by the federal government certainly should be the target of reformers. But this does not justify extremist tactics, civil disobedience, and violence. Nor does this justify ignoring the balance that must be struck between ecological concerns and economic development. It is neither humane nor does it serve the public good to shut businesses needlessly, to restrict the supply of housing by prohibiting construction of new homes, or to drive up the costs of energy by reducing electrical generating capacity. There are ways to protect the environment without paying those prices. Some of these ways include privatization and ending of federal development subsidies. Environmental policies must be designed around natural market forces which would deliver more ecological amenities at lower cost.

Americans want to preserve a clean world—to conserve their environment. Americans too want an economy that offers them increasing economic opportunities. How to balance these two goals all too often splits Washington between myopic conservationists and equally myopic developers. Out of this split comes the ecoterrorists, who believe that anything short of complete victory for "the environment" is a moral as well as a practical disaster.

Their extremist philosophy is leading to a guerrilla movement that is destroying property and injuring the innocent and one day will kill innocent workers or park employees.

To prevent this, policy makers and particularly establishment environmental groups must respond to the ecoterrorists by rebuilding the moral consensus against the use of violence. The environmental movement has a special responsibility. It must no longer tolerate, let alone encourage, the ecoteurs. In particular, environmental groups should publicize the fact that the ecoteurs' violence sabotages legitimate environmental groups. These mainstream groups thus should speak out forcefully to encourage their members to distance themselves from violent and destructive activities.

"The international environmental mess can be controlled and rolled back only if each country will do its share."

International Cooperation Can Protect the Environment

J.I. Bregman

J.I. Bregman is the president of an environmental consulting firm, Bregman & Company, Inc. He has also served as the U.S. deputy assistant secretary of the interior for water quality. In the following viewpoint, Bregman argues that immediate international cooperation is necessary to protect the environment from further damage. He maintains that special-interest political groups, such as Germany's Green Party, have good intentions, but that true change can come only through international antipollution treaties between industrial nations and their Third World counterparts. Bregman argues that since pollution knows no boundaries, the solution must be equally broad in scope.

As you read, consider the following questions:

1. What examples does Bregman give to prove that international cooperation is necessary?
2. How does the author propose that current international pollution laws be used to protect the environment?
3. What positive steps does Bregman see being taken to protect the global environment?

J.I. Bregman, "How to Clean Up the Mess." This article appeared in the June 1989 issue and is reprinted with permission from *The World & I,* a publication of The Washington Times Corporation, © 1989.

What is the international situation today vis-à-vis pollution and its control? The evidence shows that:

The historic ruins at the Acropolis in Athens are being destroyed by air pollution. The famed city of Piraeus is covered with a yellow cloud of air pollution. Beaches up and down the Greek coast are dangerous for bathing because of high fecal coliform counts, as the historic city of Athens lacks adequate treatment facilities for human sewage.

Rome is only a little better off. The third of four sewage treatment plants required to treat its sewage is about ready to start functioning. The historic beach at Ostia has been closed for years because of contamination by sewage. Roman monuments are reputed to have about 10 years left before they fall total victim to air pollution. . . .

The USSR has environmental problems galore, but none matches the Chernobyl incident. More than 135,000 persons were evacuated from communities near the plant. Their cities are now ghost towns that stand as permanent testaments to man's ineptitude.

International Pollution

Brazil is destroying its priceless Amazon forests (as well as their human protectors) as the country industrializes. The impact on world weather may be dramatic. Brazilian leaders rebel at attending international conferences where they may be asked to slow down or stop this world threat.

France has suffered from chemical factory accidents that polluted the Rhine and Loire rivers. In Lille, one of France's major population centers, accidents at chemical plants sent ammonia clouds over large parts of the city.

Large parts of Vietnam still have not recovered from the Agent Orange that was sprayed there. Nor have many U.S. soldiers and Vietnamese peasants.

The holes in the ozone layer at the earth's poles threaten humanity with melanoma, radiation illness, and other health problems. Yet, until recently, the United States hesitated to do much about the chlorofluorocarbons (CFCs) that have been indicted as helping to create the holes. Now that industrialized nations are ready to gradually stop CFC production, Third World countries are asking that we bribe them by giving them free replacement materials to get them to cooperate.

Acid rain has soured U.S.-Canadian relations for a long time. The problem is caused by the much-discussed power plant emissions on the U.S. side of the border and the little-discussed (and poorly controlled) masses of sulfur dioxide coming from paper mills on the Canadian side.

A barge full of wastes from New York's sewage roamed the seas in 1988, looking for a place to land.

The above are but a few of the international environmental horror stories one can tell. The critical question to be faced is, How are we going to clean up this mess?

There are many technological answers to that question. Each can mitigate a part of the problem, but one overriding ingredient must be present or everything else is in vain: Each government must truly want to clean up the mess and must *do* it rather than just give lip service to the concept. Far too many countries have adopted the attitude that a clean environment is a nice thing to have, but it is much more important that their people have the jobs that industry can bring to them. They take the attitude that when the standard of living rises, then they will begin worrying about cleaning up the mess being created. This attitude must be changed. Governments must stop *saying* the right things and start *doing* them.

The Logical Answer

We are today living in a global community. The actions of one nation in cutting its forests, or spewing industrial waste into the air, or in building unsafe nuclear power plants that can accidentally release deadly radiation, can potentially affect neighboring nations directly and many others indirectly.

There is only one logical answer: international cooperation.

Peter Ditzel, *The Plain Truth*, February 1990.

In March 1989, more than 100 nations meeting in Switzerland concluded a treaty controlling toxic waste exports. The pact requires the government of an exporting country to obtain a prior written permit from the government of the country to which dangerous residue is to be shipped. This tiny step has been hailed. Egypt's Mostafa Tolba, executive director of the United Nations Environment Program, has said that "it has signaled the international resolve to eliminate the menace that hazardous wastes pose to the welfare of our shared environment and to the health of all the world's peoples." Those are beautiful words, but the pact merely says that "you need my OK before you can put your poison on my land."

New Priorities

What about the poisons that are presently being generated by the host country? The air in Cairo, for example, is just about permanently polluted. And Cairo turned its last small park into a parking lot a few years ago. Infected drinking water is more common than uncommon in Egypt. Wouldn't Tolba's native

263

country be much better off if it spent the largess it receives from the United States on environmental protection and health programs for its people instead of on factories to build tanks? The sad part of this story is that similar accusations could be directed at 30 or 40 other countries.

There are signs of popular revolts against pollution. Green parties in France, West Germany, and other Western European countries have swept ecological activists into political office. In France, the Greens captured about 1,800 city council seats, including one in Paris, causing Paris' Mayor Jacques Chirac to say that he is "very attentive to the messages transmitted by ecologists" and Prime Minister Michel Rochard to say that his party, like the Greens, is in the battle for the environment.

Small minority parties that may be captured or become allied with other forces that have their own axes to grind are not the best way to go, however. Rather, the major parties must be bipartisan (multipartisan in some countries) in their approach to a cleaner environment. The concept of a clean planet must be shared by all political parties, since people of all political persuasions want a better world.

Enforceable Laws

When the improbable recruitment of most of the world's leaders to the cause of preserving the environment, rather than just talking about it, occurs, a variety of tools will be available to do the work. Laws tailored to each country's problems are attainable *and enforceable.* Many countries have laws on their books that are either too weak or too strong and, most important of all, are enforced laxly or not at all. Such laws should deal with the following:

• *Air pollution emissions.* Particulates, sulfur dioxide, and nitrogen oxides *can* be controlled and minimized.

• *Water quality.* Discharges of pollutants and toxics from industrial plants can be controlled.

• *Sewage treatment.* In many Third World countries, just enforcing primary treatment requirements—the removal of solids and about 40 percent of the organics—would be a major step forward. In the more "civilized" countries, secondary treatment—removal of at least 85 percent of the organics—must be enforced.

• *Hazardous and toxic wastes.* Abandoned or active dumping sites can be identified. Further dumping can be stopped, and work on cleanup can get under way. Countries that lack the funding that the United States puts into this effort can develop their own streamlined, cost-effective techniques that, in practice, may clean up sites faster and more effectively than the cumbersome procedures the United States follows.

- *Chemical hazards.* The use of certain very hazardous pesticides like DDT can be banned, as can aerosol containers containing CFCs.

Recycling

Recycling is another major technology that can be employed by almost any country. It requires the goodwill of the people or industries doing the recycling, as well as reasonable, attainable programs being set up and enforced. Applied at the household level, this approach can be simplicity itself. It merely requires separation of paper, plastics, and metal for pickup or purchase by local authorities.

International Collaboration

The individual environmental problems that have come to public attention are intricately and inescapably interlinked, both scientifically and politically. Scientifically, their resolution requires an understanding of the physical, chemical, and biological processes that govern the Earth, and of the interaction of these processes in the entire Earth system. Politically, policy options to address these problems converge on the need for internationally accepted actions relating to energy, technology, land use, and economic development. Their implementation will require U.S. commitment and the development of improved mechanisms for international collaboration.

Robert N. Stavins, *Environment,* January/February 1989.

In the case of industry, recycling is accompanied by reuse. Although initiating such procedures is expensive, in the end the firm saves money and protects the environment. In the United States, the National Association of Manufacturers is stressing recycling and reuse to its member industries as a practical and economical way of being a good neighbor.

Ocean dumping of industrial wastes, municipal sewage, and sludge should be prohibited by every country that now allows these practices.

A strong tool used in the United States and a few other countries to prevent environmental damage is the environmental impact statement process. In this approach, the possible environmental effects of any proposed major activity are examined *before* permits for the activity are granted. In addition, similar studies are done on alternatives to the proposed action, which may include moving the project a few hundred yards to avoid environmental problems, redesigning it, or even studying the "no-action" alternative—that is, what happens if you don't carry through the project. These studies are placed before the permit-gathering agencies prior to the evaluation process. The result, not infrequently, is a change—minor or major—in the plans that results in much less negative environmental impact, while preserving the jobs or housing that the project would bring.

Natural Resources

Wetlands must be protected. Too many countries still look upon them as useless swampy areas that are better filled in and developed. The wetlands in one country may be the breeding place for the birds and fish that are important to another country. Policies similar to that adopted by the United States—of no net loss of wetlands—should be adopted and enforced.

Alternative clean energy sources should be utilized where practical. Many underdeveloped nations are blessed with enough sunlight to warrant its use as an energy source for at least part of their electrical needs. In other lands, a constantly blowing wind can be harnessed to turn huge windmills that produce electricity. Some countries, such as Mexico, Italy, and New Zealand, already use geothermal resources for energy production.

The provision of safe drinking water is an inherent responsibility of every government. Water can and should be disinfected with chlorine or ozone prior to distribution. If money is to be spent anywhere, it should be spent on providing pure drinking water.

Positive Steps

There are a number of positive developments that bode well for the future, such as the following:

The treaty on the export of hazardous waste, while only a minor achievement, means that most countries are at least talking to each other about pollution control.

Two important European meetings were held in March 1989. The first, on "Saving the Ozone Layer," was organized by British Prime Minister Margaret Thatcher and brought 700 senior delegates from 123 countries. The second meeting, in The Hague, was hosted by the prime ministers of France, the Netherlands, and Norway, and attended by leaders of 24 countries. A declaration promoting a new UN agency to fight global warming was the key result.

Waste associations of seven European countries have formed the European Federation of Special Waste Industries.

In the Netherlands, specially designed trucks pick up paints, solvents, and motor oils from communities for regular disposal at supervised facilities, much as paper and glass are collected.

Denmark has two furnaces that incinerate about 100,000 metric tons of organic and oily waste annually at an efficiency of more than 99 percent. Some 540 municipal incinerators throughout the European Community dispose of about 25 percent of the member countries' wastes each year. Discussions now under way could result in each of the member countries setting emission standards on the release of acids, dioxins, sulfur dioxide, and heavy metals.

West Germany has set a mandatory deposit fee on plastic containers for all kinds of drinks.

The Netherlands is providing fiscal incentives to buyers of small and medium-sized cars fitted with catalytic converters. The UK has preferential pricing on unleaded gasoline.

American congressmen have been talking to the Brazilian government about possibly instituting a program through the World Bank that would trade some debt forgiveness for saving portions of the Amazon forests.

International Cooperation

The glaring absence of most developing countries from the list of countries taking the corrective actions cited above should be noted.

This article has stressed what individual nations should be doing. Obviously, international agreements can and should be signed and observed with regard to problems that affect the world as a whole—ocean dumping, the ozone layer, destruction of rain forests, and acid rain, to name a few.

The international environmental mess can be controlled and rolled back only if each country will do its share instead of just having its representatives make beautiful speeches that cover the lack of action. We've all been alerted to the problem by many tragically visible signs. Now is the time to insist that each country take strong action to protect itself and its neighbors. As far as pollution is concerned, this is one world that has no boundaries. The approach to overcoming pollution must follow the same philosophy.

"Local organizations form a sort of ragtag front-line in the worldwide struggle to end poverty and environmental destruction."

Citizen Action Can Protect the Environment

Alan B. Durning

In the following viewpoint, Alan B. Durning, an environmental writer for the Worldwatch Institute, a research organization, writes that only through local activism can the environment be rescued. Durning profiles numerous organizations made up of local citizens whose tactics have successfully stopped corporations from polluting or destroying the environment.

As you read, consider the following questions:

1. What forces does the author believe have helped create the grass-roots movement?
2. Why does Durning say that community action in industrial nations must differ from that in Third World countries?
3. In the author's opinion, what one thing must people do to protect the environment?

Alan B. Durning, "Groundswell at the Grassroots," *Worldwatch*, December 1989. Reprinted with permission.

Women living on the banks of India's Ganges River may not be able to calculate an infant mortality rate, but they know all too well the helplessness and agony of holding a child as it dies of diarrhea. Residents along the lower reaches of the Mississippi River may not be able to name the mutagens and carcinogens that nearby petrochemical factories pump into their air and water, but they know how many of their neighbors have miscarried or died of cancer. Forest dwellers in the Amazon basin cannot quantify the mass extinction of species now occurring around them, but they know what it is to watch their primeval homeland go up in smoke before advancing waves of migrants and developers.

These men and women understand global degradation in its rawest forms. To them, creeping destruction of ecosystems has meant lengthening workdays, failing livelihoods, and deteriorating health. And it has pushed many of them to act. In villages, neighborhoods, and shantytowns around the world, people are coming together to strike back at the forces of environmental and economic decline that threaten communities and the planet.

In the face of such enormous threats, isolated grass-roots initiatives appear minuscule—10 women plant trees on a roadside, a local union strikes for a nontoxic workplace, an old man teaches neighborhood children to read—but from a global perspective, their scale and impact are monumental. Those who endure economic and environmental decline are beginning to chart the course to sustainability. Local organizations form a sort of ragtag front-line in the worldwide struggle to end poverty and environmental destruction.

The battle to save the planet needs more than a front-line, though. National governments and international agencies, which all too often have excluded or sought to control popular organizations, must learn to work with them. Forming equal partnerships between local organizations and government bodies, built on mutual respect and shared goals, is a prerequisite to resolving many of the tenacious problems confronting the earth. To succeed, progress toward a sustainable society will have to come from both the bottom and the top.

The Grass-Roots Movement

The birth of Third World grass-roots movements is a dramatic departure from historical precedent. Kinship, social hierarchies, and religious structures form the scaffolding of human community in traditional societies all over the world. Yet traditional organizations have been stretched and often dismantled in this century by rapid population growth, urbanization, and the spread of modern technology.

In the resulting vacuum, a new generation of community and

269

grass-roots groups has been steadily, albeit unevenly, developing since mid-century, particularly over the past two decades. This emergence is driven by a shifting constellation of forces, including stagnant or deteriorating economic and environmental conditions for the poor; the failure of governments to respond to basic needs; the spread, in some regions, of new social ideologies and religious doctrines; and the political space opened in some countries as tight-fisted dictatorships give way to frail democracies. Unlike traditional organizations and mass political movements, this rising tide of community groups is generally pragmatic, focused on development, and concerned above all with self-help.

Global Grass-Roots Action

Grass-roots pressure plays an important role in pushing governments to give environmental concerns a higher priority. Environmental groups have sought not only to influence the policies of their own governments and corporations but, by linking up with their counterparts abroad, those of foreign governments and of the World Bank and International Monetary Fund. Greenpeace, for instance, has developed a truly globe-spanning network of activists mobilized on a wide range of issues.

Michael G. Renner, *Worldwatch*, November/December 1989.

Outside the Third World, grass-roots movements are just as much on the rise. In industrial nations of both East and West the concerns of these groups increasingly align them with the goal of creating sustainable societies in which current generations satisfy their needs without diminishing the prospects for future ones. In the Soviet Union and Eastern Europe, where officially sanctioned local organizations are numerous but largely controlled by state and party hierarchies, the political openness of this decade has brought the genesis of independent citizens' groups. In Western industrial nations, environmental movements have experienced an extraordinary renaissance, especially at the grass-roots level, over the past few years. No longer a concern primarily of the well-to-do or of educated elites, environmental activism is springing from working-class and minority communities. . . .

Community Action

Communities are both more apt and better able to protect their environments against outsiders who exploit it. A visible adversary brings out defense instincts that local groups can tap. Traditional fishers of northeastern Brazil, the Philippines, and the Indian states of Goa and Kerala, for example, have organized sustained campaigns, including massive protest marches, against commercial trawlers and industrial polluters who deplete ocean fisheries. From the Congo to Kalimantan, the people of the world's disappearing tropical forests have begun defending their homes, despite a pace of destruction that makes their task daunting.

The world's most acclaimed community forest-protection movement, Chipko, shows how grass-roots action to defend a resource can grow into something much greater. Born in the Garhwal hills of Uttar Pradesh, India, Chipko first drew fame for its sheer courage. In March 1973, as a timber company headed for the woods above impoverished Gopeshwar village, desperate local men, women, and children rushed ahead of them to *chipko* (literally "hug" or "cling to") the trees, daring the loggers to let the axes fall on their backs.

Resource Protection

Since its initial success, the movement has deepened its ecological understanding and, in the words of follower Vandana Shiva, "widened from embracing trees to embracing mountains and waters." In 1987, activists formed a seven-month blockade at a limestone quarry that was recklessly destroying the ecosystem of an entire valley. Chipko has gone beyond resource protection to ecological management and restoration. The women who first guarded trees from loggers now plant trees, build soil-retention walls, and prepare village forest plans.

Most of the world's hundreds of local movements for resource protection never draw the international attention accorded Chipko, but that doesn't diminish their effectiveness. A representative case comes from a rudimentary settlement called Zapocó in one of Bolivia's most isolated regions. There, 170 Ayoréode and Chiquitano Indians have built a small sawmill and learned the fundamentals of sustainable forestry in a bid to fend off the commercial timber companies encroaching on their lands.

Convoluted Bolivian forest laws, which simply write off the Ayoréodes and Chiquitanos as "savages," mean the only way the tribes can assert control over their forests is to legally establish themselves as timber contractors. Ironically, a sawmill is in this case the best defense against the chain saw. . . .

First World Problems

People in wealthy nations live in radically different circumstances than their impoverished brethren to the south: the long chains of commerce and industrial production buffer their dependence on natural systems. The industrial economy is too new and too complex to be regulated by traditional practices; its environmental side-effects can only be controlled by law. The

271

environmental threats of industrialization, moreover, are not typically resource depletion but pollution. All of these factors make community action in industrial countries markedly different from Third World concepts of self-help. Yet, the fundamental principle of joining together to protect lives, livelihood, and the prospects for the next generation is universal.

Individual Determination

So many of the big problems—coastal water pollution, pesticides in ground water, urban smog and municipal garbage—aren't simply caused by large power plants and refineries. And many can't be solved by national legislation alone.

Millions of small, diverse sources contribute to these problems, including the everyday behavior of people at work and at home. Such overwhelming environmental challenges can be solved by individual determination that we can do better.

George Bush, *Los Angeles Times*, September 20, 1989.

Stretching along the banks of the Mississippi River for 85 miles north of New Orleans lies America's "Petrochemical Corridor," producer of one-fifth of the nation's oil-based chemicals. Hundreds of tons of toxic materials leak into groundwater, are pumped into the river, and spew from rows of smokestacks. In national cancer registries, the region juts out like a red flag. Still, regulation has been lax.

To protect themselves, neighborhoods up and down the corridor have organized. The predominantly black residents of Revelletown, Louisiana, a two-street working-class community in the shadows of a mammoth chemical facility, grew alarmed in the mid-1980s when they began waking up gasping for air. Plant representatives were uncooperative when pressed for an explanation. "No one ever told us what was going on over there," says community activist Janice Dickerson. Local organizers had all 75 residents' blood tested and found that many had vinyl chloride—a potent carcinogen and the main product of the chemical plant—coursing through their veins.

A Partial Victory

The residents brought suit but, faced with the prospect of continuing to live under the smokestacks through years of litigation, most accepted a substantial sum to settle out of court and relocate. Revelletown's people are out of danger, although the factory keeps making vinyl chloride and other toxic substances.

Revelletown's partial victory has added momentum to the organizing efforts in dozens of nearby communities. Residents of these towns and others marched the length of the chemical corridor to draw attention to the region's plight and to unify their disparate efforts.

The United States has hundreds of Revelletowns that are together forging the basis of a new environmentalism, a movement of working-class communities concerned about local issues. In the Bronx, New York, Patricia Nonnon and her neighbors, alarmed at the high incidence of various diseases, are demanding that a nearby abandoned hazardous waste dump be cleaned up. In the pesticide-saturated San Joaquin Valley of California, where cancer rates among children are eight times the expected incidence, Connie Rosales of McFarlane township and other mothers have demanded action from state officials. In Seattle, Washington, plans to construct a waste incinerator ignited such opposition from community groups that city hall opted for an ambitious recycling program instead. Within a year, Seattle was recycling more of its solid waste than any other urban area in the country. . . .

Shaping the Future

At base, grass-roots action on poverty and the environment comes down to a question of the rights of people to shape their own destiny. The United Nations-sponsored World Commission on Environment and Development is unequivocal on this. Its landmark report, *Our Common Future,* states that "the pursuit of sustainable development requires a political system that secures effective citizen participation in decision making."

Around the world, community organizations are doing their best to put this participatory vision into practice. Simultaneously, they pose a deeper question. In the world's impoverished South, it is phrased, "What is development?" In the industrial North, "What is progress?" Behind the words, however, is the same profoundly democratic refrain—what kind of society shall our nation be? What kind of lives shall our people lead? What kind of world shall we leave to our children?

The rethinking that the world's grass-roots movements are doing brings fresh hope, for who, if not these millions of local organizations, can build the institutional foundations and define the guiding values for sustainable societies?

Whether these scattered beginnings rise in a global groundswell depends only on how many more individuals commit their creativity and energy to the challenge. The inescapable lesson for each of us is distilled in the words of Angeles Serrano, a grandmother and community activist from Manila's Leveriza slum: "Act, act, act. You can't just watch."

Ranking Environmental Concerns

Toles. Copyright 1990 *The Buffalo News.* Reprinted with permission of Universal Press Syndicate. All rights reserved.

The authors in this chapter offer several suggestions on how best to protect the environment. This activity will allow you also to explore the different values you, your classmates, and others consider important in protecting the environment. Many people disagree on specific priorities for protecting the environment. Often the differences reflect their occupations. Loggers in the U.S. Northwest, for example, may oppose restrictions on cutting down forests because of fear of losing their jobs. A naturalist may call for limiting the number of people allowed to visit Yellowstone National Park, saying that too many visitors are damaging the fragile environment. Other economic and social concerns can clash with the pursuit of environmental protection.

As the cartoon indicates, some people may be unwilling to change their lifestyles to protect the environment. Additional concerns are listed below.

Step 1: The class should break into groups of four to six students. Group members should rank the concerns listed below. Decide what you believe to be the most important concerns, and be ready to defend your answers. Use number 1 to designate the most important concern, number 2 for the second most important concern, and so on.

_____ preserving wilderness areas by preventing people from using them

_____ enabling companies to devise their own pollution reduction strategies

_____ sabotaging and vandalizing development projects if necessary to protect the environment

_____ passing laws and regulations to force businesses to reduce pollution

_____ reducing the world population

_____ promoting environmental awareness among America's schoolchildren through educational programs

_____ reducing the amount of materials and energy people in developed countries consume

_____ discouraging the use of plastics and other materials that are not biodegradable or easily recycled

_____ establishing international treaties to force countries to protect the rain forests

_____ promoting grass-roots movements to battle large corporations and environmental destruction

_____ using more undeveloped wilderness areas for planting crops, raising cattle, logging, and other projects to feed and house the world's population

Step 2: After your group has agreed on the rankings, compare your answers with those of other groups in a classwide discussion. Discuss the differences and similarities of the groups' rankings.

Periodical Bibliography

The following articles have been selected to supplement the diverse views presented in this chapter.

David Brooks	"Saving the Earth from Its Friends," *National Review*, April 1, 1990.
Lester R. Brown, Christopher Flavin, and Sandra Postel	"A Global Plan to Save Our Planet's Environment," *USA Today*, January 1990.
Business Week	"Let's Not Stall on Cleaner Gasoline," June 11, 1990.
Gregg Easterbrook	"Cleaning Up," *Newsweek*, July 24, 1989.
David R. Gergen	"Collisions Ahead for Environmentalists," *U.S. News & World Report*, May 7, 1990.
Meg Greenfield	"The Word's Too Big," *Newsweek*, April 30, 1990.
Robin Knight	"The Greening of Europe's Industries," *U.S. News & World Report*, June 5, 1989.
Thomas R. Kuhn	"Striving for Balanced Growth," *Vital Speeches of the Day*, August 1, 1989.
Wesley Marx	"Environmental Countdown: Where We're Losing—and Winning," *Reader's Digest*, May 1990.
Robert H. Nelson	"Tom Hayden, Meet Adam Smith and Thomas Aquinas," *Forbes*, October 29, 1990.
The New Republic	"Grime and Punishment," February 20, 1989.
Jim Robbins	"Saboteurs for a Better Environment," *The New York Times*, July 7, 1989.
Dick Russell	"Earth Last!" *The Nation*, July 17, 1989.
Dick Russell	" 'We Are All Losing the War,' " *The Nation*, March 27, 1989.
Kirkpatrick Sale	"Deep Ecology and Its Critics," *The Nation*, May 14, 1988.
Thomas A. Sancton	"The Fight to Save the Planet," *Time*, December 18, 1989.
Murray Weidenbaum	"Protecting the Environment," *Society*, November/December 1989.
Michael Weisskopf	"Environmental Groups Sail the Mainstream," *The Washington Post National Weekly Edition*, April 30-May 6, 1990.

Organizations to Contact

The editors have compiled the following list of organizations that are concerned with the issues debated in this book. All of them have publications or information available for interested readers. The descriptions are derived from materials provided by the organizations. This list was compiled upon the date of publication. Names and phone numbers of organizations are subject to change.

Accuracy in Media (AIM)
1275 K St. NW, Suite 1150
Washington, DC 20005
(202) 371-6710

Accuracy in Media is a conservative watchdog organization dedicated to detecting bias in media reports on major social issues, including the environment. AIM does not support costly government cleanup measures such as the Clean Air Act or Superfund and believes too many journalists have crossed the line into advocacy journalism when reporting environmental stories. AIM also claims that the environmental crisis is exaggerated. It publishes the bimonthly *AIM Report*.

The Acid Rain Foundation, Inc.
1410 Varsity Dr.
Raleigh, NC 27606
(919) 828-9443

The Foundation was established to raise the level of public awareness about acid rain. It publishes the newsletter *Update* quarterly and the *Resource Directory* annually.

American Council on Science and Health
1995 Broadway, 16th Floor
New York, NY 10023-5860
(212) 362-7044

The Council is an association of scientists and doctors concerned with public health. It works to calm the fears of American citizens who believe their air, water, and food are contaminated. The Council believes that regulatory controls protect the public from harm and that the environmental crisis is exaggerated. It publishes a series of pamphlets, including *Pesticides and Food Safety*, and occasional special reports.

American Farm Bureau Federation
225 Touhy Ave.
Park Ridge, IL 60068
(312) 399-5700

The Federation analyzes farm problems such as weed control and pest eradication for its members and formulates appropriate action. It has a Natural and Environmental Resources division and its forty-nine state farm bureaus maintain speakers' bureaus, sponsor education programs, and operate libraries. The Federation publishes the weekly *Farm Bureau News*.

American Water Works Association (AWWA)
6666 W. Quincy Ave.
Denver, CO 80235
(303) 794-7711

The AWWA is an association of water utility managers, engineers, chemists, bacteriologists, and other individuals interested in public water supply and quality. It develops and supports research programs in waterworks design, construction, operation, and water quality control. The Association publishes booklets, manuals, reference materials, and the monthlies *AWWA Journal, Mainstream, Washington Report,* and the bimonthly *Waterworld News.*

Chemical Manufacturers Association (CMA)
2501 M St. NW
Washington, DC 20037
(202) 887-1108

The Association sponsors research in areas crucial to chemical manufacturers, including air and water pollution. It promotes plant safety, education, and the need for chemicals in modern society. The organization believes that industrial chemical production can be environmentally responsible. It publishes *ChemEcology* and *CMA News* ten times a year and makes available various booklets promoting safe chemical use.

Earth First!
PO Box 7
Canton, NY 13617
(315) 379-9940

Earth First! uses civil disobedience and direct action to preserve wilderness and natural diversity. Some of its best-known actions include spiking trees to make them more difficult to cut down and dressing as bears in order to protest the destruction of forests. It publishes *Earth First! The Radical Environmental Journal* eight times a year.

Friends of the Earth
218 D St. SE
Washington, DC 20003
(202) 544-2600

This organization works globally to influence public policy in order to protect the environment. It has successfully opposed the construction of nuclear power plants and helped preserve wildlife sanctuaries. It publishes the bimonthly magazine *Not Man Apart.*

Greenpeace
1436 U St. NW
Washington, DC 20009
(202) 462-1177

Greenpeace opposes nuclear energy and the use of toxins and supports ocean and wildlife preservation. It uses controversial direct action techniques and strives for media coverage of its actions in an effort to educate the public. It publishes the bimonthly magazine *Greenpeace* and many books, including *Radiation and Health, Coastline,* and *The Greenpeace Book on Antarctica.*

The Heritage Foundation
214 Massachusetts Ave.
Washington, DC 20002
(202) 546-4400

The Heritage Foundation is a conservative think tank that examines current social and political topics, including the environmental crisis. It opposes excessive governmental involvement in reducing pollution and advocates a free-market approach to environmental preservation. The Foundation publishes the quarterly *Policy Review*. Its *Backgrounder* series of occasional papers and its *Lectures* series of speeches often cover environmental issues.

Minnesota Mining and Manufacturing (3M)
Environmental Engineering and Pollution Control Department
PO Box 33331
Building 21-2W
St. Paul, MN 55133
(612) 733-1110

3M has implemented various toxic-waste reduction measures that have saved the company several hundred million dollars. Numerous environmental leaders have singled out 3M as a positive example of corporate environmental responsibility. It makes available an information packet on its "Pollution Protection Pays" program.

National Agricultural Chemicals Association (NACA)
1155 15th St. NW, Suite 900
Washington, DC 20005
(202) 296-1585

NACA is an association of firms that produce agricultural chemical products like herbicides, pesticides, defoliants, and soil disinfectants. It contains legislative and regulatory departments and maintains committees on environmental management, public health, and toxicology. The Association promotes the use of chemicals in farm production. It publishes the periodic *Bulletin* and the bimonthly *Actionews*.

National Environmental Development Association
1440 New York Ave. NW
Washington, DC 20005
(202) 638-1230

The Association is a coalition of individuals from organized labor, agriculture, and industry. It promotes a balance between environmental protection and economic concerns in the development of America's resources. The Association publishes the quarterly newsletter *Balance*.

National Research Council
2101 Constitution Ave.
Washington, DC 20418-0001
(202) 334-2000

The Council was organized by the National Academy of Sciences in 1916 to promote broader participation by American scientists and engineers in the work of the Academy. It is a private, independent research organization that examines questions of science and technology at the request of the federal government. The Council publishes briefing papers and reports, some relevant to the environment, including *Alternative Agriculture*.

National Solid Wastes Management Association
1730 Rhode Island Ave. NW, Suite 1000
Washington, DC 20036
(202) 659-4613

The Association is a trade organization of industries involved in garbage collection, recycling, landfills, and treatment and disposal of hazardous and medical wastes. It lobbies for laws that are environmentally sound but still allow communities to dispose of their waste. It publishes the monthly magazine *Waste Age* and the newsletter *Recycling Times*.

National Wildlife Federation
1400 16th St. NW
Washington, DC 20036-2266
(202) 797-6800

With over six million members, the Federation is one of the largest environmental organizations in the country. It encourages the intelligent management of natural resources, awards fellowships for graduate studies in conservation, publishes classroom education materials, and produces the daily radio show "Nature NewsBreak." The Federation's publications include the bimonthlies *International Wildlife, National Wildlife,* the monthlies *Ranger Rick, Your Big Backyard, The Leader,* and the annual *Environmental Quality Index.*

Natural Resources Defense Council
40 W. 20th St.
New York, NY 10011
(212) 727-2700

The Council is a nonprofit activist group of scientists, lawyers, and citizens working to promote environmentally safe energy sources, protection of the environment, and American-Soviet understanding of global issues. It publishes a quarterly, *The Amicus Journal,* the newsletter *Newsline,* and a bibliography of books concerning air quality, water resources, and land preservation.

Sierra Club
530 Bush St.
San Francisco, CA 94108
(415) 981-8634

Since 1892, the Sierra Club has been working to protect and conserve the natural resources of the Sierra Nevada, the United States, and the world. It publishes the weekly *National News Report;* a bimonthly, *Sierra;* and numerous books and newsletters.

STAPPA/ALAPCO
444 N. Capitol St. NW
Washington, DC 20001
(202) 624-7864

The State and Territorial Air Pollution Program Administrators (STAPPA) is the national association of state air quality officials in the fifty-four states and territories of the United States. The Association of Local Air Pollution Control Officials (ALAPCO) is the national association representing air pollution control officials in over 150 major metropolitan areas across the nation. The associations serve to encourage the exchange of information among air pollution control officials, to enhance communication among federal, state, and local regulatory agencies, and to promote good management of air resources. It makes available position papers on the Clean Air Act, smog, acid rain, and pollution control legislation.

Union of Concerned Scientists (UCS)
26 Church St.
Cambridge, MA 02138
(617) 547-5552

The Union of Concerned Scientists is an organization of scientists and other citizens concerned about the impact of advanced technology on society. It is a nationally known advocate of arms control and safe energy. The UCS conducts independent research, sponsors and participates in conferences and panels, and testifies at congressional and regulatory hearings. The UCS publishes a quarterly newsletter, *Nucleus*, as well as books, reports, and briefing papers.

United Nations Environment Programme (UNEP)
New York Liaison Office
Two UN Plaza, Room 803
New York, NY 10017
(212) 963-8093

The Programme promotes environmental awareness among America's youth and provides educational material suitable for classroom use. UNEP publishes the free booklets *Youth Environmental Agenda* and *Global Environmental Monitoring System* and the bimonthly *UNEP North America News.*

Water Education Foundation
717 K St., Suite 517
Sacramento, CA 95814
(916) 444-6240

The Foundation is a nonprofit, nonbiased organization that provides material on water-related issues, including quality control and conservation, to legislators, educators, and the general public. It sponsors seminars, supplies brochures, and promotes water-use education. The Federation publishes the *Layperson Guides* series and the bimonthly *Western Water.*

The Wilderness Society
900 17th St. NW
Washington, DC 20006-2596
(202) 833-2300

Founded in 1935, the Wilderness Society is a national, nonprofit organization devoted to preserving America's forests, parks, rivers, deserts, and shorelands. It initiates citizen action, lobbies Congress, and sponsors coalitions between various environmental groups so they can work together to protect the nation's natural resources. The Society provides technical assistance to land managers and congressional decision makers and works to educate the public. It publishes an annual report as well as sponsors nature specials on television.

Worldwatch Institute
1776 Massachusetts Ave. NW
Washington, DC 20036
(202) 452-1999

The Worldwatch Institute is a nonprofit research organization created to analyze and focus attention on global problems, including environmental concerns. The Institute, which is funded by private foundations and United Nations organizations, has a mailing list that includes the names of political decision makers, scholars, and the general public. It publishes the Worldwatch Paper Series, including *Air Pollution, Acid Rain and the Future of Forests, Mining Urban Wastes: The Potential for Recycling,* and *Defusing the Toxics Threat: Controlling Pesticides and Industrial Waste.*

Bibliography of Books

Roger Batstone,
James E. Smith Jr.,
and David Wilson, eds.
The Safe Disposal of Hazardous Wastes. Washington, DC: The World Bank, 1989.

James Bellini
HighTech Holocaust. San Francisco: Sierra Club Books, 1989.

Louis Blumberg and
Robert Gottlieb
War on Waste: Can America Win Its Battle with Garbage? Covelo, CA: Island Press, 1989.

Murray Bookchin
Remaking Society: Pathways to a Green Future. Edison, NJ: South End Press, 1990.

Murray Bookchin
and Dave Foreman
Defending the Earth: A Dialog Between Murray Bookchin and Dave Foreman. Edison, NJ: South End Press, 1990.

Peter Borrelli
Crossroads: Environmental Priorities for the Future. Covelo, CA: Island Press, 1988.

Lester R. Brown, et al.
State of the World: A Worldwatch Institute Report on Progress Toward a Sustainable Society. New York: W.W. Norton, 1990.

David K. Bulloch
The Wasted Ocean. New York: Lyons & Burford, 1989.

Ruth Caplan
Our Earth, Ourselves. New York: Bantam Books, 1990.

Lee Clarke
Acceptable Risk? Berkeley, CA: University of California Press, 1989.

Gary Cohen and
John O'Connor, eds.
Fighting Toxics. Covelo, CA: Island Press, 1990.

Andree Collard
Rape of the Wild. Bloomington, IN: Indiana University Press, 1989.

T. Allan Comp, ed.
Blueprint for the Environment: A Plan for Federal Action. Salt Lake City: Howe Brothers, 1989.

John D. Connor Jr.,
Lawrence S. Ebner,
Charles A. O'Connor,
and Christian Volz
Pesticide Regulation Handbook. New York: Executive Enterprises Publications, 1987.

Czech Conroy and
Miles Litvinoff, eds.
The Greening of Aid: Sustainable Livelihoods in Practice. London: Earthscan, 1988.

The Conservation
Foundation
State of the Environment: A View Toward the Nineties. Washington, DC: The Conservation Foundation, 1987.

Joseph F. DiMento
Environmental Law and American Business. New York: Plenum Publishing, 1986.

Alan B. Durning
Action at the Grassroots. Washington, DC: Worldwatch Institute, 1989.

Robert Finch and
John Elder, eds.
The Norton Book of Nature Writing. New York: W.W. Norton, 1990.

L.E. Friday and
R.A. Laskey, eds.
The Fragile Environment. New York: Cambridge University Press, 1989.

Anne Witte Garland
For Our Kids' Sake: How to Protect Your Child Against Pesticides in Food. New York: Resources Defense Council, 1989.

Richard H. Gaskins	*Environmental Accidents*. Philadelphia: Temple University Press, 1989.
Robert Gottlieb	*A Life of Its Own: The Politics and Power of Water*. San Diego: Harcourt Brace Jovanovich, 1988.
David G. Hallman	*Caring for Creation*. Oroville, WA: Wood Lake Books, 1989.
D. Mark Harris	*Embracing the Earth*. Chicago: The Noble Press, 1990.
Floyd Hasselriis	*Refuse-Derived Fuel Processing*. Stoneham, MA: Butterworth Publishers, 1986.
Thorkil Kristenson and Johan Peter Paludan	*The Earth's Fragile Systems: Perspectives on Global Change*. Boulder, CO: Westview Press, 1988.
Michael Kronenwetter	*Managing Toxic Wastes*. Englewood Cliffs, NJ: Julian Messner, 1989.
H. Jeffrey Leonard	*Pollution and the Struggle for the World Product*. New York: Cambridge University Press, 1988.
Christopher Manes	*Radical Environmentalism and the Unmaking of Civilization*. Boston: Little, Brown, and Company, 1990.
Anthony J. Marro	*Rush to Burn: Solving America's Garbage Crisis*. Covelo, CA: Island Press, 1989.
John M. Mendeloff	*The Dilemma of Toxic Substance Regulation: How Overregulation Causes Underregulation*. Cambridge, MA: MIT Press, 1988.
Lawrie Mott and Karen Snyder	*Pesticide Alert*. San Francisco: Sierra Club Books, 1987.
Arne Naess	*Ecology, Community and Lifestyle: An Outline of Ecosophy*. London: Cambridge University Press, 1988.
Roderick Fraser Nash	*The Rights of Nature: A History of Environmental Ethics*. Madison: University of Wisconsin Press, 1989.
Homer A. Neal and J.R. Schubel	*Solid Waste Management and the Environment*. Englewood Cliffs, NJ: Prentice Hall, 1987.
Gary Null	*Clearer, Cleaner, Safer, Greener*. New York: Villard Books, 1990.
Robert Ornstein and Paul Ehrlich	*New World, New Mind: Moving Toward Conscious Evolution*. New York: Doubleday, 1989.
Bruce W. Piasecki and Gary A. Davis	*America's Future in Toxic Waste Management*. Westport, CT: Greenwood Press, 1987.
Sharon L. Roan	*Ozone Crisis*. New York: John Wiley & Sons, Inc., 1989.
Mostafa Kamal Tolba	*Sustainable Development: Constraints and Opportunities*. Stoneham, MA: Butterworth Publishers, 1987.
U.S. Environmental Protection Agency	*Pesticide Fact Handbook*. Park Ridge, NJ: Noyes Publications, 1988.
Jonathan Weiner	*The Next One Hundred Years: Shaping the Fate of Our Living Earth*. New York: Bantam Books, 1990.
The World Commission on Environment and Development	*Our Common Future*. London: Oxford University Press, 1987.

Index

Greenpeace, 29, 30, 116, 165, 248, 249-250, 270
groundwater
  advantages of drinking, 195
  definition of, 194-195
  pollution
    has increased, 45-46
    toxins causing, 201-205
  uses of, 193
  see also water supply
Guttman, Erica, 138
Guzzo, Lou, 25

Ham, Robert K., 120, 126
hazardous waste. *See* toxic waste
herbicides
  cause cancer, 50-51
    myth of, 57-58
  see also toxic chemicals
The Heritage Foundation, 239
Hershkowitz, Allen, 143, 145
Hildyard, Nicholas, 161
Hinchey, Maurice, 130
Hirschhorn, Joel S., 185
human beings
  cancer in, 50-51
  improved health of, 37-38, 199
  toxic chemicals in, 46, 49, 51-53, 79, 117-118
  unique qualities of, 26-28, 32
hydrocarbons, 112, 117, 161, 207, 218
Hynes, H. Patricia, 23, 142

incineration of wastes, 235
  alternatives to, 121
  and recycling, 109
  ash from
    is hazardous, 116-117, 150, 169-170
    myth of, 111-112, 162
    toxins in, 116, 170
  benefits of, 110, 161
  emissions from
    amount of, 168
    are hazardous, 117-118, 150, 168-169
    myth of, 112-113
    toxins in, 113, 120, 168-169
  government sponsorship of, 118
  in Europe, 119-120, 266-267
  method of, 119, 160, 170
  misconceptions about, 109, 113
  public opinion on, 125, 162-163
  U.S. inexperience in, 120, 167-168,

170-171
  versus landfills, 110-111
  see also toxic waste
Ingram, Helen, 230
Institute for Local Self-Reliance, 115, 121, 129
Institute for Policy Studies, 30

Jeffreys, Kent, 243
Jensen, Alan, 51, 52
Jensen, Holly, 152
Journal of Chromatography and Science, 117

landfills
  growth of, 149-150
  harms of, 112
  incineration perpetuates, 120
  need for more, 124, 142
  public opinion on, 125, 147-148
  shortage of, 115, 130-131
  toxic ash in, 116-117
  versus incineration, 110-111
  water pollution from, 150
  will solve garbage crisis, 122-127
  see also garbage
lead, 117, 169, 178, 207, 213, 223
  diseases from, 203
Lehrburger, Carl, 134, 136
Love Canal, 60, 161, 179, 180
Lovitz, Toby, 223
Low-Input, Sustainable Agriculture (LISA). *See* farming
Lyman, Francesca, 133

Martin, Nicolas S., 54
Meadows, Donella H., 91, 152
Merchant, Carolyn, 45
mercury, 117, 129, 151
Merline, John W., 215
methanol, 220
  diseases from, 222
  health costs of, 223
  is unsafe for car fuel, 222-223
monkeywrenching, 251-253, 256
Monsanto, 58, 71, 173
Montague, Peter, 183
Morris, David, 115, 129
Morton, James, 47
Muir, John, 238, 250
Murphy, Larry, 97

Naar, Jon, 170
Naj, Amal Kumar, 172
Napier, Kristine M., 194

287